Learn BlackBerry 10 App Development

Development

A Cascades-Driven Approach

Anwar Ludin

apress
open

Learn BlackBerry 10 App Development: A Cascades-Driven Approach

Anwar Ludin

Copyright © 2014 by Apress Media, LLC, all rights reserved

ISBN-13 (pbk): 978-1-4302-6157-5

ISBN-13 (electronic): 978-1-4302-6158-2

President and Publisher: Paul Manning
Lead Editor: Steve Anglin
Lead Technical Reviewer: Levon Levonian
Project Editor: Ryan McDonald
Editorial Board: Steve Anglin, Mark Beckner, Ewan Buckingham, Gary Cornell, Louise Corrigan, Jim DeWolf, Jonathan Gennick, Jonathan Hassell, Robert Hutchinson, Michelle Lowman, James Markham, Matthew Moodie, Jeff Olson, Jeffrey Pepper, Douglas Pundick, Ben Renow-Clarke, Dominic Shakeshaft, Gwenan Spearing, Steve Weiss
Coordinating Editors: Anamika Panchoo and Melissa Maldonado
Copy Editor: Kimberly Burton
Compositor: SPi Global
Indexer: SPi Global
Artist: SPi Global
Cover Designer: Anna Ishchenko

Distributed to the book trade worldwide by Springer Science+Business Media New York, 233 Spring Street, 6th Floor, New York, NY 10013. Phone 1-800-SPRINGER, fax (201) 348-4505, e-mail orders-ny@springer-sbm.com, or visit www.springeronline.com. Apress Media, LLC is a California LLC and the sole member (owner) is Springer Science + Business Media Finance Inc (SSBM Finance Inc). SSBM Finance Inc is a Delaware corporation.

For information on translations, please e-mail rights@apress.com, or visit www.apress.com.

Apress and friends of ED books may be purchased in bulk for academic, corporate, or promotional use. eBook versions and licenses are also available for most titles. For more information, reference our Special Bulk Sales–eBook Licensing web page at www.apress.com/bulk-sales.

Any source code or other supplementary material referenced by the author in this text is available to readers at www.apress.com. For detailed information about how to locate your book's source code, go to www.apress.com/source-code/.

About ApressOpen

What Is ApressOpen?

- ApressOpen is an open access book program that publishes high-quality technical and business information.

- ApressOpen eBooks are available for global, free, noncommercial use.

- ApressOpen eBooks are available in PDF, ePub, and Mobi formats.

- The user friendly ApressOpen free eBook license is presented on the copyright page of this book.

To Bibijan.

At 85 she has no interest in smartphones but constantly encouraged me to finish this book.

To this world's naysayers.

They give us the drive to achieve what they will never attempt.

Contents at a Glance

Contents

About the Author

Anwar Ludin is a freelance software engineer located in Geneva, Switzerland. He studied Electrical Engineering at the Swiss Federal Institute of Technology in Lausanne. After having fried a chip too many, he decided to switch to software engineering and never looked back. Anwar has spent the past decade in IT in the financial services sector where he tried to figure out the meaning of life amongst men in gray. His current interests, and the road ahead, include sensors-aware mobile app design, Cascades programming, data visualization, data science and high performance computing. He considers himself as a hardcore developer and is so happy he no longer needs to do the pencil pushing wearing a gray suit and a navy blue tie.

About the Technical Reviewers

Paul Bernhardt

David Clayworth

Shadid Haque

Tim Howie

Anthony Hu

Levon Levonian

Rodrigo Peixoto

Jonathan Ross

Bob Roth

Roy Sarkar

Suavek Zajac

Brian Zubert

Acknowledgments

I would like to first and foremost express my gratitude to my tech reviewers who are part of the amazing BlackBerry Developer Relations team. Thanks to their diligence and feedback, the book you are currently holding in your hands is by an order of magnitude better than the initial drafts. They helped me avoid huge embarrassments by specifically pinpointing inaccuracies in the successive drafts. They also helped me focus on the most important aspects of Cascades programming and made sure I addressed them. Dear tech reviewers, thank you so much for helping me get this book past the finishing line despite your own work schedule and commitments. I was very lucky having you all on board.

I am also immensely indebted to Ryan McDonald who is the Learning Program Manager at BlackBerry Developer Relations. Ryan has been coordinating the project on BlackBerry's behalf and has always made sure my questions were addressed promptly. Thank you so much Ryan.

This book would not exist without the amazing help provided by the Apress team. Steve Anglin was the book's acquisition editor. Steve helped me crystallize a rough idea into a concrete book proposal. Jeffrey Pepper was the book's project editor. Jeff was a constant encouragement to get the book passed the finishing line despite me missing my deadlines. Matt Moodie and Douglas Pundick were the book's development editors. Matt in particular helped me break up some of the content in manageable chunks in order to keep the reader on track. Anamika Panchoo and Melissa Maldonado were the book's coordinating editors. Ana made sure I got my tech reviews on time. She also tried very hard to make me deliver my own drafts on time. Ana I hope your newborn baby is doing well and that I did not stress you out too much by constantly missing my deadlines. Melissa took over when Ana left on maternity leave and helped me get the book passed the finishing line. Kimberly Burton was the book's copy editor. She cleaned up my broken English and made sure the book's overall style was kept in synch. Dhaneesh Kumar handled the book's compositing. Last but not least, Anna Ishchenko designed this book's cover. Thank you so much team Apress.

Introduction

BlackBerry 10 is the latest incarnation of the mobile operating system developed by BlackBerry for its new line of smartphones. As you can imagine, mobile platforms have experienced exponential growth in the recent years and BlackBerry has invested tremendous efforts in order to build a rock solid operating system fuelling its future generations of devices. BlackBerry 10 is also amazingly powerful and includes tons of enhancements compared to its predecessors. First of all, the heart of BlackBerry 10 ticks with the QNX hard real-time microkernel, which is used in safety critical systems such as nuclear power plants, medical devices, and also increasingly in automotive systems. BlackBerry 10 adds to rock-solid QNX a wealth of new APIs for accessing a mobile device's sensors (such as its camera, accelerometer and gyroscope) and also includes the Cascades UI framework for building beautiful mobile applications. In essence, the new range of APIs propel BlackBerry 10 to the next level of mobile computing and give you the tools for developing truly innovative apps.

The purpose of this book is to introduce you to the amazingly cool features of BlackBerry 10 and give you a solid foundation in Cascades application development. As I mentioned it in the previous paragraph, Cascades is first and foremost the new UI framework for building native BlackBerry 10 applications. Cascades is also based on QML, which is a powerful declarative language for designing UIs. Because QML is tightly integrated with JavaScript and C++, you have the choice between using JavaScript for the UI layer of your app and, if necessary, rely on C++ for the performance critical aspects of the app. In essence, Cascades gives you an efficient way of creating native applications with beautiful UIs optimized for the BlackBerry 10 line of mobile devices. From a consumer perspective Cascades provides a very rich and visually enticing user experience based on beautiful controls and animations.

After having read this book, you will be able to develop BlackBerry 10 native apps based on the Cascades framework and leverage the BlackBerry 10 platform services in your own apps. The book will also show you how to integrate your apps with the core BlackBerry 10 productivity apps in order to create the tools required by the professional user in order to get his job done. The only perquisite to get the most out of this book is some prior knowledge of OOP and perhaps a little experience with other mobile platforms such as iOS or Android (you will be introduced to all the key concepts required for building native apps using Cascades, including C++, in a progressive manner).

BlackBerry 10 is also a land of opportunity. As I write this introduction, new markets are opening up and new devices, more powerful with wider screens than my year-old Z10 companion, are rolling out. Secure platforms designed for enterprise users and, increasingly, cloud services users are still BlackBerry's forte. As a developer you can tap into this largely unexploited world of opportunities by designing the next killer app. I hope this book will help you pave the way and that you will enjoy the same sense of fun and excitement I have using Cascades.

Should you want to share anything about the book with me, please feel free to reach me through my website (http://www.aludin.com). You will also find on the site some advanced material about BlackBerry 10 and Cascades programming that did not make the cut in the book's current release. Finally I have also kept an up-to-date errata list on the book's page. So if you feel at any point that the sample code ziggs when it should have zagged, make sure to check the list.

The eBook version of this book is free for all users under the license found on the copyright page of this book. You are therefore encouraged to share the ebook version with your friends, colleagues and BlackBerry developer enthousiasts. It can be downloaded for free from any major book reseller's website, and from Apress using the following URL: www.apress.com/9781430261575 (you can also download from that location the code included with the book).

—Anwar Ludin,
la Muse coworking center,
Geneva,
3.14.2014

Chapter

1

Getting Started

This chapter will show you how to set up your BlackBerry 10 development environment and deploy your first application on the BlackBerry 10 simulator and on a physical device. You will also get a broad perspective of the Cascades programming model, as well as its most essential features. In setting up your environment, I will walk you through the following steps:

- Getting your code signing keys and generating debug tokens.
- Using the Momentics IDE to create your first Cascades project.
- Building and deploying your application on a simulator and a physical device.

Cascades Programming Model

BlackBerry 10 is a major mobile operating system overhaul. It's the third release built on top of the extremely reliable QNX operating system, which is used in critical applications ranging from medical devices to nuclear power plants. QNX is also *POSIX compliant*, meaning that if you're familiar with a UNIX programming API, you will feel just at home with the operating system's calls. Another big advantage of building BlackBerry 10 on top of a POSIX system is the availability of a myriad of open-source libraries that you can include in your own projects.

A key feature of BlackBerry 10 is that it is built using a multilayered architecture where QNX is the backbone providing essential services such as multithreading, memory management, and security, to name a few (see Figure 1-1). The layer on top of QNX includes the BlackBerry Platform Services (BPS) as well as several modules from the Qt framework.

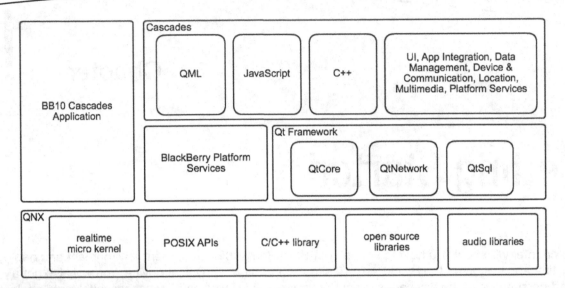

Figure 1-1. BlackBerry 10 platform

BPS is an API written in C, giving low-level access to the BlackBerry 10 device. It's mostly used when you need to write high-performance applications such as games that require the most effective way of accessing the hardware. BPS is not the main subject of this book. I will nevertheless give you examples of how to use it, but I will mostly concentrate on the higher-level modules built on top of BPS.

Qt is a C++ framework providing an abstraction layer to the lower-level POSIX APIs. It also adds many classes and components essential to C++ programming. The following modules from the Qt framework have been ported to the BlackBerry 10 platform and can be used in your own applications:

- *QtCore*: Provides the core framework elements for building C++ applications. In particular, QtCore defines the Qt object system, an event handling mechanism called *signals and slots*, memory management, and collection classes, to name a few.

- *QtNetwork*: Provides APIs for building networked applications. In particular, for HTTP applications, it provides the QNetworkAccessManager class.

- *QtSql*: Includes drivers and data access logic to relational databases.

- *QtXml*: Includes SAX and DOM parsers for handling XML documents.

The Qt modules mostly provide non-GUI functionality for your application. To build rich native applications with an engaging UI, you need to rely on the Cascades layer of the BlackBerry 10 architecture. In fact, Cascades is much more than a GUI framework; it also includes the following nonexhaustive list of services and APIs:

- *User interface*: Provides the core components for building rich native user interfaces using QML/JavaScript, C++, or a mix of all three technologies.

- *Application integration*: APIs that integrate platform applications and functionality such as e-mail and calendar into your own apps.

■ *Data management*: High-level APIs abstracting data sources and data models. The supported data formats include SQL, XML, and JSON.

■ *Communication*: APIs for enabling your apps to communicate with other devices by using, for example, Bluetooth, Wi-Fi, and NFC.

■ *Location*: APIs for using maps and managing location services in your application.

■ *Multimedia*: APIs for accessing the camera, audio player, and video player in your apps.

■ *Platform*: Additional APIs for managing platform notifications and home screen functions.

When developing native applications, you will notice that there is some overlap between the functionality provided by Cascades and the underlying modules. At first this might seem confusing but you should keep in mind that Cascades often provides a richer and easier-to-use API. Therefore, as a good rule of thumb, always try to implement a functionality with the Cascades API first, and if it is not possible, use the underlying Qt or BPS modules. Networking is a good example where you will use the QtNetwork module essentially.

QML

When building user interfaces with Cascades, you can proceed in two distinct ways: you can either write imperative code in C++ or create your UI declaratively with the Qt Modeling Language (QML). Most examples in this book use the latter approach for the following reasons:

■ Thanks to the Cascades Builder tool, you get immediate feedback on the way your UI will look in QML.

■ When it comes to designing UIs, writing C++ code can quickly become unmanageable, especially if you consider many nested components. In contrast, QML keeps the code much more tractable.

■ Once you get the hang of QML, it is way faster to create a polished UI within a few minutes than in C++.

■ Behind the scenes, you are still using C++ objects exposed to QML by Cascades. QML simply makes your life easier during the entire application development life cycle by avoiding numerous compile-build-deploy cycles until you get the UI right.

■ QML is a much friendlier language than C++ for people with a programming background in JavaScript. You will therefore have a greater chance of sharing your UI designs with other members of your team if they are written in QML.

To illustrate the previous points, let's design a very simple UI using both approaches: one UI design in QML and another one in C++. As shown in Figure 1-2, the UI isn't very fancy; it's simply a text field stacked on top of a slider. Whenever the slider moves, the text field is updated with the slider's new position.

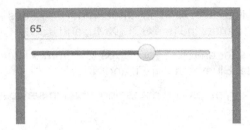

Figure 1-2. Stacked TextField and Slider

Listing 1-1 shows the QML markup version.

Listing 1-1. main.qml

```
import bb.cascades 1.0
Page {
    Container {
        TextField {
            id: texfield
        }
        Slider{
            id: slider
            fromValue: 0
            toValue: 100
            onImmediateValueChanged: {
                texfield.text = Math.round(immediateValue)
            }
        }
    }
}
```

The equivalent C++ version of the code for creating the same UI is given in Listings 1-2 and 1-3.

Don't worry if you have never programmed in C++, we will cover the basics in Chapter 3. As a matter of fact, you will also see in Chapter 2 that you can build relatively complex Cascades applications using QML/JavaScript only, without ever writing a single line of C++ code.

Listing 1-2. applicationui.hpp

```
class ApplicationUI : public QObject
{
    Q_OBJECT
public:
    ApplicationUI(bb::cascades::Application *app);
    virtual ~ApplicationUI() { }
```

```
public slots:
    void onImmediateValueChanged(float value);

};
```

Listing 1-3. applicationui.cpp

```cpp
ApplicationUI::ApplicationUI(bb::cascades::Application *app) : QObject(app) {
    Page *page = new Page();

    Container *contentContainer = new Container();
    contentContainer->setLayout(StackLayout::create());

    TextField* textfield = TextField::create();
    Textfield->setObjectName("textfield");
    Slider* slider = Slider::create();
    slider->setFromValue(0);
    slider->setToValue(100);

    contentContainer->add(textfield);
    contentContainer->add(slider);

    QObject::connect(slider, SIGNAL(immediateValueChanged(float)), this,
                    SLOT(onImmediateValueChanged (float)));

    page->setContent(contentContainer);
    app->setScene(page);
}

void ApplicationUI::onImmediateValueChanged(float value) {
    value = round(value);
    QString stringValue = QString::number(value);
    Application* app = static_cast<Application*>(this->parent());
    TextField* textField = app->scene()->findChild<TextField*>("textfield");
    textField->setText(stringValue);
}
```

ApplicationUI is the "application delegate" in charge of creating the user interface and wiring together the application's controls' event handling. You have to provide this class and it is instantiated during the application bootstrap process.

As you can see, the declarative way of building the UI in QML is very concise compared to the imperative C++ approach. This is also because Cascades takes care of a lot of the plumbing work for you behind the scenes when you're using QML.

Signals and Slots

In Cascades terminology, event handling is done using signals and slots, which are basically a loosely coupled notification mechanism between controls. Whenever something interesting happens to a control, such as a state change, a predefined signal is emitted for notifying that change. If you're interested in receiving that notification, then you have to specify some application logic in JavaScript or C++, which will be called in the corresponding Cascades predefined signal handler. Signals and slots are part of the QtCore module. The Cascades framework uses them in order to build a high-level event handling mechanism. This section will expand on the topic in order to give you a firm grip on the way signals and slots work. As noted previously, the most important property of signals is their ability to let you bind objects together without them knowing about each other.

Signals and Slots in QML

For a given predefined `signal` signal, Cascades also provides a corresponding predefined `onSignal` handler (which is also called equivalently a slot). You can write JavaScript code in your QML document to tell Cascades what to do when the handler is triggered and how the control should respond to the signal. For example, in order to handle the slider's position updates, Cascades defines a predefined `onImmediateValueChanged` signal handler called when the slider emits the `immediateValueChanged` signal. In Listing 1-1, the predefined handler will execute the `texfield.text = Math.round(immediateValue)` JavaScript code in order to update the textfield. You will also notice that the JavaScript code references an `immediateValue` parameter. Signals usually include extra parameters that provide additional information about them. In QML, they are implicitly available to the JavaScript execution context and you can use them in order to retrieve further information about the change that just occurred.

You can refer to the Cascades API reference found at `http://developer.blackberry.com/cascades/reference/user_interface.html` for a list of all predefined signals and corresponding slots organized by GUI control. Look under the core controls section.

Signals and Slots in C++

Looking at Listing 1-2, you will notice that I've used the `slots:` annotation to declare an `onImmediateValueChanged(float value)` slot in the application delegate class. In Listing 1-3, I've connected the slider's `onImmediateValueChanged(float value)` to the application delegate's `onImmediateValueChanged(float value)` slot using the `QObject::connect(source, SIGNAL(signal), destination, SLOT(slot))` method.

> The `Q_OBJECT`, `signals:` and `slots:` "annotations" are Qt extensions to the C++ language.

Signals and slots are implemented in Qt using the following constructs:

- A class must inherit from `QObject`.
- You must add the `Q_OBJECT` macro at the beginning of the class definition. The `Q_OBJECT` macro marks the class as managed by the Meta Object Compiler (MOC). During compilation, the MOC generates additional code for the class in a file called `moc_classname.cpp`, which adds support for signals and slots, metaprogramming, and other features for runtime introspection. Note that the entire process is completely transparent and you don't need to worry about it during compilation.

> If you intend on extending the class, you must also repeat the Q_OBJECT macro in all of its subclasses.

- You must declare the class signals using the `signals:` annotation.
- You must declare the class slots using the `slots:` annotation.
- You must define the class slots as regular member functions.
- Finally, you must wire signals and slots using `QObject::connect()`.

As an example, let us consider the case of a temperature sensor. We would like to build a system where we can chart and log temperature readings over time. We would also want to decouple the system by separating the charting logic from the temperature logging. A very simplified design can be implemented using three classes (see Figure 1-3). The `TempSensor` class is responsible for the temperature readings through the `setTemp(float newValue)` function, which could be triggered by a hardware interrupt. The function would then update `TempSensor`'s internal state, and then emit a `tempChanged(float)` signal. The `TempChart` and `TempLogger` classes would respectively handle the signal with a corresponding onTempChanged(float) slot.

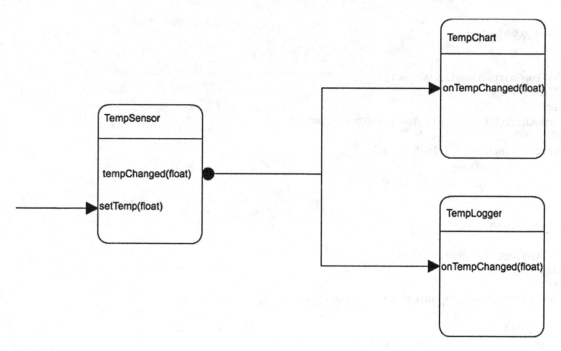

Figure 1-3. Sensor system

The C++ implementation is given in Listings 1-4 and 1-5.

Listing 1-4. TempSensor.hpp

```cpp
#include <QObject>

class TempSensor : public QObject{
Q_OBJECT
public:
    TempSensor(QObject* parent=0) : QObject(parent), m_value(0) {};
    virtual ~TempSensor(){};

    void setTemp(float newValue){
        if(m_value == newValue) return;
        m_value = newValue;
        emit(tempChanged(m_value));
    }

signals:
    void tempChanged(float)

private:
    float m_value;
};

#include <QObject>


class TempChart : public QObject{
Q_OBJECT
public:
    TempChart(QObject* parent=0) : QObject(parent){};
public slots:
    void onTempChanged(float value){
        // do charting
    }
};

#include <QObject>

class TempLogger : public QObject{
Q_OBJECT
public:
    TempLogger(QObject* parent=0) : QObject(parent){};

public slots:
    void onTempChanger(float value){
        // do logging
    }
};
```

Listing 1-5. main.cpp

```cpp
#include "TempSensor.hpp"
int main(){
    TempSensor sensor;
    TempLogger logger;
    TempChart chart;

    QObject::connect(sensor, SIGNAL(tempChanged(float)), logger, SLOT(onTempChanged(float)));
    QObject::connect(sensor, SIGNAL(tempChanged(float)), chart, SLOT(onTempChanged(float)));

    // do temperature readings here.
}
```

Here are a few things to keep in mind when implementing signals and slots:

- Signals are triggered in your code using the emit `signalName()` syntax (see Listing 1-4).

- Signals must always have a void return value. In other words, you can't get a return value from a signal once it has been emitted.

- As illustrated in the previous example, one signal can be connected to many slots. When the signal is emitted, the slots are called one after the other.

- The opposite is also true; many signals can be connected to the same slot.

- You can also connect a signal to another signal. When the first signal is emitted, the second one is also emitted.

- Slots are normal member functions. You can call them directly if you wish. They can also be virtual functions if you wish.

- The signature of a signal must match the signature of the receiving slot. A slot can also have a shorter signature than the signal (in this case the slot drops the extra arguments).

Meta-Object System

Qt extends C++ with a meta-object system in order to introduce runtime introspection features that would not be available with a statically compiled language such as C++. Behind the scenes, Qt uses the meta-object compiler (MOC) to generate the extra C++ plumbing code for the functions declared by the Q_OBJECT macro and for the class signals. Finally, the QObject::connect function uses the MOC-generated introspection functions to wire signals and slots together. When building Cascades applications, the MOC is called transparently by the build system.

Cascades Application Bootstrap Process

The entry point for all Cascades applications is the main function shown in Listing 1-6.

Listing 1-6. main.cpp

```cpp
#include <bb/cascades/Application>
#include <QLocale>
#include <QTranslator>
#include "applicationui.hpp"

#include <Qt/qdeclarativedebug.h>

using namespace bb::cascades;

Q_DECL_EXPORT int main(int argc, char **argv)
{
    Application app(argc, argv);

    // Create the Application UI object, this is where the main.qml file
    // is loaded and the application scene is set.
    new ApplicationUI(&app);

    // Enter the application main event loop.
    return Application::exec();
}
```

The first step in main is to create an instance of a bb::cascades::Application class, which provides the application's run loop, and all the boilerplate functionality required by a Cascades application. At this point, you will have a "bare bones" Cascades app but the run loop has not kicked in yet. To further customize the application, the following properties of the bb::Cascades::Application instance have to be specified:

- *Scene property*: Specifies the instance of bb::cascades::AbstractPane to use as the scene for the application's main window. A scene is basically a layout of controls which will be displayed in the application's main window.

- *Cover property*: Specifies the instance of bb::cascades::AbstractCover to be used when the application is in cover mode.

- *Menu property*: An instance of a bb::cascades::Menu accessible by the user with a swipe from the top of the screen.

In practice, you will not update the bb::cascades::Application's properties directly in the main function but instead rely on an application delegate object, which will take care of loading or creating the main scene and wiring all the events using signals and slots. You've already seen an implementation of an application delegate in Listing 1-2 and Listing 1-3 given by the ApplicationUI class. In Listing 1-3, we customized the application delegate in order to build the scene graph using C++. Listing 1-7 shows the default version generated by the Momentics IDE's New BlackBerry Project wizard (more on installing your development environment later in the chapter).

Listing 1-7. applicationui.cpp

```cpp
ApplicationUI::ApplicationUI(bb::cascades::Application *app) :
        QObject(app)
{
    // prepare the localization. Code omitted
```

```
    // Create scene document from main.qml asset, the parent is set
    // to ensure the document gets destroyed properly at shut down.
    QmlDocument *qml = QmlDocument::create("asset:///main.qml").parent(this);

    // Create root object for the UI
    AbstractPane *root = qml->createRootObject<AbstractPane>();

    // Set created root object as the application scene
    app->setScene(root);
}
```

I've removed the code related to localization in order to concentrate on the scene graph creation logic. Here an instance of a bb::cascades::QmlDocument is created by reading the main.qml QML file containing the declarative UI description. This is the same QML you will design using the Cascades Builder tool.

Finally, once the application delegate has been initialized, the application's main event loop kicks in through a call to bb::cascades::Application::exec().

Parent-Child Ownership

If you take a close look at Listing 1-3, you will notice that I haven't released the objects allocated with the new operator at any point in the code. This might seem as a memory leak but it's not. Cascades widgets are organized in a parent-child relationship that also handles object ownership and memory management. In the case shown in Listing 1-3, the root parent of the entire object hierarchy is the bb::cascades::Application app object. The memory associated with the child controls will be released when this object is deleted by the runtime. I will cover memory management in detail in Chapter 3, but for the moment you can safely assume that there are no memory leaks in Listing 1-3.

Native SDK Setup

To build Cascades applications, you need to set up the native SDK using the following steps:

1. Download and install the latest version of the Momentics IDE from
    http://developer.blackberry.com/native/downloads (the page will also
    provide you with a link to the latest BlackBerry 10 simulator). You can either
    download the simulator directly or let Momentics handle the download at a
    later stage when you configure a simulator target.

2. Request a BlackBerry ID from http://blackberryid.blackberry.com. You
    will need your BlackBerry ID to create a BlackBerry ID *token*, which is
    used in turn for generating debug tokens (debug tokens are deployed on
    a BlackBerry device during development and enable your device to run
    development code). Note that you don't need a debug token for the simulator.

3. As soon as you have created your BlackBerry ID, go to
    https://www.blackberry.com/SignedKeys in order to generate a BlackBerry
    ID token. Select the first option and sign in with your BlackBerry ID
    (see Figure 1-4).

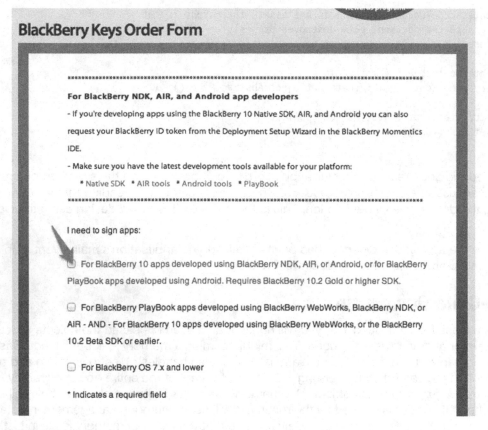

Figure 1-4. BlackBerry keys order form

4. After having signed in, you will be redirected to another page for generating your BlackBerry ID token. Enter a password for the token, accept the license agreement, and click Get Token (see Figure 1-5).

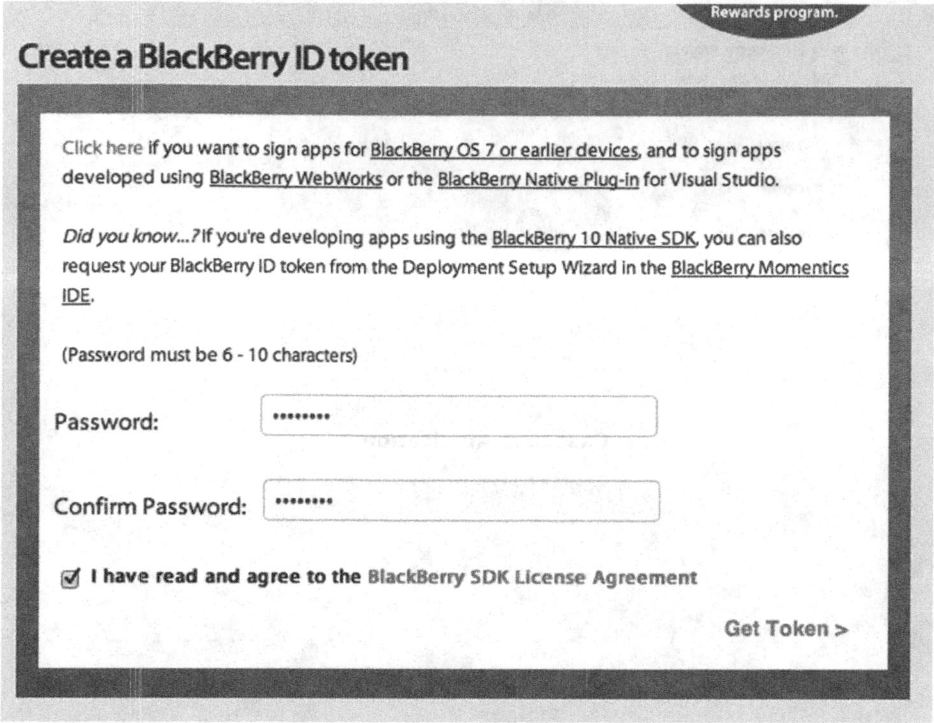

Figure 1-5. *BlackBerry ID token*

5. The token will be generated and downloaded as a file called `bbidtoken.csk`. Depending on your development platform, you will have to put the file in one of the following locations:

    a. Windows XP: `C:\Documents and Settings\Application Data\Research in Motion\`

    b. Windows Vista, Windows 7, and Windows 8: `C:\Users\AppData\Local\Research in Motion\`

    c. Mac OS X: `~/Library/Research in Motion`

Momentics IDE

To create Cascades applications, you will use the Momentics IDE, which essentially adds extra plug-ins and tools to a standard Eclipse distribution (if you've already used Eclipse in the past for Java or Android development, you will be right at home; otherwise, don't worry—this section will guide you through the IDE). This section explains how a Cascades project is organized in Momentics and reviews the most important features of the IDE that you will be using frequently. First start by creating a new Cascades project using the following steps:

1. Launch the Momentics IDE and choose File ➤ New ➤ BlackBerry Project… This will start the New BlackBerry Project wizard shown in Figure 1-6.

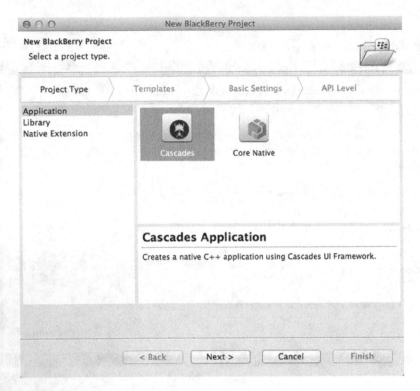

Figure 1-6. BlackBerry 10 Platform

2. Select Cascades as the project type and click Next.

3. Select Standard Empty Project from the templates page and click Next.

4. On the Basics Settings page, change your project's name from the default CascadesProject to HelloCascades, and then click Next. Don't change any of the other default settings.

5. Keep the default settings on the last wizard page API Level and click Finish.

6. If you're not in the QML Editing perspective, a prompt will appear, asking you if you want to switch to it. Click Yes.

Workspace

Momentics stores your projects in a *workspace*, which is essentially a collection of projects located in the same directory on your file system. Once you've finished creating the HelloCascades project, your workspace should look similar to Figure 1-7.

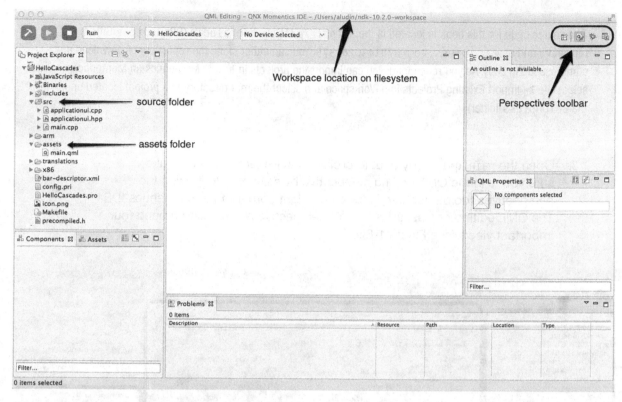

Figure 1-7. Momentics workspace

Perspectives

A *perspective* is a task-oriented collection of views and editors. When designing Cascades applications, you will mostly use the QML Editing, C/C++, and Debug perspectives. You can easily switch from one perspective to another using the perspectives toolbar or the Window ➤ Open Perspective navigation menu. Some views, such as the Project Explorer, will appear in multiple perspectives.

In the Project Explorer view, the src subfolder contains the following C++ source files:

- main.cpp: Defines the application entry point main.

- applicationui.hpp and application.cpp: You will find the wizard-generated application delegate declaration and definition.

You've already seen simplified versions of these files in the examples in Listing 1-7. For the moment, you can simply ignore them. The assets subfolder contains the main.qml defining your application's UI.

Let's spice up the default version of the app generated by the Cascades wizard.

1. Create a new folder called images under the assets folder of your project (see Figure 1-5).

2. Copy the swissalpsday.png and swissalpsnight.png from the book's resources in your project's images folder.

The source code for this book is located in the https://github.com/aludin/BB10Apress GitHub repository and at www.apress.com/9781430261575. You can either clone the repository or download a compressed Zip copy. As you read along, you can import the projects in turn in Momentics (in Momentics, select File ➤ Import Existing Projects into Workspace and select the root directory of a project located under the BB10Apress folder).

3. Open the main.qml file by double-clicking it in Project Explorer. Make sure you're in the QML editing perspective by switching to it using the perspectives toolbar located in the upper-right corner of the Momentics IDE. The QML editing or Cascades Builder perspective is organized around four important views (see Figure 1-8):

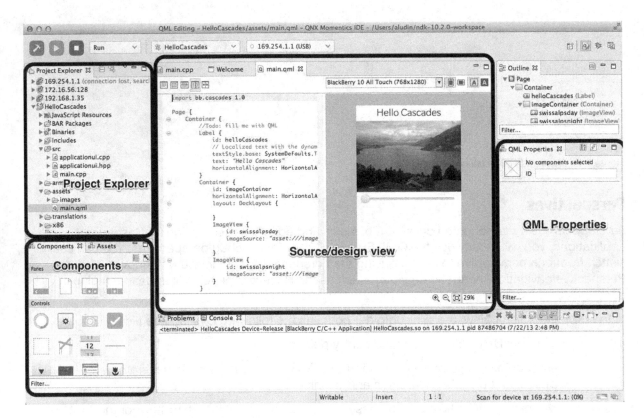

Figure 1-8. Momentics IDE, QML perspective

■   The Project Explorer shows you all the resources available in your project, including source folders, asset folders, and targets.

■   The Components view located on the lower-left section of the screen displays core Cascades controls that you can drag and drop in the Source view located at the center of your screen.

- The QML Properties view is displayed on the right side of the screen. You can use this view by selecting a QML element in the Source view.

- The main design area is located in the middle of your screen. You can switch between source only, design only, and source-design split modes.

4. In the Source view, remove the `text: qsTr(Hello World) + Retranslate.` `onLocaleOrLanguageChanged` property from the Label control.

5. Select the Label in the Source view by double-clicking it, and then update the QML Properties view by doing the following:

   - Add "helloCascades" in the id field.

   - Add "Hello Cascades" in the text field.

   - Scroll down until you reach the Horizontal Alignment property of the label and change it to `Center`.

`main.qml` should now look like Listing 1-8.

Listing 1-8. main.qml

```
import bb.cascades 1.0

Page {
    Container {
        //Todo: fill me with QML
        Label {
            id: helloCascades
            // Localized text with the dynamic translation and locale updates support
            textStyle.base: SystemDefaults.TextStyles.BigText
            text: "Hello Cascades"
            horizontalAlignment: HorizontalAlignment.Center
        }
    }
}
```

6. Drag a Container control from the Components view and drop it under the label's closing brace in the Source view.

7. Double-click the second Container control:

   - Change the id to imageContainer.

   - Change the Horizontal Alignment property to Center.

   - Change the Layout property to DockLayout.

8. Drag an ImageView control from the Components view and drop it after the DockLayout control's closing brace in the Source view.

9. Select the ImageView control:

    ■   Change the id property to "swissalpsday".

    ■   Click the Image Source button and select the `swissalpsday.png` file in the `assets/images` folder.

10. Add another ImageView control under the previous one in the Source view.

    ■   Change the id property to "swissalpsnight".

    ■   Click the Image Source button and select the `swissalpsnight.png` file in the `assets/images` folder

    ■   Set the opacity property to 0.

11. Drag a Slider control from the Components view and drop it in the Source view after `imageContainer`'s closing brace. Change the slider Horizontal Alignment to Center.

12. In the Source view, add the following code in the body of the Slider control:

```
onImmediateValueChanged: {
    swissalpsnight.opacity = immediateValue
}
```

The final version of the QML markup should look like Listing 1-9. If not, try to repeat the previous steps until you reach the same result, or simply update the QML directly in the Source view.

Listing 1-9. main.qml

```
import bb.cascades 1.0

Page {
    Container {
        //Todo: fill me with QML
        Label {
            id: helloCascades
            // Localized text with the dynamic translation and locale updates support
            textStyle.base: SystemDefaults.TextStyles.BigText
            text: "Hello Cascades"
            horizontalAlignment: HorizontalAlignment.Center
        }
        Container {
            id: imageContainer
            horizontalAlignment: HorizontalAlignment.Center
            layout: DockLayout {

            }
            ImageView {
                id: swissalpsday
                imageSource: "asset:///images/swissalpsday.png"
```

```
        }
        ImageView {
            id: swissalpsnight
            imageSource: "asset:///images/swissalpsnight.png"
        }
    }
    Slider {
        horizontalAlignment: HorizontalAlignment.Center
        onImmediateValueChanged: {
            swissalpsnight.opacity = immediateValue
        }
    }
}
}
}
```

Congratulations! You've just finished designing your first Cascades application!

Build Configurations

There are four build configurations to consider when creating Cascades application:

- Simulator debug
- Device debug
- Device profile
- Device release

A build configuration defines a set of rules and settings for building your application for a given processor or target (for example, the "Simulator debug" configuration will build your project with debug symbols enabled for a Simulator target, whereas "Device release" will build a release version of your project for a physical device with an ARM processor). At any point, you can set the active build configuration, as explained in the following paragraph.

To build the project for the simulator, select HelloCascades in Project Explorer, and then set Project ➤ Build Configurations ➤ Set Active ➤ Simulator-Debug from the Momentics main menu. Next, select Project ➤ Build Project. The build starts immediately and the build output is displayed in the Console View.

When the build finishes, a new folder called x86/o-g containing the build results will be created under your project's root folder.

Note that another extremely convenient way of selecting a build configuration is by using the BlackBerry Toolbar, as shown in Figure 1-9 (you will also see in the next section how to use the BlackBerry Toolbar to set up targets). To build the project, select Debug for the build type and then click the Hammer button.

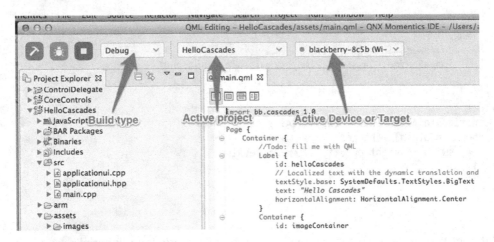

Figure 1-9. BlackBerry Toolbar

Targets

Before testing HelloCascades, you need to define a deployment target. On the BlackBerry Toolbar, select the Manage Devices… option located in the Active Device drop-down (this will display the Device Manager wizard; see Figure 1-10 and Figure 1-11).

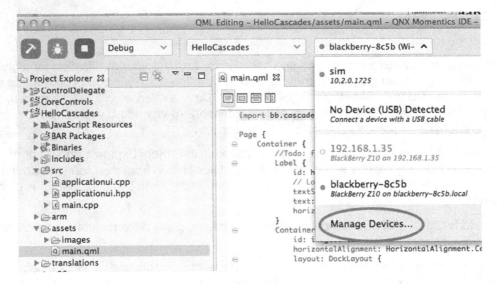

Figure 1-10. Manage devices

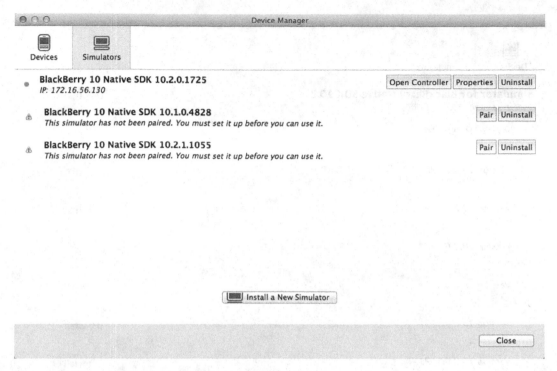

Figure 1-11. Device Manager (figure also shows installed simulators)

Simulator

To configure a new simulator using the Device Manager wizard, follow these steps:

1. Click Install a New Simulator. Choose the most recent simulator from the list and install it (see Figure 1-12). (Note that if you are developing for a specific API level, you can select a different simulator. I will tell you more about API levels at the end of this Chapter.)

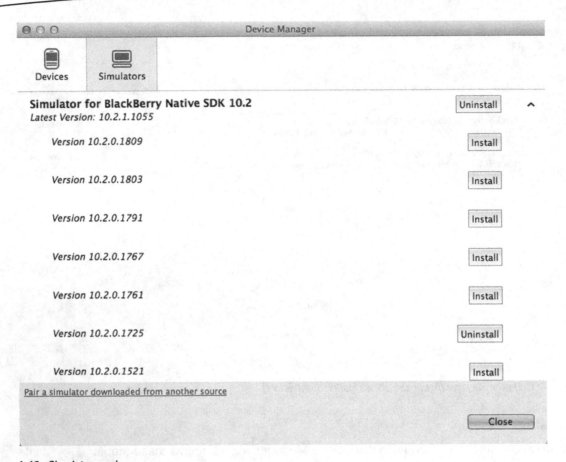

Figure 1-12. Simulator versions

2.   As soon as you have selected the simulator, the Device Manager wizard will start its download.

3.   When the download has completed, the simulator will be launched and the final step will be to pair Momentics with the simulator (see Figure 1-13).

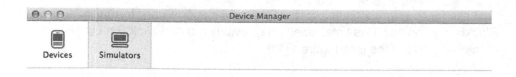

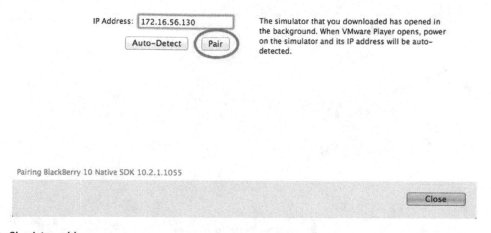

Figure 1-13. Simulator pairing

4. The simulator will now appear in the Device Manager's list of simulators and
    you can connect to it (see Figure 1-11). (Note that you might need to restart
    Momentics for the new simulator to appear in the BlackBerry Toolbar's Active
    Device list.)

You can now try to launch HelloCascades on the simulator using the green Debug button on the
BlackBerry Toolbar (if you haven't built the project previously, click the Hammer button; see Figure 1-9).

Device

Configuring a new physical device for testing purposes is accomplished by pairing the device with
Momentics. You will also have to generate a debug token, which will be saved on the device by
Momentics. Once again, the BlackBerry Toolbar streamlines the process:

1. Make sure to turn on Development Mode on your device using
    Settings ➤ Security and Privacy ➤ Development Mode.

2. Connect your device to your computer with the USB cable provided by
    BlackBerry.

3. Just like for the simulator, launch the Device Manager wizard from the BlackBerry Toolbar. This time, select the Devices tab and click Set Up New BlackBerry 10 Device (see Figure 1-14).

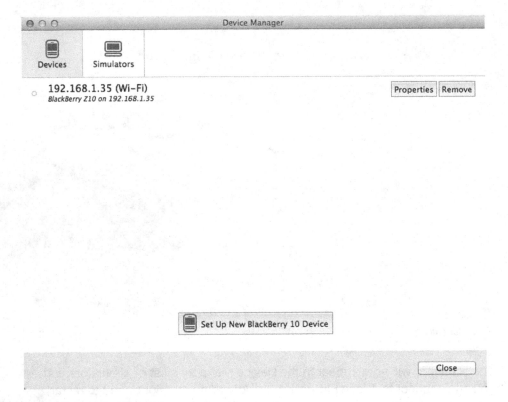

Figure 1-14. Set up new BlackBerry 10 device

4. You will have to pair your device during the first step of the configuration. To pair your device, you can either use the USB cable or a Wi-Fi connection. Select Pair Using USB and then click Next. (Note that if your device is protected by a password, enter it in the password field; see Figure 1-15.)

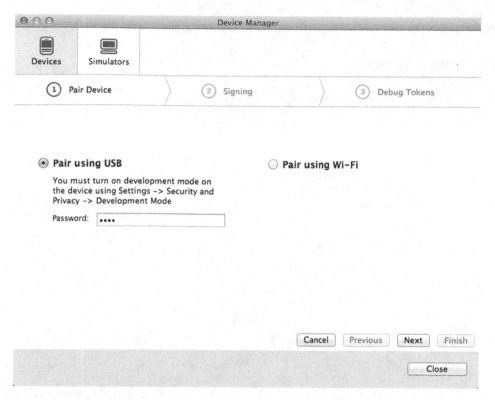

Figure 1-15. *Pair device using USB*

5. If you have already generated your BlackBerry ID token as explained in the SDK configuration section, the wizard will skip the second step; otherwise, follow the wizard's instructions.

6. On the next wizard page, select Create Debug Token and click Finish. You will finally be asked to provide the password used to create your BlackBerry ID token (see Figure 1-5) before a new debug token is deployed on your device (see Figure 1-16).

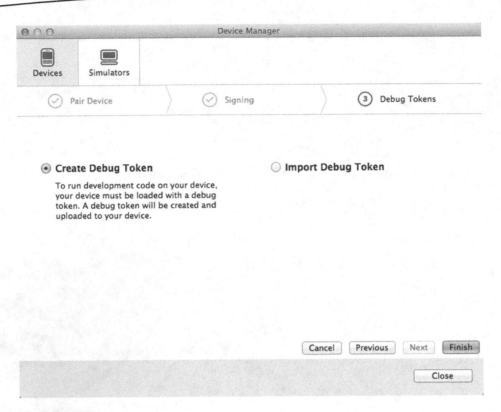

Figure 1-16. Create Debug Token

This time, you can try to launch HelloCascades on the device by selecting it as the Active Device on the BlackBerry Toolbar.

Launch Configurations

The purpose of this section is to explain what's happening behind the scenes when you use the BlackBerry Toolbar, which essentially creates launch configurations for you. A launch configuration is purely an Eclipse concept and not at all specific to Momentics; it associates a build result with a target. You must create it in order to run your application on a simulator or a device. There are two kinds of launch configurations that you can create: the Run Configuration and the Debug Configuration. In this section, I will show you how to create a Debug Configuration for the Simulator target. (The steps for creating a Run Configuration are identical to a Debug Configuration. A Run Configuration will simply launch your application on the target, whereas a Debug Configuration will launch it under Momentics' debugger control.)

1. Select Run ➤ Debug Configurations… from the Momentics main menu to display the Debug Configurations Dialog (see Figure 1-17).

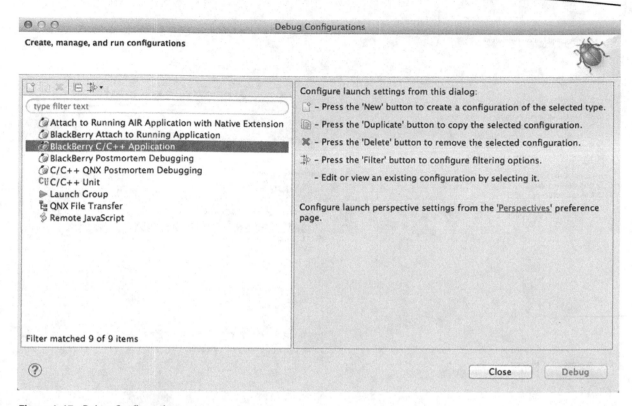

Figure 1-17. *Debug Configurations*

2. Select BlackBerry C/C++ Application from the list and press the New button in the upper-left corner of the dialog box. The settings for the new launch configuration will be displayed (see Figure 1-18).

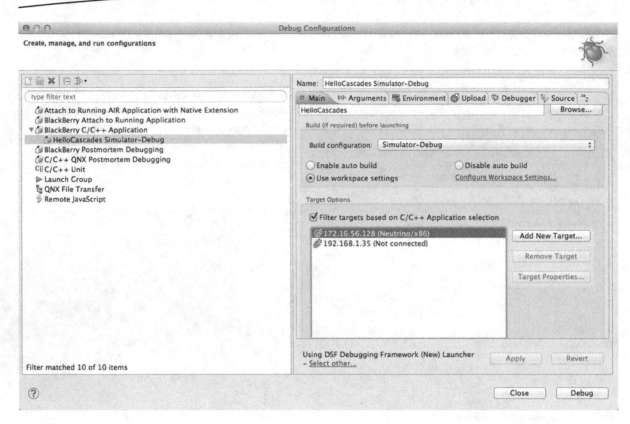

Figure 1-18. Simulator launch configuration

3. Make sure that the build configuration is Simulator Debug and the selected target is Neutrino/x86, which corresponds to the simulator. Press Apply and then press Debug (note that the simulator name might be different, depending on how you have configured it).

4. HelloCascades will now be launched in debug mode on the simulator. The Momentics IDE will also switch from the QML Editing perspective to the Debug perspective, and the program execution will stop at the beginning of the main function (see Figure 1-19) .

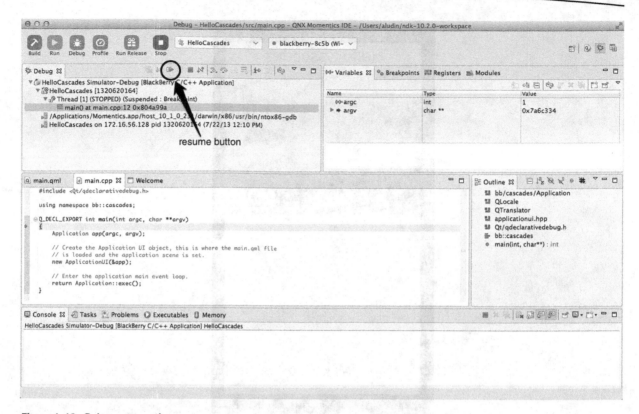

Figure 1-19. Debug perspective

5. Press the Resume button to continue the program execution. The Hello
Cascades application should now be running on the simulator (see Figure 1-20).

Figure 1-20. Hello Cascades on the simulator

6. Try moving the slider and notice how the scene changes from day to night.

To create a debug Launch configuration for the device, you basically need to repeat the same steps, with the following differences:

1. Set the active build configuration to Device-Debug.

2. Build the HelloCascades project.

3. Create a new launch configuration (see Figure 1-17 and Figure 1-18).

4. Give a name to your launch configuration (for example, HelloCascades Device-Debug).

5. Select the device target.

6. Press Debug.

Once again, launch configurations can be completely ignored by using the BlackBerry Toolbar, but it is always a good idea to have a basic understanding of their functionality.

API Levels

An API level is a set of APIs and libraries that your application builds against. It also corresponds to a version of the BlackBerry 10 OS. API levels are backward compatible. (Higher API levels include APIs from the previous releases, although some APIs could be deprecated. In other words, this is identical to the way Java manages its APIs.) If for some reason you need to compile against a specific API level, you can change the setting in Momentics using Momentics ➤ Preferences ➤ BlackBerry ➤ API Level.

QNX System Information Perspective

Before finishing this chapter, I want mention the Momentics QNX System Information perspective, which can be used for navigating your device's or simulator's filesystem (you can open the perspective by selecting Windows ➤ Open Perspective ➤ QNX System Information; see Figure 1-21). As you develop Cascades applications, you will realize that the possibility to access your device will be extremely useful for retrieving logs from the target file system or for monitoring your application's memory and CPU usage.

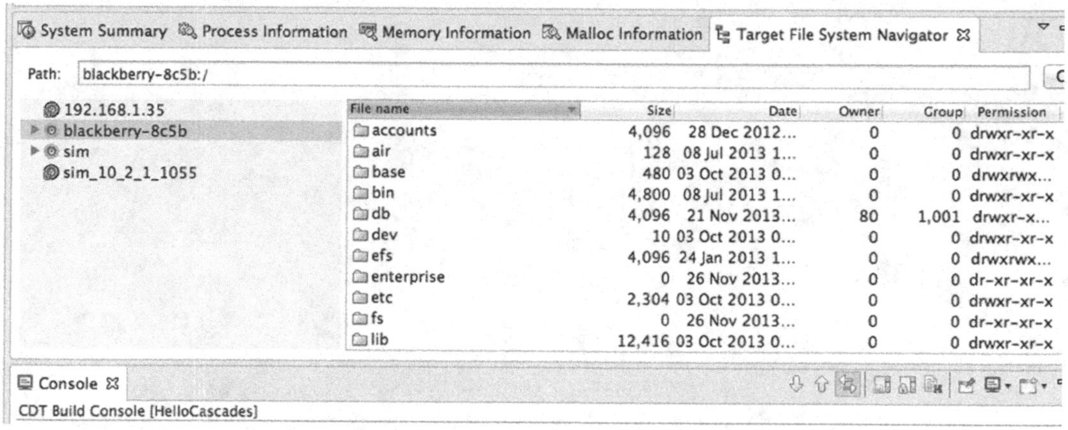

Figure 1-21. QNX System Information perspective

Summary

This chapter gave you a bird's-eye view of the BlackBerry 10 platform and the Cascades programming model. I showed you how to declaratively design your UI using QML, which is much more efficient than using imperative C++ code. QML is therefore the preferred approach—not just because the Cascades framework takes care of a lot of the plumbing work for you, but also because you can rely on the Cascades Builder tools to visually design your UI. You can nevertheless still rely on C++, something that we will further discuss in Chapter 3, for the performance-critical aspects of your application. Signals and slots were introduced as a high-level mechanism used by Cascades for event handling and I explained how to use them in your own code for reacting to events generated by UI controls.

You discovered how the Momentics IDE was organized in Perspectives, giving a task-centric view of your work. The three most important ones are the QML Editing, C/C++ Editing, and Debug perspectives. You will be using them time and again when creating Cascades applications. We also went through the configuration of a BlackBerry device for development purposes, as well as the generation of the debug tokens required for application deployment on a device. Finally, you learned how to create, build, and launch configurations for your application in order to deploy it on a simulator or device.

Chapter 2

QML and JavaScript

QML and JavaScript are the cornerstones of Cascades declarative user interface design. Both technologies, while amazingly easy to master, pack an enormous amount of punch when it comes to creating user interfaces quickly and effortlessly. QML, being a declarative language, lets you describe your user interface much like HTML would describe a web page. JavaScript then adds programmatic logic in event handlers, slots in Qt/Cascades parlance, and essentially ties your UI together with some behavior.

I've deliberately kept C++ out of the mix because I want to exclusively concentrate on QML and JavaScript for the moment, but you will see in Chapter 3 that C++ also transparently integrates with QML. As a good rule of thumb, you should always rely on C++ whenever you need to access core platform services or do some heavy lifting, such as computationally intensive tasks.

If you are a core JavaScript programmer and would like to quickly get a taste of Cascades programming, you can read this chapter, and then skip to Chapters 4 and 5 (this will provide you with the essential building blocks for creating Cascades applications using QML and JavaScript). At a later stage, you can return to Chapter 3 to understand what is happening behind the scenes in the C++ world.

QML, despite being a small language, is nevertheless extremely flexible, and by mastering the language's nuances, you will be able to build rich and enticing user interfaces. QML is also extensible: you can add to the core system your own types or "custom controls." You should consider this chapter as a review of the building blocks of QML, where you will learn how to assemble the language constructs and types to design your UI. Once you have mastered the basic elements of QML, you will be ready to apply them in full throttle in the following chapters. You will also have a firm grip on how Cascades uses the same language constructs for its own core controls (the topic of Chapters 4 and 5).

Syntax Basics

You have already seen in Chapter 1 an example of a QML document. I did not go into the details of explaining the QML syntax and I informally presented concepts such as properties, signals, and slots (or *signal handlers*, if you prefer). It is now time to dig a bit deeper and give you a description of the various QML syntactical elements.

QML Documents

A QML document is the basic building block for creating Cascades UIs. The QML syntax resembles JSON, except that you don't need to use quotes for defining attributes and that the QML language, combined with inline JavaScript, is much more expressive than JSON. Another big advantage of QML over other XML-based languages for designing UIs is that QML has been created from the ground up. The resulting language is very concise and expressive with advanced features, such as dynamic loading of components and transparent interoperability with C++ (you will see in Chapter 3 that you can very easily expose C++ objects to QML).

A QML document is a self-contained piece of QML source code that consists of the following:

- Import statements
- A root object declaration (the root object can also in turn declare children and JavaScript functions)

An example of a minimal `main.qml` document is given in Listing 2-1.

Listing 2-1. main.qml

```
import bb.cascades 1.0

Page {

}
```

As you saw in Chapter 1, the `main.qml` QML document is typically loaded during application start-up. The loading process is orchestrated behind the scenes by the QML declarative engine. When the engine encounters the `import bb.cascades 1.0` statement, it will also search through its import paths for the `bb.cascades` *namespace* and load the Cascades core controls and types registered with that namespace. By the time it reaches the `Page` object declaration, the QML engine already knows about the Page type definition, properties and signals, and is in measure to validate the Page element within the document.

Another interesting aspect of QML documents is that they provide an extension mechanism for defining new object types. In fact, a QML document implicitly defines a new type. For example, a document called `MyType.qml` will implicitly define the corresponding `MyType` QML type. The engine will also validate custom types declarations against their definition whenever you import them in other QML documents.

Import Statements

Import statements tell the declarative engine which libraries, resources, and component directories are used in a QML document. An import statement will then do any of the following:

- Load a versioned module containing QML registered types. This is how you import the Cascades core controls module in the global namespace (this is also how C++ types are exposed to QML through the `qmlRegisterType` method, as we will see in Chapter 3).

- Specify a directory relative to your application's assets directory, which contains type definitions in QML documents. As a result, all the QML object types defined in the directory will be imported in the global namespace.

- Load a JavaScript file containing functions that you want to use in your QML document.

When using an import statement, you can further use a qualifier as a local namespace identifier. This is mostly used when importing a JavaScript file or when you want to make sure that there will be no clashes with types declared in the global namespace. Listing 2-2 shows a few examples:

Listing 2-2. imports

```
import bb.cascades 1.2

import "mycontrols"
import "mycontrols/core" as MyCoreControls
import "parser.js" as Parser
```

The first line imports the versioned `bb.cascades` library (or module) in the global QML document namespace. The second line imports all the QML types defined in the `mycontrols` directory in the global QML namespace. The third example imports the QML types defined in the `mycontrols/core` directory and binds them to the local `MyCoreControls` namespace. A type `SomeType` will then be accessible using `MyCoreControls.SomeType`. This is essentially a way of avoiding clashes when importing controls with the same name from different modules (for example, if you have defined your own Label control in `mycontrols/core`, then it will not clash with the Cascades control with the same name and yours will be accessible using `MyCoreControls.Label`).

Object Declarations

In `main.qml`, a block of QML code defines a scene graph of objects to be created by the runtime engine. An object is declared in QML using the name of its object type followed by a set of curly braces. The object's attributes are then declared in the body. An object's attribute can in turn be another object declaration. In this case, you simply need to reapply the same rules for declaring that attribute. Listing 2-3 extends the example given in Listing 2-1 to show you how this works in practice.

Listing 2-3. main.qml

```
import bb.cascades 1.2

Page {
    id: mainscreen
    content: Container {
        id: maincontainer
        controls: [
            Button {
                id: first
                text: "Click me!"
            },
            Button {
                id: second
                text: "Not me!"
            }
        ]
    }
}
```

The `import bb.cascades 1.2` statement in Listing 2-3 tells the QML engine to import version 1.2 of the Cascades library, which is provided in BlackBerry API level 10.2. If you are targeting a different API level, the import statement should reflect the corresponding Cascades library version (for example, `import bb.cascades 1.0` provided in BlackBerry API level 10.0).

The Page control represents a device's screen. Its content property, the root control, is usually a cascades Container core control. A Container can in turn include child controls as well as other Containers by setting its `controls` *property* (note that the property values are specified in brackets ([ ]), indicating that this is a QML list). As you will see later in this chapter, QML objects also have a predefined id property, which is useful when you want to reference them from JavaScript code. The page declaration in Listing 2-3 is a bit verbose and you can actually make it shorter by avoiding explicitly declaring *default properties*. A property can be marked as "default" in the QML object type *definition*, and whenever you declare an object without assigning it to a property, the QML engine will try to assign it to the parent object's default property (the default property for the Page control is content and the default one for Container is controls). Listing 2-4 gives an updated version of main. qml using default properties.

Listing 2-4. main.qml with Default Properties

```
import bb.cascades 1.2

Page {
    id: mainscreen
    Container {
        id: maincontainer
        Button {
            id: first
            text: "Click me!"
        }
```

```
    Button {
            id: second
            text: "Not me!"
    }
  }
}
```

QML Basic Types

This section reviews some of the most important QML basic types that you will often use when writing Cascades applications.

- ▣ string, int, bool, real, double: The "standard" types supported by most programming languages. A real is a number with a decimal point. A double is a number stored in double precision.

- ▣ *list*: A list type contains a list of objects. In JavaScript, you can use the standard array notation to access the list elements. For example, myList[0]. You can also use the length property for iteration: for (int i=0; i < myList.length; i++) {...}.

- ▣ *enumeration*: An enumeration type consists of a set of named values. For example, the LayoutOrientation enumeration, which dictates how controls are displayed on the screen, can take values such as LayoutOrientation. TopToBottom or LayoutOrientation.LeftToRight.

- ▣ *variant*: A generic type that can contain any of the other basic types.

Creating a Custom Control

The best way to learn QML is by designing a custom type or control. This will give you the opportunity to see how the different QML syntactical elements fit together and will also give you some insight on how they are used by the Cascades framework.

If you've worked in a large corporation, chances are that you have already relied on an intranet for locating a person in your organization. This information is usually stored in LDAP directories and accessed by using a client application over an intranet. When you look up a person's entry, you will usually be presented with his surname, first name, job title, employee number, and so forth. You will also be presented with the person's picture so that you can easily recognize him when you attend one of those boring corporate meetings. Now let us imagine that your organization has decided to maintain this information using BlackBerry devices. You have been tasked to design a reusable custom control for displaying and updating a person's entry. Let us start by defining a new QML type called PersonEntry.

1. Create a new standard empty Cascades project and call it CorpDir.

2. In the assets folder of your project, where main.qml is located, create a new QML file called PersonEntry.qml using the Container template (right-click the assets folder, and then select New ➤ QML File).

3. Set the Container control's id to root (see Listing 2-5).

Listing 2-5. PersonEntry.qml

```
import bb.cascades 1.0

Container{
    id: root

}
```

4.   PersonEntry is now a new, albeit minimal, custom type recognized by the QML declarative engine. Also, because PersonEntry's root control is a Container, you can add it to a QML page. Go ahead and modify main.qml as shown in Listing 2-6.

Listing 2-6. main.qml

```
import bb.cascades 1.0

Page {
   PersonEntry {

   }
}
```

Attributes

Let's go over the attributes used in the example.

The id Attribute

As mentioned previously, object declarations can specify an id attribute that must start with a lowercase letter or an underscore. You will usually assign a value to the id attribute whenever you want to uniquely reference that object instance in your QML document.

Property Attributes

Let us now flesh out our PersonEntry type by adding some *properties* to it. We want to be able to add extra information such as a person's surname, first name, login, e-mail, and so forth. We will also eventually have to implement business rules such as "a person's login is the first letter of his first name concatenated to his surname with all letters in lowercase" and "a person's e-mail is his login followed by the at symbol and the company's domain name."

In QML, this kind of information is provided by object properties.

A *property* is an attribute that can be assigned a static value or bound to a dynamic expression provided by some JavaScript code. Properties are used to expose to the "outside world" an object's state by hiding its implementation at the same time. The syntax for defining properties is given by

```
property <propertyType> <propertyName>
```

Listing 2-7 adds the surname, first name, login, and e-mail properties to PersonEntry.qml.

Listing 2-7. PersonEntry.qml

```
import bb.cascades 1.0

Container{
    id: root
    property int employeeNumber
    property string surname
    property string firstname
    property string login
    property string email

}
```

You can in turn set the properties in `main.qml` as shown in Listing 2-8.

Listing 2-8. main.qml

```
import bb.cascades 1.0

Page {
    PersonEntry {
        employeeNumber: 100
        surname: "Smith"
        firstname: "John"
        login: "jsmith"
        email:"jsmith@mycompany.com"
    }
}
```

The `PersonEntry` control is visually not very interesting at the moment. The most glaring problem is that it's missing a screen representation. If you try to build the project and run it on the simulator, you will just get a blank screen (you will notice the same thing in the "Cascades builder" design view if you try to display `main.qml`). What we need to do is display the properties on the screen after they have been set. In order to achieve this, let's use Cascades Labels (a Label is a core control with a displayable text property on the screen). Listing 2-9 gives an updated version of `PersonEnty.qml` using Labels for displaying the object's properties.

Listing 2-9. PersonEntry.qml

```
import bb.cascades 1.0

Container{
    id: root
    property int employeeNumber
    property string surname
    property string firstname
    property string login
    property string email

    Label{
        text: "MyCompany Employee Details"
        textStyle.base: SystemDefaults.TextStyles.TitleText
        horizontalAlignment: HorizontalAlignment.Center
    }
```

```
Label{
    text: "Employee number: " + employeeNumber;
}

Label{
    text: "Last name: "+surname;
}

Label{
    text: "First name:"+ firstname;
}

Label{
    text: "Login: "+ login;
}
Label{
    text: "Email: "+ email;
}

}
```

You can now build the CorpDir project and run on it on the simulator (see Figure 2-1).

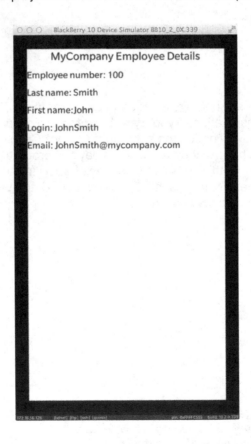

Figure 2-1. Employee view

So far so good, but we still need to be able to set the person's job title. This kind of information usually comes from a list of predefined values such as Software Engineer, Manager, Director, Consultant, Technician, and so forth. In order to achieve this, we can use a Cascades DropDown control. The control will be selectable so that if a person's entry needs to be updated, a new job title can be selected from the list. See Listing 2-10 for the updated `PersonEntry.qml` control.

Listing 2-10. PersonEntry.qml

```
import bb.cascades 1.0

Container {
    id: root
    property int employeeNumber
    property string surname
    property string firstname
    property string login
    property string email
    property string jobTitle

    Label{
        text: "Employee Details"
        textStyle.base: SystemDefaults.TextStyles.TitleText
        horizontalAlignment: HorizontalAlignment.Center
    }

    Label {
        text: "Employee number: " + employeeNumber;
    }

    Label {
        text: "Last name: " + surname;
    }

    Label {
        text: "First name:" + firstname;
    }

    Label {
        text: "Login: " + login;
    }
    Label {
        text: "Email: " + email;
    }
    DropDown {
        id: jobs
        title: "Job Title"
        enabled: true
        Option{
            text: "Unknown"
        }
```

```
        Option {
            text: "Software Engineer"
        }
        Option {
            text: "Manager"
        }

        Option {
            text: "Director"
        }

        Option {
            text: "Technician"
        }

    }

}
```

Listing 2-11 shows `main.qml` with the job property set.

Listing 2-11. main.qml

```
import bb.cascades 1.0

Page {
    PersonEntry {
        employeeNumber: 100
        surname: "Smith"
        firstname: "John"
        login: "jsmith"
        email:"jsmith@mycompany.com"
        jobTitle: "Software Engineer"
    }
}
```

At this point, we are still facing a couple of issues. For one thing, we need to be able to synch the `jobTitle` property with the corresponding option value in the DropDown control. Also, instead of setting the e-mail and login properties, they should be generated using the business rules described at the start of this section. Whenever you need to add this kind of programmatic logic, you will have to rely on JavaScript.

JavaScript

JavaScript is not an object attribute per se, but is still tightly integrated and can be used in the following scenarios:

- A JavaScript expression can be bound to QML object properties. The expression will be reevaluated every time the property is accessed in order to ensure that its value stays up-to-date. Typically, the one-liners you have seen until now for setting a Label's property are JavaScript expressions (for example, "Login" + login;). The expressions can be as complex as you wish as long as their result is a value whose type can be assigned to the corresponding property. You can even include multiple expressions between open and close braces.

- Signal handlers can contain JavaScript code that is automatically evaluated every time the corresponding QML object emits the corresponding signal.

- You can define custom JavaScript methods within a QML object (this can be considered as an object attribute).

- You can import JavaScript files as *modules* that you can use in your QML document.

- And finally, you can wire a signal directly to a JavaScript function.

You have already encountered the first two methods of using JavaScript, and by time you finish this chapter, you will have seen all the different ways of incorporating JavaScript in your QML documents.

JavaScript Host Environment

The QML engine includes a JavaScript host environment, giving you the possibility of building extremely complex applications using JavaScript/QML only. There are some restrictions, however; for example, the environment does not provide the DOM API commonly available in browsers. If you think about it, this makes complete sense since a QML application is certainly not an HTML browser app and the DOM would be irrelevant. Also, the environment is quite different from server-side technologies such as Node.js. The runtime does, however, implement the ECMAScript language specification, so this effectively means that you have a complete JavaScript programming environment at your disposal. The host environment also provides a set of global objects and functions that you can use in your QML documents:

- The Qt object, which provides string utility functions for localization, date formatting functions, and object factories for dynamically instantiating Qt types in QML.

- The qsTr() family of functions for providing translations in QML.

- The console object for generating logs and debug messages from QML (using console.log() and console.debug()).

- And finally, the XMLHttpRequest object. This basically opens the door to asynchronous HTTP requests directly from QML!

Let us now return to our PersonEntry type and spice it up with some JavaScript behavior (see Listing 2-12).

Listing 2-12. PersonEntry.qml

```
import bb.cascades 1.0
Container {
    id: root
    property int     employeeNumber
    property string surname
    property string firstname
```

```
property string jobTitle

function getLogin(){
    return root.firstname.charAt(0).toLowerCase() + root.surname.toLowerCase();
}

function getEmail(){
    return root.firstname.toLowerCase() +"."+root.surname.toLowerCase()+"@mycompany.com";
}

onCreationCompleted: {
    switch (jobTitle) {
        case "Software Engineer":
            jobs.selectedIndex = 1;
            break;
        case "Manager":
            jobs.selectedIndex = 2;
            break;
        case "Director":
            jobs.selectedIndex = 3;
            break;
        case "Technician":
            jobs.selectedIndex = 4;
            break;
        default:
            jobs.selectedIndex = 0;
            break;
    }
}

Label{
    text: "Employee Details"
    textStyle.base: SystemDefaults.TextStyles.TitleText
    horizontalAlignment: HorizontalAlignment.Center
}

Label {
    text: "Employee number: " + employeeNumber;
}

Label {
    text: "Last name: " + surname;
}

Label {
    text: "First name:" + firstname;
}

Label {
    text: "Login: " + root.getLogin();
}
```

```
    Label {
        text: "Email: " + root.getEmail();
    }

    DropDown {
        id: jobs
        title: "Job Title"
        enabled: true

        onSelectedIndexChanged: {
            console.debug("SelectedIndex was changed to " + selectedIndex);
            console.debug("Selected option is: " + selectedOption.text);
            root.jobTitle = selectedOption.text;
        }

        Option{
            text: "Unknown"
        }

        Option {
            text: "Software Engineer"
        }

        Option {
            text: "Manager"
        }

        Option {
            text: "Director"
        }

        Option {
            text: "Technician"
        }

    }

}
```

Listing 2-13 is the updated version of main.qml.

Listing 2-13. main.qml

```
import bb.cascades 1.0

Page {
    PersonEntry {
        employeeNumber: 100
        surname: "Smith"
        firstname: "John"
        jobTitle: "Jack of All Trades"
    }
}
```

You will notice that login and email are no longer settable properties. Instead, the getLogin() and getEmail() JavaScript functions are used in order to update the corresponding labels using the business rules for generating logins and e-mails respectively. Another interesting point is that in order to synchronize the jobFunction property with the DropDown control's selected index, the onCreationCompleted: signal handler is used (the body of the handler is simply a switch statement that sets the selected index). The QML engine automatically calls this handler after a QML object has been successfully constructed. This is the ideal place to set up additional validation or initialization logic (in the example given in Listing 2-13, "Jack of All Trades" is not a valid job title and the selectedIndex will be set to 0, which corresponds to the "Unknown" job title).

Signal Attributes

In Chapter 1, you declared signals in C++ using the signals: annotation. Declaring your own signals in QML is just as simple and is given by the following syntax:

```
signal <signalName>[([<type> <parameter name>[, ...]])]
```

If your signal does not take any parameters, you can safely ignore the "()" brackets in the declaration.

Here are two examples:

- signal clicked
- signal salaryChanged(double newSalary)

There are also a couple of things that the QML engine provides you "for free:"

- The QML engine generates a slot for every signal emitted by your controls. For example, the onSalaryChanged slot will be generated for the salarayChanged signal (you will see this in action in Listing 2-15).

- Property change signals. The QML engine automatically generates these signals for your custom control's properties. They are emitted whenever a control's property value is updated.

- Property change signal handlers. For a given property <Property>, they take the form on<Property>Change. This is where you can define your own business logic when the property change signals are emitted.

Let's add the salaryChanged signal to the PersonEntry control and the corresponding handler in main.qml. The signal will be emitted with an updated salary whenever a person's job title changes. The first step is to define the signal in the root QML object. You can then emit the signal using root.salaryChanged() from the DropDown control's onSelectedIndexChanged handler. The final version of the PersonEntry custom control also includes a new property for setting the person's picture. (Note that I am using a *property alias* in this case. A property alias is a reference to an existing property. In other words, the picture property is a reference to the employeeImage.imageSource property, and by setting the picture property, you are actually updating the referenced property.)

Listing 2-14. PersonEntry.qml Final

```
import bb.cascades 1.0
Container {
    id: root
    property int employeeNumber
    property string surname
    property string firstname
    property string jobTitle
    property alias  picture: employeeImage.imageSource

    signal salaryChanged(double newSalary)

    function getLogin(){
        return root.firstname.charAt(0).toLowerCase() + root.surname.toLowerCase();
    }

    function getEmail(){
        return root.firstname.toLowerCase() +"."+root.surname.toLowerCase()+"@mycompany.com";
    }

    onCreationCompleted: {
        switch (jobTitle) {
            case "Software Engineer":
                jobs.selectedIndex = 1;
                break;
            case "Manager":
                jobs.selectedIndex = 2;
                break;
            case "Director":
                jobs.selectedIndex = 3;
                break;
            case "Technician":
                jobs.selectedIndex = 4;
                break;
            default:
                jobs.selectedIndex = 0;
        }
    }

    ImageView {
        id: employeeImage
        horizontalAlignment: HorizontalAlignment.Center
    }

    Label{
        text: "Employee Details"
        textStyle.base: SystemDefaults.TextStyles.TitleText
        horizontalAlignment: HorizontalAlignment.Center
    }

    Label {
        text: "Employee number: " + employeeNumber;
```

```qml
}

Label {
    text: "Last name: " + surname;
}

Label {
    text: "First name:" + firstname;
}

Label {
    text: "Login: " + root.getLogin();
}
Label {
    text: "Email: " + root.getEmail();
}
DropDown {
    id: jobs
    title: "Job Title"
    enabled: true

    onSelectedIndexChanged: {
        console.debug("SelectedIndex was changed to " + selectedIndex);
        console.debug("Selected option is: "+selectedOption.text);
        root.jobTitle = selectedOption.text;
        switch (selectedOption.text){
            case "Software Engineer":
                root.salaryChanged(90000);
                break;
            case "Manager":
                root.salaryChanged(100000);
                break;
            case "Director":
                root.salaryChanged(150000);
                break;
            case "Technician":
                // yes technicians should be more rewarded than Managers
                // as they are more useful.
                root.salaryChanged(160000);
                break;
            default:
                root.salaryChanged(0.0);
        }
    }

    Option{
        text: "Unknown"
    }

    Option {
        text: "Software Engineer"
    }
```

```
        Option {
            text: "Manager"
        }

        Option {
            text: "Director"
        }

        Option {
            text: "Technician"
        }

    }

}
```

And Listing 2-15 gives the final version of main.qml. You will notice that now the root control is no longer a PersonEntry object but a Container. The reason for this is because we have also added a Label that will display a person's updated salary whenever the salaryChanged signal is emitted.

Listing 2-15. main.qml Final

```
import bb.cascades 1.0

Page {
    Container{
        PersonEntry {
            employeeNumber: 100
            surname: "Smith"
            firstname: "John"
            jobTitle: "Jack of All Trades"
            picture: "asset:///johnsmith.png"

            onSalaryChanged: {
                salaryLabel.text = "Salary: "+newSalary;
            }
        }
        Label{
            id: salaryLabel

        } // Label
    } // Container
} // Page
```

You can now finally build the CorpDir application and run it on the simulator (see Figure 2-2).

Figure 2-2. Employee view

XMLHttpRequest Example

In this section, I want to show you how easily you can use the XMLHttpRequest object from QML. The sample code provided here is a quick and dirty REST client for the Weather Underground weather forecast service (www.wunderground.com/weather/api/d/docs). To call the REST service, you will need to register and obtain a free development key. Listing 2-16 shows you how to use the service to get a weather forecast for a given city. The application is quite basic at the moment and simply "dumps" the result of the query in a TextArea (see Figure 2-3; you will see in Chapter 7 how to enhance the app by building a full-fledged weather service client). The most important point to keep in mind is that the call to the weather service is completely *asynchronous* and will not block the UI thread.

Listing 2-16. main.qml

```
import bb.cascades 1.0

Page {
    id: root
    function getWeather(apikey, city, state) {
        var getString = "http://api.wunderground.com/api/"+apikey+"/conditions/q/";
        if("".valueOf() != state.valueOf()){
            getString = getString+state;
        }
```

```
            getString = getString + "/"+city+".json";
            var request = new XMLHttpRequest();
            request.onreadystatechange = function() {
                // Need to wait for the DONE state or you'll get errors
                if (request.readyState === XMLHttpRequest.DONE) {
                    if (request.status === 200) {
                        result.text = request.responseText
                    } else {
                        // This is very handy for finding out why your web service won't talk to you
                        console.debug("Status: " + request.status + ", Status Text: " + request.
statusText);
                    }
                }
            }
            request.open("GET", getString, true); // only async supported
            request.send()
        }
    Container {
        Container {
            layout: StackLayout {
                orientation: LayoutOrientation.LeftToRight
            }
            TextField {
                id: locationField
                layoutProperties: StackLayoutProperties {
                    spaceQuota: 2
                }
            }
            Button {
                text: "Get City!"
                layoutProperties: StackLayoutProperties {
                    spaceQuota: 1
                }
                onClicked: {
                    var values = locationField.text.split(",")
                    if(values.length > 1){
                        root.getWeather("75cfd4c741088bfd", values[0], values[1]);
                    }
                    else
                    root.getWeather("75cfd4c741088bfd", values[0],"");
                }
                verticalAlignment: VerticalAlignment.Center
            }

        }
        ScrollView {
            TextArea {
                id: result

            }
        }
    }
}
```

Figure 2-3. Weather service

When the user touches the Get City! button, its `onClicked` slot calls the `getWeather()` JavaScript function defined at the Page level. The function in turn uses the standard `XMLHttpRequest` object to asynchronously call the weather service. An anonymous callback function is also provided in order to handle the `HTTP` response and update the `TextArea` (note that this the standard `AJAX` way of handling requests and responses).

SCalc, the Small Calculator

Before wrapping up this chapter, I want to illustrate how QML and JavaScript can be used for developing a slightly more complex application than the ones shown up to this point. This will also give me the opportunity to explain your application's project structure, something that I skimmed over in Chapter 1 (if you want to give the application a try right away, you can download it from BlackBerry World).

> To import the SCalc project in Momentics, you can clone the `https://github.com/aludin/BB10Apress` repository.

SCalc is a simple calculator app written entirely in JavaScript and QML (see Figure 2-4). The application's UI is built in QML and the application logic is handled in JavaScript using Matthew Crumley's JavaScript expression engine (`https://github.com/silentmatt/js-expression-eval`). The engine is packaged as a single JavaScript file that I have dropped in the project's `assets` folder (`parser.js`, located at the same level as `main.qml`).

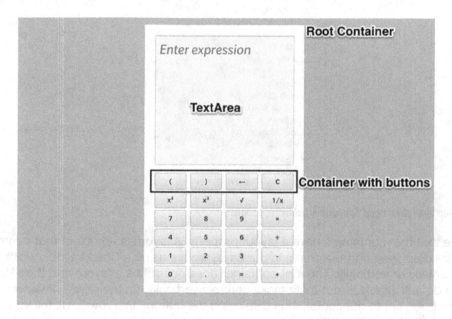

Figure 2-4. SCalc

As illustrated in Figure 2-4, a root Container contains a TextArea and six child containers, which in turn hold Button controls. Finally, the parent of the root Container is a Page control that represents the UI screen. Another way of understanding the control hierarchy is by looking at the outline view in the QML perspective in Momentics (see Figure 2-5).

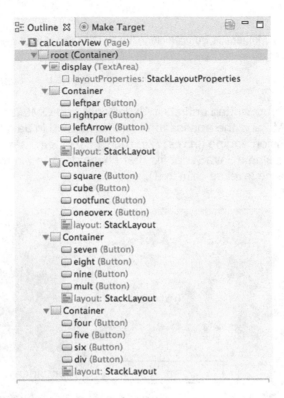

Figure 2-5. Outline view (four child Containers below root shown)

You will notice that the containers have a layout property. A layout is an object that controls the way UI elements are displayed on the screen. In our case, we are using a StackLayout, which stacks controls horizontally or vertically. The root container does not define a layout and therefore Cascades will assign it a default StackLayout that stacks controls vertically. (In the child containers, the layout orientation has been set to horizontal, thus displaying the buttons in a row. I will tell you more about layout objects in Chapter 4.) Listing 2-17 is an outline of main.qml.

Listing 2-17. main.qml

```
import bb.cascades 1.2
import "parser.js" as JSParser
Page {
    id: calculatorView
    // root containter goes here
}
```

The second import statement imports the JavaScript expression engine as a module and assigns it to the JSParser identifier (because the file is located in the same folder as main.qml, you don't need to provide a path to the file). Now that the library has been imported, you will be able to use it in your QML document (the expression engine provides a Parser object that you can call using JSParser.Parser.evaluate(expression, "")).

As mentioned previously, the root container contains a TextArea and six child Containers (see Listing 2-18).

Listing 2-18. root Container

```
Container {
       id: root
       // padding properties omitted.
        layout: StackLayout {
           orientation: LayoutOrientation.TopToBottom
       }
        // background properties and attached object omitted.
       TextArea {
           bottomMargin: 40
           id: display
           hintText: "Enter expression"
           textStyle {
               base: SystemDefaults.TextStyles.BigText
               color: Color.DarkBlue
           }
           layoutProperties: StackLayoutProperties {
               spaceQuota: 2
           }
       }
       Container{ // 1st row of Buttons, see Figure 2-4
               Button{id: lefpar ...}
               Button{id: rightpar ...}
               Button{id: leftArrow ...}
               Button{id: clear ...}
}
       ... // 5 more Containers
}
```

The application logic is implemented by handling the clicked signal emitted by the Buttons and by updating the TextView with the current expression. For example, Listing 2-19 shows the implementation for the clicked signal when Button "7" is touched by the user.

Listing 2-19. Button "7"

```
Button {
    id: seven
    text: "7"
    onClicked: {
        display.text = display.text + 7;
    }
}
```

Finally, the JavaScript expression library's Parser.evaluate() method is called when the user touches the "=" button (the TextView is also updated with the result of the evaluation).

Listing 2-20. Button "="

```
Button {
    id: equal
    text: "="
    onClicked: {
```

```
        display.text = JSParser.Parser.evaluate(display.text, "");
    }
}
```

The current input handling logic is quite crude and you can easily enter invalid expressions. As an exercise, you can try to make it more robust.

Project Structure

Figure 2-6 illustrates SCalc's project structure in the Momentics Project Explorer view.

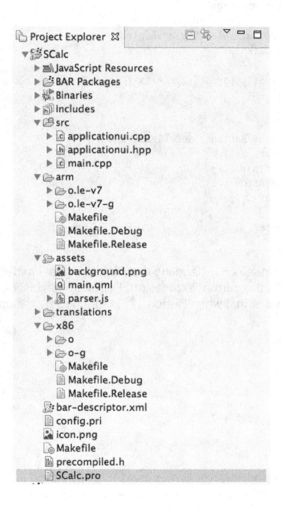

Figure 2-6. Project Explorer

You will find the same structure in all of your applications and you should therefore take some time to get familiar with it. Here is a quick overview of the most important project elements:

- src: You will find the C++ source code of your project in this folder.

- assets: This folder contains your QML documents. You can also create subfolders and include additional assets such as images and sound files. You will generally load at runtime the assets located in this folder.

- x86, arm: Folders used for the build results of your application for the simulator and device respectively. The folders include subfolders, depending on the build type (debug or release). For example, a debug build for the simulator will be located under \x86\o-g (and the corresponding Device folder is \arm\o.le-v7-g).

- SCalc.pro: This is your project file and includes project settings. You can add dependencies such as libraries in this file (you will see how this works in Chapter 3).

- bar-descriptor.xml: This file defines important configuration settings for your application. In particular, it also defines your application's permissions. You will have to update this file for certain projects in following chapters. The easiest way to proceed is to work with the General and Permissions tabs when the file is open in Momentics (see Figure 2-7).

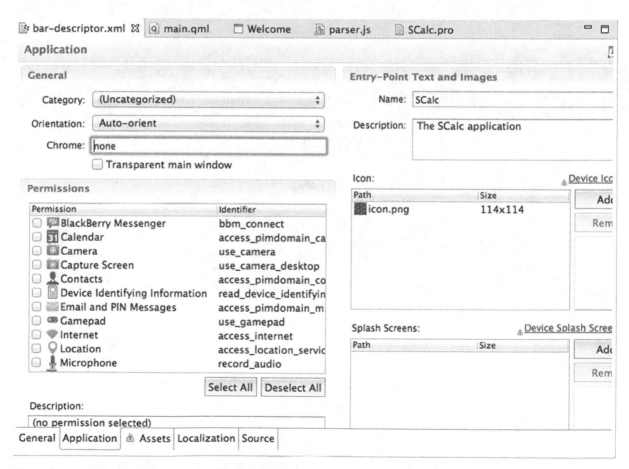

Figure 2-7. bar-descriptor.xml view

- `icon.png`: Your application's icon.

Summary

This chapter dissected the core elements of the QML language. You discovered how the different elements of QML fit together by designing your own custom control. You also saw that QML, despite its simplicity, is an extremely powerful programming environment. Most importantly, this chapter gave you some insight on how Cascades uses those same QML constructs, and hopefully unveiled some of the magic involved in Cascades programming.

JavaScript is the glue giving you the tools for adding some programmatic logic to your controls. The environment provided by QML runtime is ECMAScript compliant. This means that at this point you can build full-fledged Cascades applications using QML and JavaScript.

Chapter 3

C++, Qt, and Cascades

I have avoided discussing C++ until now and given you mostly a "QML/JavaScript" perspective of Cascades programming. My goal was to show you how easily you could quickly build applications using QML and JavaScript only, without even writing a single line of C++ code. By now you know enough about the Cascades programming model and it is time to look at what's happening behind the scenes in the C++ world.

QML and JavaScript provide a quick and efficient way of declaratively designing your application's UI and wiring some behavior for event handling. You will, however, reach a point where you will need to do some heavy lifting and implement core business logic in C++. The reasons for this can be manifold but they will almost certainly revolve around the following:

- Your application's business logic is complex and you don't want it scattered in QML documents.

- You need to achieve maximum performance, and JavaScript will simply not scale as well as C++ (for example, it would make no sense writing a physics engine in JavaScript).

- You need tight platform integration provided by Qt modules or BPS.

- You need to reuse third-party libraries written in C/C++.

C++ has the reputation of being a large and complex language, but the purpose of this chapter is to teach just enough so that you can efficiently build Cascades applications. I am actually going to make the bold assertion that all that you need to build Cascades applications is entirely covered in this chapter. The only prerequisite to understanding the material presented here is that you already have some OOP knowledge by having written applications in Java or Objective-C, and I will show you the equivalent C++/Qt way.

Note that the material will also strongly focus on the Qt C++ language extensions for writing applications. Cascades is heavily based on the Qt framework and therefore it is important that you have a good understanding of the underlying Qt framework. For example, I will tend to favor the Qt types, memory management, and container classes even if the standard C++ library provides equivalent functionality. (Another important reason is that the Qt containers are tightly integrated with QML and this will save us the pain of writing glue code to access standard C++ containers from QML.)

After having read this chapter, you will have a C++ perspective of Cascades programming and a good understanding of

- The Qt object model.

- Qt memory management techniques.

- The Qt container classes that you can access from QML.

- The different mechanisms for exposing C++ classes to QML.

C++ OOP 101

C++ has naturally evolved a great deal over the years and its current incarnation includes all the features required for modern software design. For example, memory management has been greatly simplified with smart pointers, and frameworks such as Qt drastically improve a programmer's productivity. The purpose of this section is to get you up and running with the OOP aspects of C++—namely support for classes, member functions, inheritance and polymorphism—so that you can quickly build Cascades applications without spending a couple of hours on a C++ tutorial.

C++ Class

Just like Java and Objective-C, C++ is a class-based language. A class serves as an abstraction for encapsulating functions and data (or in other words, a class is used to create new types in C++). Instances of the class are the objects that you pass around in your application and act upon by calling their methods. Usually, the class is separated between a header file providing the class definition, which includes the class's public interface, and an implementation file, which provides member function definitions (for example, in Cascades the application delegate definition is given by applicationui.hpp, and its implementation is given by applicationui.cpp). To illustrate C++ classes, let's consider the case of a financial instrument's pricing library. Pricing libraries are usually used by investment banks on Wall Street in order to price financial products such as options, bonds, and other kinds of derivative instruments (the pricing problem can actually become quite complex and is done by "rocket scientists" called *quants*). Quite naturally, the very first abstraction provided by a pricing library is the Instrument class, which will be the root abstraction for managing all financial products (see Listing 3-1).

Listing 3-1. Instrument.h

```
#ifndef INSTRUMENT_H_
#define INSTRUMENT_H_
#include <QObject>

class Instrument : public QObject {
    Q_OBJECT
    Q_PROPERTY(QString symbol READ symbol WRITE setSymbol NOTIFY symbolChanged)
    Q_PROPERTY(double price READ price NOTIFY priceChanged)
```

```
public:
    Instrument(QObject* parent = 0);
    virtual ~Instrument();

    QString symbol() const;
    void setSymbol(const QString& symbol);

    virtual double price() const=0;
signals:
    void symbolChanged();
    void priceChanged();

private:
    QString m_symbol;
};
```

> **Note**   C++, unlike Java, does not define or mandate a base class from which all classes must derive.
> However, in the following examples, I will be using QObject as a base class in order to illustrate its properties
> and emphasize its central role in Cascades programming.

Listing 3-1 is called a class definition. As mentioned previously, a class definition is provided in a
header file (ending with an .h or .hpp extension) that declares the class's member functions and
variables, as well as their visibility (private, protected, or public). Note that the Instrument class
declares a *constructor* and a *destructor*. The Instrument(QObject* parent=0) constructor is used to
initialize a class instance and the ~Instrument() destructor is where you release resources owned
by the object (such as dynamically allocated objects managed by the class instance). (Note that
unlike Java, where the garbage collector handles memory management, in C++ you are in charge of
memory management, and you must make sure that dynamically allocated resources are released
when no longer needed.)

Besides the constructor and destructor, the class's public interface also includes:

- The virtual double Instrument::price()=0 function, which is used to return
  the instrument's fair price. I will tell you more about this strange looking function
  in a moment.

- The symbol property, which is defined using the Q_PROPERTY macro. I will tell
  you more about the macro shortly. For the moment, simply keep in mind that it
  makes the corresponding property accessible from QML.

- The symbolChanged() signal, which is emitted when the corresponding symbol
  property is updated.

- The priceChanged() signal, which is emitted when the instrument's price
  changes.

Finally, the Instrument class inherits from QObject, which is part of the Qt framework (also note the presence of the Q_OBJECT macro, which tells the MOC compiler to generate additional code in order to support the signals and slots mechanism; see Chapter 1).

The Instrument class member function definition is given in a separate file, usually ending with the .cpp extension (see Listing 3-2).

Listing 3-2. Instrument.cpp

```cpp
#include "Instrument.h"

Instrument::Instrument(QObject* parent) : QObject(parent), m_symbol(""){

}

Instrument::~Instrument() {
    // TODO Auto-generated destructor stub
}

void Instrument::setSymbol(const QString& symbol){
    if(m_symbol == symbol) return;
    m_symbol = symbol;
    emit symbolChanged();
}

QString Instrument::symbol() const{
    return m_symbol;
}
```

We first include the Instrument.h header file and then proceed by defining the member functions. The constructor first calls the QObject(QObject* parent) base class constructor and then initializes the class members using a *member initialization list* (in this case, there is only one class member, m_symbol, to initialize). As you can see, the file also defines the accessor functions for the m_symbol member variable. Finally, note how the symbolChanged() signal is emitted when m_symbol is updated. As you will see later in this chapter, the signal is used by the QML declarative engine to update properties bound to Instrument's symbol property.

We can now try to use the newly created instrument class by creating a simple test application with a main function, which is the entry point of all C/C++ applications (see Listing 3-3).

Listing 3-3. main.cpp

```cpp
int main()
{
    Instrument instrument;
}
```

If you try to compile the previous code, the compiler will complain with the following message:

```
../src/main.cpp:15:16: error: cannot declare variable 'instrument' to be of abstract type
'Instrument'
../src/Instrument.h:13:7: note: because the following virtual functions are pure within
'Instrument':
../src/Instrument.h:21:17: note: virtual double Instrument::price()
```

The compiler essentially tells you that it cannot instantiate the Instrument class because it contains a *pure virtual function*. You must be wondering what kind of a beast this is! Well, it is just a fancy way of saying that the method is abstract and that we have not provided an implementation. Also, marking a member function virtual tells the C++ compiler that a child class can override it. This is very important. By default, methods are statically resolved in C++. If you intend *polymorphic behavior*, then you need to flag the function as virtual. By appending the =0 to the method declaration, you are telling the compiler that the method is abstract and you are not providing a default implementation. In effect, the class also becomes an abstract base class.

Note   Listing 3-3 creates the Instrument instance on the stack as an automatic variable (in other words, the instrument will be automatically deleted as soon it runs out of scope). In C++ you can also dynamically allocate an object using the new operator. In that case, you will have to reclaim the memory when the object is no longer needed using the delete operator.

C++ Inheritance

So far so good; the Instrument class provides us with a convenient abstraction for managing financial instruments. However, for the pricing library to be useful, you need to extend it by building a hierarchy of concrete types. In finance you can literally synthesize any instrument with a desired payoff (that's what quants do). However, the basic building blocks are bonds, stocks, and money accounts. You can use these instruments to create more or less complex derivatives such as options and swaps (that's why they are called derivatives, because their price derives from an underlying instrument). Let's extend the hierarchy to include stocks (see Listing 3-4).

Listing 3-4. Stock.h

```
#define STOCK_H_
#include "Instrument.h"

class Stock: public Instrument {
Q_OBJECT
Q_PROPERTY(double spot READ spot WRITE setSpot NOTIFY spotChanged)
public:
    Stock(QObject* parent = 0);
    virtual ~Stock();

    double spot();
    void setSpot(double spot);

    double price() const;
```

```
signals:
    void spotChanged();
private:
    double m_spot;
};

#endif /* STOCK_H_ */
```

As illustrated in the previous code, Stock inherits from the Instrument class and adds a new spot property, which corresponds to the stock's market price. The member function definitions are given by Stock.cpp (see Listing 3-5).

Listing 3-5. Stock.cpp

```
#include "Stock.h"

Stock::Stock(QObject* parent) : Instrument(parent), m_spot(0) {

}

Stock::~Stock() {
    // for illustration purposes only. Show that the destructor is called
    std::cout << "~Stock()" << std::endl;
}

double Stock::price() const{
    return spot();
}

double Stock::spot() const{
    return m_spot;
}

void Stock::setSpot(double spot){
    if(m_spot == spot) return;
    m_spot = spot;
    emit spotChanged();
}
```

The Stock constructor calls the Instrument base class constructor in order to initialize the base class object correctly (and once again, a constructor initialization list is used in order to initialize the Stock object's member variables). The Stock.cpp file also includes a concrete implementation of the Instrument::price() method, which simply returns the current spot or market price of the stock.

An option is a slightly more complex beast. A vanilla equity option gives you the right, but not the obligation, to buy (in the case of a call option) or sell (in the case of a put option) the underlying stock for a specific agreed-upon price sometime in the future. The parameters defining the current price of the option (i.e., the right to buy or sell the underlying stock in the future according to the terms of the option contract) are given by the following:

- The current spot price of the stock.

- The future agreed-upon *strike* price of the stock.

- The stock's *volatility*, which is a measure of its riskiness.

■ The time to *maturity* of the contract expressed in years.

■ The *risk-free rate*, which usually represents the interest rate on a three month US Treasury bill.

Using the previous input parameters, a neat little thing called the Black-Scholes formula gives you the option's fair value. Putting all of this together, our Option class definition is given in Listing 3-6.

Listing 3-6. Option.h

```
#ifndef OPTION_H_
#define OPTION_H_
#include "Instrument.h"

class Option: public Instrument {
    Q_OBJECT
    Q_ENUMS(OptionType)

    Q_PROPERTY(OptionType type READ optionType WRITE setOptionType NOTIFY typeChanged)
    Q_PROPERTY(double riskfreeRate READ riskfreeRate WRITE setRiskfreeRate NOTIFY
                riskfreeRateChanged)
    Q_PROPERTY(double spot READ spot WRITE setSpot NOTIFY spotChanged)
    Q_PROPERTY(double strike READ strike WRITE setStrike NOTIFY strikeChanged)
    Q_PROPERTY(double maturity READ timeToMaturity WRITE setTimeToMaturity
                NOTIFY maturityChanged)
    Q_PROPERTY(double volatility READ volatility WRITE setVolatility NOTIFY volatilityChanged)

public:
    enum OptionType {
        CALL, PUT
    };

    Option(QObject* parent = 0);
    virtual ~Option();

    double price() const;

    double riskfreeRate() const;
    void setRiskfreeRate(double riskfreeRate);

    double spot() const;
    void setSpot(double spot);

    double strike() const;
    void setStrike(double strike);
    double timeToMaturity() const;
    void setTimeToMaturity(double timeToMaturity);

    OptionType optionType() const;
    void setOptionType(OptionType type);
```

```
    double volatility() const;
    void setVolatility(double volatility);

signals:
    void priceChanged();
    void typeChanged();
    void spotChanged();
    void volatilityChanged();
    void strikeChanged();
    void riskfreeRateChanged();
    void maturityChanged();

private:
    OptionType m_type;
    double m_strike;
    double m_spot;
    double m_volatility;
    double m_riskfreeRate;
    double m_timeToMaturity;
};

#endif /* OPTION_H_ */
```

Here again, the Option class adds its own set of properties and notification signals. An option type is also defined using the OptionType enumeration, which is used to differentiate between put and call options (depending on the option type, the Black-Scholes price is different). Also note how the Q_ENUMS macro is used to export the enumeration to QML. Here again, the virtual price method is overridden to provide the option's Black-Scholes fair value (see Listing 3-7). You can simply skim over the implementation, which is only provided to illustrate how the different option parameters are used in the pricing. (Note that the CND function, which is an implementation of the cumulative distribution function, is not shown here.)

Listing 3-7. Option::price()

```
double Option::price() const {
    double d1, d2;

    d1 = (log(m_spot / m_strike)
                + (m_riskfreeRate + m_volatility * m_volatility / 2)
                * m_timeToMaturity)
                / (m_volatility * sqrt(m_timeToMaturity));
    d2 = d1 - m_volatility * sqrt(m_timeToMaturity);

    switch (m_type) {
    case CALL:
        return m_spot * CND(d1)
                - m_strike * exp(-m_riskfreeRate * m_timeToMaturity) * CND(d2);
    case PUT:
        return m_strike * exp(-m_riskfreeRate * m_timeToMaturity) * CND(-d2)
                - m_spot * CND(-d1);
```

```
        default:
            //
            return 0;
    }
}
```

The methods used for updating the option's properties are straightforward. For example, Listing 3-8 illustrates how the spot property is updated:

Listing 3-8. Spot Property

```
double Option::spot() const {
    return m_spot;
}

void Option::setSpot(double spot) {
    if(m_spot == spot) return;
    m_spot = spot;
    emit spotChanged();
    emit priceChanged();
}
```

Also note that when a property is updated, besides emitting the corresponding property change signal, the priceChanged() signal is also emitted. This will play an important role when you will use the Option instance in QML bindings.

At this point, we have defined three abstractions in our class hierarchy: Instrument, Stock, and Option. Let's try to use them in practice. A small test program is given in Listing 3-9.

Listing 3-9. main.cpp

```
#include <iostream>
#include "Stock.h"
#include "Option.h"

int main()
{

    Stock stock;
    stock.setSymbol("orcl");
    stock.setSpot(50);

    Option option;

    option.setSymbol("myOption");
    option.setSpot(50);
    option.setStrike(55);
    option.setMaturity(0.5);
    option.setVolatility(0.2);
    option.setRiskfreeRate(.05);
```

```
std::cout << "Stock price is: "  << stock.price() << std::endl;
std::cout << "Option price is: " << option.price() << std::endl;
```

```
}
```

To display the program's output, I am using the standard C++ library by including the `iostream` header (`std::cout` is the standard output stream, which displays characters in a text console by default). The program's output is given as follows:

```
Stock price is: 50
Option price is: 1.45324
```

Polymorphism

We defined the `Stock` and `Option` class, but for our class library to be truly useful, we need to be able to manipulate them using the common base class `Instrument` interface. In practice, we care about being able to price instruments no matter the concrete type; whether it is a `Stock` or an `Option`. In other words, we want to be able to manipulate financial instruments using the base class `Instrument` abstraction. If the instrument is a `Stock`, it will return its market spot price, and if it's an `Option`, it will return the Black-Scholes price. This is exactly what we imply by polymorphism: the ability to implement the pricing logic differently depending on the underlying concrete type and being able to call at runtime the correct implementation using the `Instrument` base class abstraction. In C++, runtime polymorphic behavior is achieved using two mechanisms: references and pointers.

Using References

A reference is essentially an alias to an existing variable. Listing 3-10 shows you how to use a reference when pricing an option.

Listing 3-10. Using References

```
Option option;
option.setOptionType(Option::CALL);
option.setSymbol("myOption");
option.setSpot(50);
option.setStrike(55);
option.setTimeToMaturity(0.5);
option.setRiskfreeRate(.05);
option.setVolatility(.2);

Instrument& instr = option;

std::cout << "Instrument symbol is: " << instr.symbol().toStdString() << std::endl;
std::cout << "Instrument price is: " << instr.price() << std::endl;
```

As shown in Listing 3-10, `instr` is defined as a reference to an `Instrument` by adding an ampersand (&) after the type declaration (note that because a reference is an alias to an existing object, the definition must also include the referenced `Option` object). Finally, the `price()` method is called polymorphically using the Instrument base class interface (remember that price is a pure virtual function in Instrument's class definition). The program's output is given as follows:

```
Instrument symbol is: myOption
Instrument price is: 1.45324
```

Another way of using references is by taking them as function parameters. For example, Listing 3-11 defines a showInstrumentPrice() function taking a reference to an Instrument (note the & indicating a pass-by-reference of the instrument parameter).

Listing 3-11. showInstrumentPrice

```cpp
void showInstrumentPrice(const Instrument& instrument) {
    std::cout << "Instrument symbol is: " << instrument.symbol().toStdString() <<
                 " Instrument price is: " << instrument.price() << std::endl;
}

int main(){
    Stock stock;
    stock.setSymbol("myStock");
    stock.setSpot(50);

    Option option;
    option.setOptionType(Option::CALL);
    option.setSymbol("myOption");
    option.setSpot(50);
    option.setStrike(55);
    option.setTimeToMaturity(0.5);
    option.setRiskfreeRate(.05);
    option.setVolatility(.2);

    showInstrumentPrice(stock);
    showInstrumentPrice(option);
}
```

The showInstrumentPrice function takes a reference to an Instrument object. It does not know if the actual object is a Stock or an Option, but it knows that it can call the base class Instrument::price() method in order to get the instrument's price. Because Instrument::price() has been declared as virtual, the C++ runtime determines the correct price method to call using virtual function dispatch. The output of the application is given as follows:

```
Instrument symbol is: myStock, Instrument price is: 50
Instrument symbol is: myOption, Instrument price is: 1.45324
```

In other words, the Instrument::price() call is polymorphic and returns a different price depending on whether you pass a Stock or an Option. This only works because you are passing a reference to the showInstrumentPrice() method. If you try to change the showInstrumentPrice signature by removing the reference operator to showInstrumentPrice(Instrument instrument), the C++ compiler will try to pass the Instrument parameter *by value*. The value semantics imply that a *copy* of the variable is passed to the function. The copy operation is done by calling a *copy constructor*, which is a special class constructor used for making a copy of a class instance. If you don't specify a copy constructor, the C++ compiler will generate one implicitly for you, which will do a member-wise copy of the source object.

There are several reasons why this will not work in the previous case:

- As explained, the compiler will try to generate a copy constructor. However, because Instrument is an abstract class, the C++ compiler cannot generate a copy.

- Let's suppose that Instrument did provide a default implementation for the price() method, always returning 0. Something more serious, called *object slicing*, would occur: only the base Instrument part of the object, whether it is a Stock or an Option, would be copied and passed to the showInstrumentPrice() function (the overridden price method would therefore be "sliced-off" and you would lose all polymorphic behavior. In other words, the function call would always return 0, no matter the concrete type passed to the function).

- There is a third reason why you can't pass an Instrument instance by value: Instrument's base class is QObject, which does not support value semantics. (I will tell you more about value semantics when we discuss QObject identities. For the moment, suffice to say that because a QObject's copy constructor is private, you cannot use it in order to make a copy of the class instance.)

Using Pointers

Now let's look at how polymorphism can be achieved using pointers. Listing 3-12 gives you an updated version of the test application using pointers (in other words, the objects are dynamically allocated on the heap).

Listing 3-12. Pointers

```
Stock* stock = new Stock;
stock->setSymbol("myStock");
stock->setSpot(50);

Option* option = new Option;
option->setSymbol("myOption");
option->setSpot(50);
option->setStrike(55);
option->setTimeToMaturity(0.5);
option->setVolatility(.2);
option->setRiskfreeRate(.05);

Instrument* instrument;

instrument = stock;
std::cout << "Instrument symbol is: " << instrument->symbol().toStdString() << std::endl;
std::cout << "Instrument price is: " << instrument->price() << std::endl;
```

```
delete instrument;

instrument = option;
std::cout << "Instrument symbol is: " << instrument->symbol().toStdString() << std::endl;
std::cout << "Instrument price is: " << instrument->price() << std::endl;

delete instrument;
```

This time we allocate the Stock and the Option on the *heap* using the new operator, which returns a pointer to the dynamically allocated object (in all of the examples until now we were allocating *automatic* objects on the *stack*). We also use an Instrument pointer (Instrument*) in order to polymorphically call the price method, which is resolved at runtime. The program's output is given as follows:

```
Instrument symbol is: myStock
Instrument price is: 50
Instrument symbol is: myOption
Instrument price is: 1.45324
```

Also note that the objects must be deleted when no longer needed, otherwise you will face a memory leak.

> **Note**   As illustrated in Listing 3-11, you must use the -> operator when accessing a class member with a pointer (accessing class members of a stack variable is done using the dot (.) operator).

This concludes our condensed overview of C++'s OOP features. The next sections will further concentrate on the Qt extensions to C++.

Qt Object Model

I very briefly mentioned the Qt object model when I presented the signals and slots mechanism in Chapter 1. The model extends standard C++ with runtime type introspection and metatype information, among other things.

> **Note**   C++ provides a limited form of runtime introspection with the typeid and dynamic_cast keywords. The Qt framework extensions provide a much richer version based on QObject and the MOC compiler.

The Qt object model adds the following features to standard C++ (your class must inherit from QObject and declare thee Q_OBJECT macro):

- Runtime type introspection using the QMetaObject class.
- A dynamic property system giving you the possibility to add properties at runtime to an instance of a QObject class.

- The signals and slots notification and interobject communication mechanism.

- A form of memory management using parent-child relationships. At any point you can set a child object's parent (this will effectively add the object to the parent's list of children). The parent will then take *ownership* of the child object and whenever the parent is deleted, it will also take care of deleting all of its children.

Meta-Object Compiler (MOC)

I already mentioned the MOC tool in Chapter 1, but I will do a quick recap here. The MOC parses a C++ header file and if it finds a class declaration containing the Q_OBJECT macro, generates additional code in order to add runtime introspection, signals and slots, and dynamic properties to that class (note that you have also encountered other macros such as Q_PROPERTY, Q_ENUMS and Q_INVOKABLE used by the MOC compiler in order to "enrich" a class's functionality). Note that when using the Momentics IDE, you don't need to take any additional steps to use the MOC tool, which is automatically called during the build process; it will scan all the header files located in the source folder of your project. (You can see this happening if you carefully inspect the console view during the build phase: if the class declaration is in a header file called MyClass.h, the MOC generated output will be created in moc_MyClass.cpp and dropped in a folder of your project tree. On the Mac, it's a hidden folder.)

QObject

QObject is essential in Qt/Cascades programming because it implements most of the functionality at the heart of the Qt object model discussed in the previous section. You have already informally encountered the QObject::connect() method in Chapter 1 in order to connect signals to slots. The purpose of this section is to give you additional details by reviewing other important QObject methods.

QObject::connect()

The bool QObject::connect(const QObject* sender, const char* signal, const QObject* receiver, const char* slot, ConnectionType = AutoConnection) method connects a sender's signal to the receiver's slot. As you can see, the signal and slot parameters are C strings. You will therefore have to use the corresponding SIGNAL() and SLOT() macros in order to convert function signatures into strings. Behind the scenes, QObject::connect() compares the strings with introspection data generated by the MOC tool. Here is a simple example illustrating how to use the connect method:

```
QObject::connect(sender, SIGNAL(valueChanged(int)), receiver,
SLOT(setValue(int)).
```

Note that the connect method returns a bool value that you should always check to make sure that the connection was successful. During development, a best practice is to pass QObject::connect()'s return value to the Q_ASSERT(bool test) macro (the macro is enabled in debug builds; prints a warning message if the test fails and halts program execution). In practice, you should never ignore a failed connection because your application might behave erratically or crash in release versions.

As you might have guessed, the QObject::connect() mechanism happens at runtime without any type checking during the compilation process. In practice, this can be quite frustrating when you have to debug silently failing connections. As a general rule of thumb, if a QObject::connect() fails, check the following points:

- Make sure that the signal and slot parameter types correspond. A slot can take fewer parameters than an emitting signal and the extra parameters will be dropped; however, it is essential that the parameter types match.

- If a parameter type is defined in a namespace, make sure to use the fully qualified type name by including the namespace (see Listing 3-13).

Listing 3-13. QObject::connect()

```
QObject::connect(myImageView,
            SIGNAL(imageChanged(bb::cascades::Image*)),
            myHandler,
            SLOT(onImageChanged(bb::cascades::Image*)));
```

Finally, you can also disconnect a signal from a slot using QObject::disconnect(const QObject* sender, const char* signal, const QObject* receiver, const char* slot).

QObject::setProperty()

You can update QObject properties defined with the Q_PROPERTY() macro using the QObject::setProperty(const char* propertyname, const QVariant& value) method. A QVariant is a union of common Qt data types; however, at any time the QVariant can contain a single variable of a given type. If the property was not defined with the Q_PROPERTY() macro, QObject::setProperty() will create a new dynamic property and add it to the QObject instance. Similarly, you can get a property's value using QVariant QObject::property(const char* propertyname). As you will see later in this chapter, properties are a fundamental aspect of exchanging data between C++ and QML by using bindings (a binding can update a Cascades control's property when a corresponding C++ property changes or vice-versa, depending on the binding target).

QObject::deleteLater()

The QObject::deleteLater() method queues up your object for deletion in the Qt event thread. As a general rule of thumb, you should never delete heap-based objects in a slot if it has been passed as a parameter to the slot by the emitting signal (otherwise your application might crash because the object might still be required by other slots, for example). You might, however, face the situation where it is the slot's responsibility to discard the passed object when it is no longer needed. In that case, you can use QObject::deleteLater() to make sure that the object will be eventually deleted once control returns to the event loop (I will not get into the details of the Qt event loop, but if you apply the above-mentioned rule by not deleting heap-based objects in slots, you will always be on the safe side of the fence).

You will see examples of how to use QObject::deleteLater() in the section discussing QThread and you will also have ample opportunity to use the method in Chapter 7 when discarding QNetworkReply objects.

QObject::objectName()

The objectName property identifies an object by name. In practice, you can set a Cascades control's objectName in QML and then retrieve the object from the scene graph in C++ using the QObject::findChild<T>() method. For example, this is how the C++ code in Chapter 1 updated the TextView in Listing 1-3.

> **Note**   It is considered bad practice to directly access from C++ Cascades controls by objectName. The reason is that you will be introducing tight coupling between the UI controls and your C++ code. Instead, as you will see in the section dedicated to the model-view-controller pattern, the preferable way to interact between C++ and QML is to use signals and properties.

QObject Memory Management

QObjects organize themselves in parent-child relationships. You can always set a QObject's parent either during construction or by explicitly calling the QObject::setParent(QObject* parent). The parent then takes ownership of the QObject and adds it to its list of children. Whenever the parent is deleted, so are its children. This technique works particularly well for GUI objects, which tend to naturally organize themselves as object trees. Here are a few things to keep in mind when using the parent-child memory management technique:

- If you delete a QObject, its destructor will automatically remove itself from its parent's list of children.

- Signal and slots are also disconnected so that a deleted object cannot receive signals previously handled by the object.

- You should never mix memory management techniques when managing an object. For example, you should not manage the same object using parent-child relationships and a smart pointer (both techniques use separate reference counts and will conflict if used with the same object). You can, however, use smart pointers and parent-child relationships in the same application as long as they manage different objects (you can even use a smart pointer as a member variable of a QObject instance).

To further illustrate parent-child memory management, let's extend the Instrument class hierarchy by adding composite instruments. In finance, we usually use aggregates of instruments in order to represent things such as indices, portfolios, and funds. Let's therefore introduce a new type called CompositeInstrument (see Listing 3-14).

Listing 3-14. CompositeInstrument.h

```cpp
#ifndef COMPOSITEINSTRUMENT_H_
#define COMPOSITEINSTRUMENT_H_

#include "Instrument.h"

class CompositeInstrument : public Instrument {
    Q_OBJECT

public:
    CompositeInstrument(QObject* parent=0);
    virtual ~CompositeInstrument();

    void addInstrument(Instrument* instrument);
    bool removeInstrument(Instrument* instrument);
    const QList<Instrument*>& instruments();
    double price() const;

signals:
    void instrumentAdded();
    void instrumentRemoved();

private:
    QList<Instrument*> m_instruments;
};

#endif /* COMPOSITEINSTRUMENT_H_ */
```

If you are into design patterns, you must have recognized an implementation of the Composite pattern, which lets you manage an aggregation of objects as a single object. Quite interestingly, these aggregate instruments are also called composites in finance. (Note that another good example of a composite class is the Cascades Container. Also in the example given in Listing 3-14, I am supposing that each instrument part of the composite is equally weighted. In practice, you could have different weights attributed to the instruments. For example, the Dow Jones Industrial Average is price weighted.)

Listing 3-15 gives you the CompositeInstrument member function definitions.

Listing 3-15. CompositeInstrument.cpp

```cpp
#include "CompositeInstrument.h"
#include <iostream>
using namespace std;

CompositeInstrument::CompositeInstrument(QObject* parent) : Instrument(parent) {

}

CompositeInstrument::~CompositeInstrument() {
    // for illustration purposes only to show that the destructor is called
    cout << "~CompositeInstrument()" << endl;
}
```

```
void CompositeInstrument::addInstrument(Instrument* instrument){
    if(!m_instruments.contains(instrument)){
        m_instruments.append(instrument);
        instrument->setParent(this);
        emit instrumentAdded();
    }
}

bool CompositeInstrument::removeInstrument(Instrument* instrument){
    if(m_instruments.contains(instrument)){
        m_instruments.removeOne(instrument);
        instrument->setParent(0);
        emit instrumentRemoved();
        return true;
    }
    return false;
}

const QList<Instrument*>& CompositeInstrument::instruments(){
    return m_instruments;
}

double CompositeInstrument::price() const {
    double totalPrice = 0;
    for(int i = 0; i < m_instruments.length(); i++){
        totalPrice += m_instruments[i]->price();
    }
    return totolPrice;
}
```

The CompositeInstrument class uses a QList<Instrument*> instance in order to keep track of its instruments (a QList<T> is one of Qt's generic container classes; see the "Qt Container Classes" section).

Turning our attention to memory management, when a new Instrument is added to the composite, the composite takes ownership of the instrument using the instrument->setParent(this) method. Similarly, when an instrument is removed from the composite, the composite removes it from its list of children using instrument->setParent(0). In practice, you should always document this kind of behavior so that it is clear to your clients who owns an object at any given time (for example, the Cascades documentation will always explicitly tell you who owns a control after it is added to or removed from another control).

Finally, Listing 3-16 shows you how to use the CompositeClass in a small test application.

Listing 3-16. main.cpp

```
int main(){
    Stock* stock = new Stock;
    stock->setSymbol("myStock");
    stock->setSpot(50);
```

```
Option* option = new Option;
option->setSymbol("myOption");
option->setSpot(50);
option->setStrike(55);
option->setTimeToMaturity(0.5);
option->setVolatility(.2);
option->setRiskfreeRate(.05);

CompositeInstrument* composite = new CompositeInstrument();
composite->addInstrument(stock);
composite->addInstrument(option);

std::cout << "Composite price is: " << composite->price() << std::endl;

delete composite;

// more code goes here
}
```

The application's output is given as follows:

```
Composite price is: 51.4532
~CompositeInstrument()
Stock was deleted
Option was deleted
```

As you can see, the Stock instance and the Option instance are also deleted when the Composite instance is deleted, which illustrates how parent-child relationships work in practice.

Finally, note that parent-child relationships are distinct from the actual class hierarchy. You can set a QObject's parent to any other QObject without having the objects sharing a direct inheritance relationship.

QObject Identity

QObjects feel strongly about their identity. In other words, you cannot use them as value objects. Having value semantics means for an object that only its value counts and that any copy of the object is equivalent. However, as mentioned previously, when considering pass-by-value semantics, QObjects cannot be copied or assigned. Before explaining how this is enforced, let me quickly recap two fundamental concepts that I brushed over when I mentioned pass-by-value semantics. In C++, you can define a copy constructor and an assignment operator. The copy constructor is used, for example, to pass the object by value to a function (or return an object by value from an function). The assignment operator (=) is used to assign one object to another (for example obj1 = obj2). I am not going to show you how to implement these operators but instead simply mention their signature:

- *Copy constructor*: The typical form of the copy constructor is MyClass::MyClass(const MyClass& original) and is used for creating a new copy of an existing instance. Typically, the copy constructor is called when passing an object by value to a function. Note that the copy constructor takes a constant reference to the original object in order to create the copy. If you do not provide a copy constructor, the compiler will implicitly create one for you doing a member-wise copy of the original object. Also note that you must pass a reference to the original object. The member-wise copy is problematic if your class contains pointers to dynamically allocated resources. In this case, the compiler-generated version of the constructor simply performs a "shallow" copy of the original object—resulting in all sorts of memory ownership problems.

- *Assignment operator*: The typical assignment operator is const MyClass& MyClass::operator=(const MyClass& rhs). The assignment operator is called when you assign one object to another. Here again, if you do not provide one, the compiler will implicitly create an assignment operator for you, which does a member-wise copy of the original object.

Because a QObject is not intended to be assigned or copied, it disables the use of the copy constructor and assignment operator using the Q_DISABLE_COPY(ClassName) macro (the macro declares ClassName's copy constructor and assignment operator as private, so that you cannot use them).

To summarize, QObjects can only be used with reference semantics. In other words, you can pass around references or pointers to QObjects in your application without breaking the single identity constraint.

QVariant

A QVariant acts like a union of common Qt data types. However, at any time, a QVariant can only hold a single value of a given type (however, the value itself can be multivalued such as a list of strings). Also the type stored in a QVariant must have value semantics (in other words, it must at least define a public default constructor, a public copy constructor, and a public destructor). A QVariant is an essential component of Cascades programming because it is used in many different scenarios, such as parsing JSON and XML files or retrieving values from a database (you will see how to parse XML using the Cascades XmlDataAccess class in Chapter 6, and JSON using the Cascades JsonDataAccess class in Chapter 7). Most importantly, the QML declarative engine uses QVariants to pass C++ types to JavaScript and vice-versa (note that this happens transparently behind the scenes). You can store your own C++ type in a QVariant by registering it with the Qt type system using the Q_DECLARE_METATYPE() macro . Listing 3-17 illustrates typical QVariant usage.

Listing 3-17. QVariant

```
QVariant variant = 10;
if(variant.canConvert<int>()){
    std::cout << variant.toInt() << std::endl;
}

variant = "Hello variant";
if(variant.canConvert<QString>()){
    std::cout << variant.toString().toStdString() << std::endl;
}

// program output is
// 10
// Hello variant
```

Finally, you will often encounter the following QVariant-based types in Cascades development:

- QVariantList: A typedef for QList<QVariant>. Typically when parsing a JSON array, the JsonDataAccess class will return a QVariantList. You can also reference a QVariantList in QML as a JavaScript array.

- QVariantMap: A typedef for QMap<QString, QVariant>. Typically when parsing JSON objects, the JsonDataAccess class will return a QVariantMap. You can then access individual object attributes using the QVariantMap's key.

The next section will give you more information about QList and QMap.

Qt Container Classes

C++ comes with the standard library, which is a collection of generic containers and algorithms for manipulating them. However, Qt also includes its own set of container classes that can be transparently accessed from QML. Note that the Qt container classes, just like their standard library counterparts, are *class templates* (in other words, you have to pass as a template parameter the type T stored in the container; you should be familiar with this if you have already used Java generics).

In Cascades programming, you will mostly use the QList and QMap containers. A QList<T> is a templated class for storing a list of values and provides fast index-based access as well as fast insertions. A QMap<Key, T> is a container for storing (key, value) pairs and provides fast lookup of the value associated with a key. You have already seen a QList in action in Listing 3-15, and Listing 3-18 gives you a quick overview of how to use a map in practice (you will also have the opportunity to see both containers in action in the code examples given in this book).

Listing 3-18. QMap

```
QMap<QString, int> integers;
integers["one"] = 1;
integers["ten"] = 10;
integers["five"] = 5;

QList<QString> keys = integers.keys();
for(int i=0; i< keys.length(); i++){
    cout << integers[keys.at(i)] << endl;
}
```

Note that you can store any value type in a QMap, including QVariants and pointers to QObjects.

Smart Pointers

I usually prefer to not worry about deleting objects; I would rather delegate the task. Like most difficult problems in programming, you can solve memory management by adding a level of indirection, which in this case is called *smart pointers*. Smart pointers are actually part of the new C++11 standard, but I am going to concentrate on the QSharedPointer, which is part of the Qt core framework. QSharedPointer is a *reference counting* smart pointer, meaning that it holds a shared reference to a dynamically allocated object. The pointee will be deleted once the last QSharedPointer pointing to it is destroyed or goes out of scope. Obviously, QSharedPointers must be automatic objects and you cannot allocate them on the heap. (Automatic objects are created on the stack and are destroyed when they get out of scope. To use a QSharedPointer, simply initialize it with a dynamically allocated resource, as shown in Listing 3-19.)

Listing 3-19. QSharedPointer

```
//don't forget to #include <QSharedPointer>

{ // start of scope

    QSharedPointer<MyClass> m_variable(new MyClass);
    m_variable->method1();  // calls MyClass::method1()
    m_variable->method2();  // calls MyClass::method2()

}  // end of scope. MyClass instance gets deleted here
```

As you can see, by automatically assigning a dynamically allocated object to a smart pointer, you don't need to worry anymore about deleting the object when it is no longer required. You can also assign a smart pointer to another one or return a smart pointer from a function (the reference count will be automatically handled for you in both cases). In other words, smart pointers make memory management as hassle free as in garbage-collected languages such as Java. Note that initializing a smart pointer, as illustrated previously, is a special case of the C++ "resource acquisition is initialization" (RAII) programming paradigm. RAII is particularly important in order to avoid memory leaks when exceptions happen during class construction. Listing 3-20 illustrates this by first using raw pointers in a class instantiation.

Listing 3-20. Constructor Exception, Raw Pointers

```
Class MyClass : public QObject{
Q_OBJECT
public:
    MyClass(QObject* parent=0) : QObject(parent){
        m_var1 = new Type1;
        m_var2 = new Type2;
    }

    virtual ~MyClass() {
        delete m_var1;
        delete m_var2;
    }
private:
    Type* m_var1;
    Type2*  m_var2;
};
```

The previous code declares two pointer member variables. Let's now imagine that an exception occurs during m_var2's allocation (at this stage, m_var1 has already been allocated). When an exception occurs in a constructor, it is as if the class instance never existed, and the destructor will not be called (in other words, the call to delete m_var1 will not happen and you will face a memory leak). If you are thinking of handling the exception in the constructor, don't; your code will become unreasonably convoluted and you would still not handle all possible cases. As you might have guessed, smart pointers are the solution. Listing 3-21 gives you a smart pointer version of the previous code.

Listing 3-21. Constructor Exception, Smart Pointers

```
Class MyClass : public QObject{
Q_OBJECT
public:
    MayClass(QObject* parent=0) : QObject(parent),
      m_var1(new Type), m_var2(new Type2)
    {
    }

    virtual ~MyClass() {
    // empty destructor.
    }
private:
    QSharedPointer<Type> m_var1;
    QSharedPointer<Type2> m_var2;
};
```

As illustrated in Listing 3-21, I am using initialization lists to initialize the smart pointers (initialization lists should be preferred when dealing with non-built-in types). So what happens when an exception occurs? As previously, your destructor does not get called but the C++ standard mandates that the destructor of all successfully constructed sub-objects have to be called. (This will effectively release the memory held by m_var1 and avoid any leaks. Note that in the case of "dumb" pointers, the pointer is effectively deleted, but not the *pointee*; this is why your class needs a destructor in the first place.)

In practice, if you do not handle an exception, it is propagated up the call stack, and eventually, your program will be terminated by the C++ runtime. This could be the sensible thing to do if your application is in such a "catastrophic state" that it would be pointless to continue running (at the very least, you should create a log trace of the problem). Obviously, smart pointers would not be very helpful in such a situation, and the BlackBerry 10 OS would reclaim the memory anyway. However, if you need to write long-running applications such as headless apps, you need to make sure that your application is resilient; you cannot afford crashing when exceptions occur. Smart pointers will therefore be very useful to avoid memory leaks in exceptional cases by making sure that memory is released.

Exposing C++ Objects to QML

There are essentially four ways of exposing C++ objects to QML:

- You can use a QDeclarativePropertyMap to aggregate values in a map, and then set it as a context property of the QML document.

- You can selectively expose properties and methods from a QObject derived class, and then set the instance as a context property of the QML document.

- You can "attach" an instance of a QObject to a QML UIObject object using its UIObject::attachedObjects property in QML. Note that you will have to first register the QObject derived class with the QML type system.

- You can create a QML custom control in C++ by extending bb::cascades::CustomControl. You can then use the control as any other QML element in your document. Once again, you will have to register your control with the QML type system.

> **Note**   To make sure that the document context properties are accessible from QML bindings, you need to
> set them *before* instantiating the scene's root object in the application delegate.

Before getting into the details of exposing C++ objects in practice, let's take a detailed look at the
application delegate's constructor and explain the flow of events (see Listing 3-22). (We conveniently
skimmed over this in Chapters 1 and 2, but now it is time to get our feet wet).

Listing 3-22. ApplicationUI.h

```
ApplicationUI::ApplicationUI(bb::cascades::Application *app) :
        QObject(app)
{
    // prepare the localization
    // code omitted here

    // Create scene document from main.qml asset, the parent is set
    // to ensure the document gets destroyed properly at shut down.
    QmlDocument *qml = QmlDocument::create("asset:///main.qml").parent(this);

    // Set the qml document context properties before creating root object using:
    // void QMLDocument::setContextProperty(const QString &propertyName, QObject *object)

    // Create root object for the UI
    AbstractPane *root = qml->createRootObject<AbstractPane>();

    // Set created root object as the application scene
    app->setScene(root);
}
```

Here is a step-by-step description of the code shown in Listing 3-22:

- `QmlDocument::create(const QString &qmlAsset, bool autoload= true)` is
  called and a QML document is loaded from the assets folder of your application.
  All documents loaded with this method will share the same *QML declarative
  engine*, which is an instance of a Qt `QDeclarativeEngine`.

- A *context* is also associated to the document. Contexts allow data to be
  exposed to components instantiated by the QML declarative engine (all
  documents loaded using the `QmlDocument::create()` method share the same
  instance of the declarative engine, which is associated with the application).

- Contexts form a hierarchy and the root of the hierarchy is the QML declarative
  engine's context. The context associated with the loaded document is therefore
  derived from the root context and shares its properties. Note that these
  properties are not the ones corresponding to QObject but the ones set with `QDec
  larativeContext::setContextProperty(const QString &, QObject *)` method.
  You also have to be aware that you will override a property from the root context
  if you set it with a different value in the document context.

- A root node is instantiated for the scene graph represented by the QML document by calling the `QmlDocument::createRootObject<T>()` template method (the template T parameter must be pointer to a `UIObject` subclass).

- During the instantiation of the root node, the `UIObject::creationCompleted()` signal will be emitted for all UIObjects in the scene graph.

Now let's look at how the document context is used in practice for exposing C++ objects.

QDeclarativePropertyMap

A `QDeclarativePropertyMap` provides an extremely convenient and easy way to expose domain data or *value types* to the QML UI layer. You basically use an instance of a `QDeclarativePropertyMap` to set key-value pairs that can be used in QML bindings (the bindings are dynamic: whenever a key's value is updated, anything bound in QML to that key will also be updated). The values in the map are stored as `QVariant` instances. Using variants effectively means that you can expose to QML any type that can be "wrapped" as a `QVariant`. As mentioned previously, `QVariantList` and `QvariantMap` are two of the most interesting QVariant-based types because you can build arbitrarily complex data structures using them. Listing 3-23 illustrates this by building a person data structure.

Listing 3-23. ApplicationUI.cpp

```
QmlDocument::create("asset:///main.qml").parent(this);

QmlDocument *qml = QmlDocument::create("asset:///main.qml").parent(this);

QDeclarativePropertyMap* propertyMap = new QDeclarativePropertyMap;

QMap<QString, QVariant> person;
person["firstName"] = "John";
person["lastName"] = "Smith";
person["jobFunction"] = "Software Engineer";
person["age"] = 40;

QVariantList hobbies;
hobbies << "surfing" << "chess" << "cinema";

person["hobbies"] = hobbies;

propertyMap->insert("department", "Software Engineering");
propertyMap->insert("person", person);
qml->setContextProperty("mymap",propertyMap);
```

After having built the QVariant data structure, you simply add the QVariant to a `QDeclarativePropertyMap` instance using `QDeclarativePropertyMap::insert(const QString& keyname, const QVariant& value)`. You can then in turn add the map instance as a context property of the QML document using `QmlDocument::setContextProperty(const QString& mapName, QObject* propertyMap)`. In QML, you can finally reference the map by name, as shown in Listing 3-24.

Listing 3-24. main.qml

```
import bb.cascades 1.0

Page {
    Container {
        //Todo: fill me with QML
        Label {
            text: "Department: " + mymap.department;
            }
        }

        Label {
            // Localized text with the dynamic translation and locale updates support
            text: {
                return "last name: "+ mymap.person.lastName;
            }
        }
        Label{
            text:{
                return "Age: " + mymap.person.age;
            }
        }
        Label{
            text:{
                return "Job function: " + mymap.person.jobFunction;
            }
        }

        Label{
            text: {
                var hobbies = mymap.person.hobbies;
                var s = "Hobbies: ";
                for (var i = 0; i< hobbies.length; i++){
                    s = s + hobbies[i] + " ";
                }
                return s;
            }
        }
    }
}
```

To extract the values stored in the map, you use the mapname.keyname "dot notation" syntax (note that in the specific case of the person key, the value returned is also a map and you have to reapply the dot notation in order to retrieve the associated values).

Exposing QObjects

As explained in the previous section, using QDeclarativePropertyMap is a great way to expose data structures based on common QML "basic types." There will be times, however, where you will need to expose your own C++ objects directly so that you can achieve more complex behaviors, such as calling the object's methods or handling its signals in QML (or vice-versa, let the object handle signals emitted from QML). Typically, such objects play the role of application delegates or service façades (I will tell you more about this in the section dedicated to the model-view-controller pattern).

When exposing some functionality to QML, you should always think in terms of services and granularity. For example, if you need to access a large C++ library from QML, it is often preferable to define a set of coarse-grained services that you expose to the QML layer instead of trying to expose every single class of your library. By doing so, you will be able to define clear boundaries between the QML layer and your C++ types. This will also avoid leaking the internals of your class library to the QML layer, thus providing the additional benefit of decoupling your UI logic from the C++ application logic. Once you have decided on your services' granularity, you will be able to design your QObject based C++ service classes using the following recipe:

- Identify the class properties that you want to access from QML.

- Identify the class signals that you want to handle in QML.

- Identify any slots and class methods that should be called from QML.

- When implementing your class methods, use types that you can pass as QVariants.

In practice, in order to expose a C++ class instance to QML, you need to do the following:

- Add the Q_OBJECT macro at the start of the class declaration (and, of course, your class must inherit from QObject).

- Use the Q_PROPERTY macro in order to expose class properties to QML.

- Use the Q_INVOKABLE macro in order to expose class methods to QML.

- Signals and slots are automatically exposed using the signals: and slots: annotations, as explained in Chapter 1.

The syntax for declaring object properties with the Q_PROPERTY macro is as follows:

```
Q_PROPERTY(type name
           READ getFunction
           [WRITE setFunction]
           [RESET resetFunction]
           [NOTIFY notifySignal]
           [DESIGNABLE bool]
           [SCRIPTABLE bool]
           [STORED bool]
           [USER bool]
           [CONSTANT]
           [FINAL])
```

The only mandatory values are the property type, name, and the getter function for reading the property. In practice, you will be using a much shorter version of the macro:

```
Q_PROPERTY(type name READ getFunction WRITE setFunction NOTIFY notifySignal)
```

> **Note**   You must specify the `notifySignal` if you intend on using the property in QML bindings, which I will explain shortly (you must also emit the signal when the property changes).

Using the Document Context

If you carefully study the `Option` class given in Listing 3-6, you will notice that we have already defined the class in such a way that it can be readily used from QML. In fact, just like the QDeclarativePropertyMap instance, all you simply need to do is to add an `Option` instance to the QML document context property from C++ (see Listing 3-25 and Listing 3-26).

Listing 3-25. ApplicationUI.hpp

```
class ApplicationUI : public QObject
{
    Q_OBJECT
public:
    ApplicationUI(bb::cascades::Application *app);
    virtual ~ApplicationUI() { }
private:
    Option* m_option;
};
```

Listing 3-26. ApplicationUI.cpp

```
ApplicationUI::ApplicationUI(bb::cascades::Application *app) :
        QObject(app), m_option(new Option(this))
{

    // Create scene document from main.qml asset, the parent is set
    // to ensure the document gets destroyed properly at shut down.
    QmlDocument *qml = QmlDocument::create("asset:///main.qml").parent(this);

    qml->setContextProperty("_option", m_option);

    // Create root object for the UI
    AbstractPane *root = qml->createRootObject<AbstractPane>();

    // Set created root object as the application scene
    app->setScene(root);
}
```

The `main.qml` document referencing the Option instance is given in Listing 3-27.

Listing 3-27. main.qml

```
import bb.cascades 1.2
Page {
    Container {
        //Todo: fill me with QML
```

```
            Label {
                text: "Option Pricer"
                horizontalAlignment: HorizontalAlignment.Center
                textStyle.base: SystemDefaults.TextStyles.BigText
            }
            TextField {
                id: spotField
                hintText: "Enter spot price"
                onTextChanging: {
                    _option.spot = text;
                }
            }
            TextField {
                id: strikeField
                hintText: "Enter strike price"
                onTextChanging: {
                    _option.strike = text;
                }
            }
            TextField {
                id: maturityField
                hintText: "Enter time to maturity"
                onTextChanging: {
                    _option.maturity = text;
                }
            }
            TextField {
                id: volatilityField
                hintText: "Enter underlying volatility"
                onTextChanging: {
                    _option.volatility = text;
                }
            }
            TextField {
                id: riskfreeRateField
                hintText: "Enter risk free rate"
                onTextChanging: {
                    _option.riskfreeRate = text;
                }
            }
            Label {
                text: "Option fair price"
                horizontalAlignment: HorizontalAlignment.Center
            }
            TextField {
                id: priceField
                text: _option.price
            }
        }
    }
}
```

Here is a brief description of the code shown in Listing 3-27:

- The TextFields' textChanging signals are used to update the corresponding Option object's properties.

- As mentioned previously, when any of the option's properties is updated, an Instrument::priceChanged() signal is also emitted by the Option.

- The priceField's text property is bound to the corresponding Instrument::price property (the QML declarative engine will therefore update the QML property when the Instrument::priceChanged() signal is emitted).

The resulting application UI is given in Figure 3-1.

Figure 3-1. Option pricer UI

Using the attachedObjects Property

I am now going to show you how to use the Option class as a UIObject's attachedObjects property. You first need register the Option class with the QML type system (usually, you will do this in main.cpp; see Listing 3-28).

Listing 3-28. main.cpp

```
Q_DECL_EXPORT int main(int argc, char **argv)
{

    qmlRegisterType<Option>("ludin.instruments", 1, 0, "OptionType");

    Application app(argc, argv);

    // Create the Application UI object, this is where the main.qml file
    // is loaded and the application scene is set.
    new ApplicationUI(&app);

    // Enter the application main event loop.
    return Application::exec();
}
```

The call to qmlRegisterType<Option>("ludin.instruments", 1, 0, "OptionType") effectively
registers the Option C++ type with the QML type system and the corresponding QML type
OptionType.

To actually use the type in main.qml, you need to import the ludin.instruments namespace and
declare an OptionType object as a UIObject's attachedObjects property (see Listing 3-29).

Listing 3-29. OptionType

```
import bb.cascades 1.2
import ludin.instruments 1.0

Page {
    Container {
        //Todo: fill me with QML
        Label {
            text: "Option Pricer"
            horizontalAlignment: HorizontalAlignment.Center
            textStyle.base: SystemDefaults.TextStyles.BigText
        }
        TextField {
            id: spotField
            hintText: "Enter spot price"
        }
        TextField {
            id: strikeField
            hintText: "Enter strike price"
        }
        TextField {
            id: maturityField
            hintText: "Enter time to maturity"
        }
        TextField {
            id: volatilityField
            hintText: "Enter underlying volatility"
        }
```

```
        TextField {
            id: riskfreeRateField
            hintText: "Enter risk free rate"
        }
        Label {
            text: "Option fair price"
            horizontalAlignment: HorizontalAlignment.Center
        }
        TextField {
            id: priceField
            text: option.price
        }
        attachedObjects: [
            OptionType {
                id: option
                type: OptionType.CALL
                symbol: "myoption"
                spot: spotField.text
                strike: strikeField.text
                maturity: maturityField.text
                volatility: volatilityField.text
                riskfreeRate: riskfreeRateField.text
            }
        ]
    }
}
```

Using Bindings

You should note that unlike Listing 3-28, you are not using signals and slots to update the controls in the scene graph. In fact, everything is done using bindings and the net result is that the UI code is mostly declarative. As illustrated in the code, the QML OptionType object's properties are bound to the corresponding TextFields' text properties. Similarly, the priceField's text property is bound to the OptionType object's price property (note that the QML declarative engine automatically transforms the numeric value of the price property into a string before setting the TextField's text property). Whenever a property changes in C++, the QML declarative engine updates the corresponding bound property in QML. In other words, by using bindings, you have delegated the mundane task of updating your application's controls' to the QML declarative engine (this also results in cleaner QML requiring less maintenance).

Model-View-Controller

An important point to consider when designing Cascades applications is the way your C++ code will interact with the QML UI layer. Typically, graphical user interface frameworks promote the model-view-controller (MVC) pattern, which separates your application's logic in three distinct responsibilities (see Figure 3-2).

- Models are responsible for managing your application's data and provide an abstraction layer for accessing and updating it. Typically, they represent the domain objects in your application. Models don't know how to display themselves. However, they can notify controllers and views when their state changes.

- Views are the visual representation of your application data. The same data can be represented by multiple views in different ways, such as a chart or a list of values. Views are displayed to the user.

- A controller effectively plays the role of a mediator between the model and the view. It handles user input and updates the model and view accordingly. In simple applications, you will usually have a single controller; but in more complex scenarios, nothing stops you from having multiple task-oriented controllers.

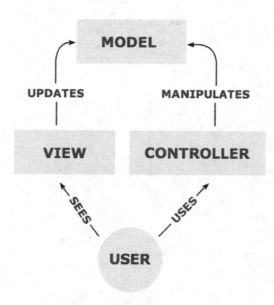

Figure 3-2. MVC interactions

When a model's state changes, it notifies its associated controllers and views so that they can handle the new state. Depending on the degree of separation you may want to achieve, you can also enforce that all model interactions go strictly through the controller. The most fundamental idea is that controllers and views depend on the model, but the opposite is not true. Models are therefore truly independent elements of your applications.

The Cascades framework does not enforce the MVC pattern. For example, there is no controller class to extend. However, Cascades is sufficiently flexible so that you design your application using the MVC pattern, should you choose so. Figure 3-3 illustrates the fundamental elements of a standard Cascades application.

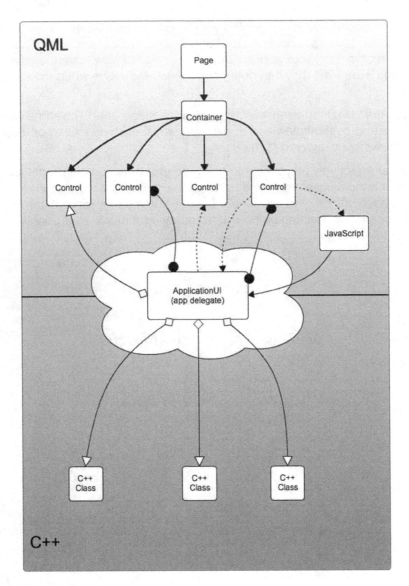

Figure 3-3. Cascades application elements

The QML layer shows a typical scene graph consisting of a root Page control and a Container with multiple children. Signals and slots are represented using dashed arrows (the signal is the start of the arrow and the corresponding slot is the end). Property bindings are the links shown with a full dot on both sides. Direct references to an element are shown as arrows with an empty diamond at their start. As illustrated in Figure 3-3, you can break up your application in a C++ layer that contains your application business logic and a QML layer that contains your application's views (typically, user interactions (such as a clicked button) is handled in the QML layer using JavaScript).

As mentioned previously, it is always a good idea to expose C++ logic to the QML layer using coarse-grained services. This is the reason why the application delegate is your central entry point to the C++ application logic (the cloud symbol represents the QML document context from which you can access the application delegate). Interactions between the application delegate and QML controls should be essentially done using signals and slots and property bindings (as shown in Figure 3-3, you can also directly access a UI control from C++ in your application delegate, but this is strongly discouraged). Mapping this to the MVC pattern, you can see that you have lots of flexibility in defining where your controllers reside. For example, you could decide that the application delegate is your sole controller that handles all interactions between UI controls and the domain model.

Alternatively, you could also split the controllers between JavaScript and the application delegate. Finally, you could also use property bindings between your application delegate and UI controls exclusively. In this case, the only interactions between the UI layer and the application delegate would happen through property updates (in other words, this is would be a form of reactive programming where the data flow between C++ and QML governs the application's state).

Application Delegate

Until now, I have used the term "application delegate" in a relatively informal way without really explaining what I meant. The application delegate is the ApplicationUI class generated for you by the New Cascades Application Wizard. The class's responsibility is to load the QML scene graph from `main.qml`, wire signals and slots between UI controls and domain objects and add itself to the QML document context if necessary. The application delegate therefore plays a central role in a Cascades application. Here again, Cascades does not enforce the presence of an application delegate and you could simply load `main.qml` in your application's main function. However, centralizing the interactions between UI controls and C++ domain objects in a dedicated object will greatly simplify your application's design in the long run. The role of the application delegate is therefore to

- Define signals reflecting the state of model objects used for updating Cascades controls.

- Define slots used by the QML layer in order to update the domain model according to user interactions.

- Define properties used in QML bindings. The properties can be used to selectively expose QObject subclasses to the QML layer of your application. There are really no limitations in what the properties can represent. For example, a property could be a DataModel used by a ListView in order to display a list of items (see Chapter 6) and another property could represent a list of contacts from the contacts database (see Chapter 8), and so on.

- Centralize all interactions between QML and C++ objects (in other words, use the application delegate as your main app controller).

To illustrate the previous points, Listing 3-30 shows you a hypothetical application delegate definition for our financial instruments. (I will not provide the member function definitions. The most important point to keep in mind is how the application delegate is used as an interface to the C++ data model. Also note that the properties' accessors are defined inline.)

Listing 3-30. Application Delegate

```
#include "Stock.h"
#include "Option.h"
#include "CompositeInstrument.h"

class ApplicationUI : public QObject
{
    // used for displaying  instruments in ListView
    Q_PROPERTY(bb::cascades::ArrayDataModel* READ instrumentsModel CONSTANT)

    Q_PROPERTY(QList<CompositeInstrument*> READ composites NOTIFY compositesChanged)
    Q_PROPERTY(QList<Option*> options READ options NOTIFY optionsChanged)
    Q_PROPERTY(QList<Stocks*> stocks READ stocks NOTIFY stocksChanged)

public:
    ApplicationUI(bb::cascades::Application *app);
    virtual ~ApplicationUI() { }

    // load financial instruments in ArrayDataModel
    Q_INVOKABLE void loadInstruments() { // code not shown};
signals:
    void compositesChanged();
    void stocksChanged();
    void optionsChanged();

private:
    bb::cascades::ArrayDataModel* dataModel() {return m_instrumentsModel};

    QList<CompositeInstrument*> composites() {return m_composites};
    QList<Option*> options() {return m_options};
    QList<Stocks*> stocks() {return m_stocks};

    QList<Stock*> m_stocks;
    QList<Option*> m_options;
    QList<CompositeInstrument*> m_composites;

    bb::cascades::ArrayDataModel* m_instrumentsModel;

};
```

The properties defined in the application delegate are accessible from QML and represent the domain model. A Q_INVOKABLE function is also provided in order to load the instruments from a database, for example (here again the function is callable from QML). Finally, the model property can be used by a ListView in order display the current list of instruments (ListViews and DataModels are covered in Chapter 6). As mentioned previously, you need to register the Stock, Option, and CompositeInstrument classes with the QML type system before being able to use them in QML. The application delegate's constructor is one possible place where you perform this. You also need to add the application delegate to the QML document context (see Listing 3-31).

Listing 3-31. Application Delegate Constructor

```
ApplicationUI::ApplicationUI(bb::cascades::Application *app) :
        QObject(app){

    // Create scene document from main.qml asset, the parent is set
    // to ensure the document gets destroyed properly at shut down.

    qmlRegisterType<Stock>("ludin.instruments", 1, 0, "Stock");
    qmlRegisterType<Option>("ludin.instruments", 1, 0, "OptionType");
    qmlRegisterType<CompositeInstrument>("ludin.instruments", 1, 0, "Composite");

    QmlDocument *qml = QmlDocument::create("asset:///main.qml").parent(this);
    qml->setContextProperty("_app", this);
}
```

And finally, Listing 3-32 shows you how to access the application delegate in your QML document.

Listing 3-32. main.qml

```
Page {
    id: page
    function optionsTotalPrice() {
        var total = 0;
        var options = _app.options;
        for (var i = 0; i < options.length(); i ++) {
            total += options[i].price();
        }
        return total;
    }

    Container {
        Label {
            text: "Options total price: " + page.optionsTotalPrice()
        }
        ListView {
            dataModel: _app.instrumentsModel
        }
    }
    onCreationCompleted: {
        _app.loadInstruments(); // loads intruments from db and popultates data model
    }
}
```

QThread

It is very important not to block the main UI thread when developing Cascades applications.
You should therefore always execute long-running operations in a secondary thread so that the main UI
thread stays as responsive as possible. A thread is simply an independent execution flow within your
application. In other words, threads can share your application's data but simply run independently

(a thread is also often called a *lightweight process*). In Qt, a thread is managed by an instance of the QThread class. This section shows you how to effectively execute a long-running operation using a QThread object. As with many things in Qt, it is mostly achieved using signals and slots.

Before starting a new thread, you need to package your workload as a worker object (see Listing 3-33).

Listing 3-33. Worker.h

```
class Worker : public QObject{
Q_OBJECT
public:
    Worker();
    virtual ~Worker();
public slots:
    void doWork();    // do the processing here
signals:
    void finished(double result);
    void error(QString error);

};
```

The worker declares a Worker::doWork() that will be called to start the processing and a finished() signal that will be emitted once the workload has been completed (in other words, the finished() signal will be emitted at the end of Worker::doWork(); see Listing 3-34).

Listing 3-34. Worker.cpp

```
Worker::doWork(){
    // do the long processing here
    emit finished(result);
}
```

Assuming that the application delegate is responsible for launching the new thread, it needs to move the Worker object to the QThread object and start the new thread to perform the workload (see Listing 3-35).

Listing 3-35. ApplicationUI.cpp

```
void ApplicationUI::doWorkAsynch() {
    QThread* thread = new QThread;
    Worker* worker = new Worker;

    worker->moveToThread(thread);
    connect(worker, SIGNAL(error(QString)), this, SLOT(errorString(QString)));
    connect(thread, SIGNAL(started()), worker, SLOT(doWork()));
    connect(worker, SIGNAL(finished(double)), this, SLOT(finished(double)));
    connect(worker, SIGNAL(finished(double)), worker, SLOT(deleteLater()));
    connect(worker, SIGNAL(finished(double)), thread, SLOT(quit()));
    connect(thread, SIGNAL(finished()), thread, SLOT(deleteLater()));
    thread->start();
}
```

As illustrated in the Listing 3-35, the `Worker::doWork()` method is called when the thread's `started()` signal is emitted (the signal is emitted when `QThread::start()` is called). When the worker object has completed the long-running task, it emits the `finished()` signal, which could be used to pass a result back to the application delegate, for example. Note also that the `Worker::finished()` and `QThread::finished()` signals are also used to handle cleanup and make sure dynamically allocated memory is reclaimed (in both cases `QObject::deleteLater()` is used to schedule the objects for deletion).

Summary

Congratulations! By now you know enough to start designing complex applications using QML, JavaScript, Qt, and C++. This chapter has been quite dense, so let's do a quick recap.

C++ is a complex language, but we got to the essentials for building object-oriented programs. In C++, you can override a function in a child class if it has been declared as virtual in the parent class. Having a pure virtual function in a class will effectively make that class abstract. Polymorphism is achieved in C++ through references or pointers to objects. C++ also makes the distinction between value types and references types, which you don't find in languages such as Java, where everything is a reference (except primitives types such int, double, float, boolean, etc.).

By using the MVC pattern, you discovered how to organize your application objects with clearly defined boundaries and responsibilities. This will help you cope with complexity and accommodate change as your application design evolves. The following chapters will build on the foundations presented here and show you how to design beautiful UIs using the Cascades framework. You will master the Cascades core controls, as well as the more advanced ones, integrate with platform services, use the device sensors—and there are many more exciting things to come. From now on, the truly fun topics begin…

Chapter **4**

Controls

Controls provide the fundamental UI building blocks of Cascades applications. By learning how to use them effectively, you will be able to design shiny applications where information is presented to the user in a polished and clear manner. This chapter will review the most essential Cascades controls and show you how to use them in your own applications. Considering that you will build your UI in QML most of the time, I will use QML exclusively in this chapter (you can also build your UI using C++, but that should rarely be the case in practice). UI best practices are another important topic that I will cover throughout the topics presented here. After having read this chapter, you will

- Understand how to use layouts in order to effectively arrange your application's controls on the screen.

- Have a broad perspective of the Cascades core set of controls that you can use in your own applications.

- Apply best practices when selecting controls and creating your UIs.

Control

Control is the base class for all UI controls and contains common properties that you can set in order to specify the control's visual appearance on the screen:

- *Preferred dimensions*: A control's preferred dimensions is specified by the preferredWidth and preferredHeight properties. Some controls, such as TextField or Button, have a fixed height. Therefore, setting the preferredHeight will have no effect. The preferredWidth and preferredHeight properties are used by the parent container's layout to position the control (I will explain containers and layouts shortly). Note that the values are indications to the layout object and could be ignored altogether.

- *Maximum and minimum dimensions*: Just like preferred dimensions, you can also set maximum and minimum dimensions using the maxWidth, maxHeight, minWidth, and minHeight properties.

- *Layout properties*: You can further refine how a control is laid out by its parent container using the control's layoutProperties property. The value must match the parent container's layout object. For example, if the parent container's layout is a StackLayout, the corresponding settable layout property for a control is StackLayoutProperties (which defines the control's relative size to other controls using space quotas).

- *Alignment*: You can set a control's vertical and horizontal alignment within a container by setting its verticalAlignment and horizontalAlignment properties (the properties are taken into account only if the parent container uses a StackLayout or DockLayout). For example, using a stack layout, you can specify that the control will be vertically centered in the parent container by setting the control's verticalAlignment property to VerticalAlignment.Center. Note that the alignment property is taken into account only if its direction is perpendicular to the current layout direction (in other words, the control's vertical alignment in the previous example will be respected only if the parent container's stack layout orientation is left to right or right to left).

- *Margins*: Margins specify some extra space around the control. The corresponding properties are leftMargin, rightMargin, topMargin, and bottomMargin. The parent container's layout manager uses these values during layout.

- *Padding*: For controls such as Container, ListView, TextArea, and TextField, you can set a padding value, which specifies space between the control's edge and its children. (Note that this is different from margins, which specify space between adjacent controls in a container.) If you don't specify paddings for a container, the child controls will be positioned at the container's edges.

The best way to understand the effects of these properties on the UI's layout is to use the QML properties view under Momentics and play with the various parameters (see Figure 4-1, where a Container control has been selected).

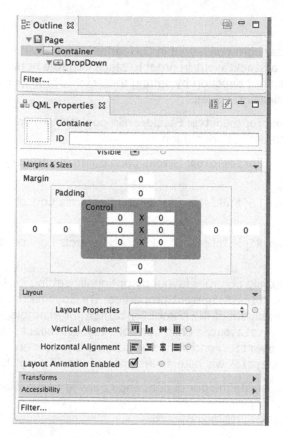

Figure 4-1. QML properties view with a Container selected

Containers and Layouts

A Container is a control for grouping other controls. A Container's layout property governs how its child controls are displayed (note that a Cascades layout is equivalent to a layout manager in Java). Because containers can be nested, you can logically regroup a subset of your UI's controls by adding them to a nested Container (there are actually no limits in the nesting depth, but for code readability reasons, it is a good idea to keep the nesting level to three at most). In practice, you can create extremely complex UIs by judiciously using the possibility to nest Containers with different layout properties.

You have three layouts to work with in Cascades: StackLayout, DockLayout, and AbsoluteLayout. The next section will review all three of them, with a particular emphasis on StackLayout, which should be preferred in most situations (a StackLayout is also used by default when no layout is specified for a Container).

StackLayout

StackLayout is by far the most common layout in Cascades. You should therefore invest some time in mastering it. You can use a StackLayout in order to stack controls horizontally or vertically in a Container. You specify the layout direction by setting the orientation property of a StackLayout, which can take one of the following values:

- LayoutOrientation.TopToBottom: Stacks child controls vertically from top to bottom. This is the default orientation.

- LayoutOrientation.BottomToTop: Stacks child controls vertically from bottom to top.

- LayoutOrientation.LeftToRight: Stacks child controls horizontally from left to right.

- LayoutOrientation.RightToLeft: Stacks child controls horizontally from right to left.

You can further customize a child control's layout by optionally setting its layoutProperties, horizontalAlignment, and verticalAlignment properties. The layoutProperties property accepts an object, which matches the layout of the parent Container (for example, if the parent Container's layout is an instance of AbsoluteLayout, a child control's layoutProperties can only accept an instance of AbsolutLayoutProperties, and if the Container's layout is an instance of StackLayout, the child control's layoutProperties will take an instance of StackLayoutProperties).

Listing 4-1 and Listing 4-2 illustrate the correspondence between layout and layoutProperties.

Listing 4-1. AbsoluteLayout and Corresponding layoutProperties

```
import bb.cascades 1.2
Page {
    Container {
        layout: AbsoluteLayout {

        }
        Button {
            layoutProperties: AbsoluteLayoutProperties {
                positionX: 200
                positionY: 500
            }
        }
    }
}
```

Listing 4-2. StackLayout and Corresponding layoutProperties

```
import bb.cascades 1.2
Page {
    Container {
        layout: StackLayout {
            orientation: LayoutOrientation.LeftToRight
        }
```

```
    Button {
        layoutProperties: StackLayoutProperties {
            spaceQuota: 1
        }
        text: "Button 1"
    }
  }
}
```

In the specific case of StackLayout, the StackLayoutProperties object defines a spaceQuota property, which specifies how space is divided amongst controls. For controls with a negative space quota, the preferredSize property is used to display the control (these "static" controls are given priority over dynamic controls with a space quota larger than 0). Controls with a space quota larger than 0 are dynamically displayed once the static controls have been positioned.

For example, Figure 4-2 illustrates a UI entirely designed using a StackLayout and space quotas.

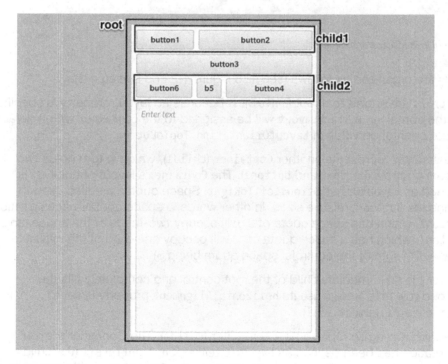

Figure 4-2. UI created with StackLayout and space quotas (portrait)

If you change the device's orientation, you will obtain the layout shown in Figure 4-3.

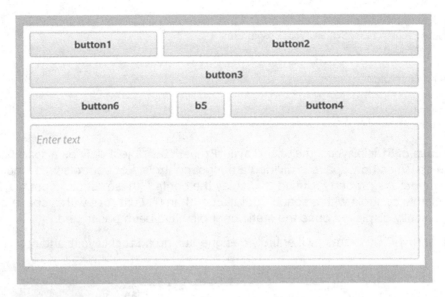

Figure 4-3. Same UI in landscape orientation

The UI controls are organized as follows (see also Figure 4-2 and Listing 4-1):

- Controls are added to a root Container. Because no layout property is specified for the container, a StackLayout will be assigned to the Container with a default layout orientation value of LayoutOrientation.TopToBottom.

- The first row represents another Container (child1), which in turn holds two Button controls (button1 and button2). The Container's layout orientation is defined as LayoutOrientation.LeftToRight. Space quotas are also used to define the Buttons' relative sizes. In other words, a space quota defines a ratio: button2, which has space quota of 2, will occupy two-thirds of the space; and button1, which has a space quota of 1, will occupy one-third of the available space (the sum of the controls' space quota being 3).

- button3 is an immediate child of the root control and completely fills the second row (this is because its horizontalAlignment property is set to HorizontalAlignment.Fill).

- The third row again represents a Container (child2). The Container's layout orientation has been defined as LayoutOrientation.RightToLeft (the child controls will therefore be laid out starting from the Container's rightmost corner). The buttons' relative sizes have been once again set using space quotas. button4's space quota is 4, b5's is 1, and finally, button6's space quota is 3. The sum of the controls' space quotas being 8, button4 occupies half of the space (4/8=1/2), b5 occupies one-eighth, and button6 occupies three-eighths.

- The last row is a TextArea. By specifying a space quota, the TextArea fills the remaining vertical space in the UI.

- Finally, note that when the UI orientation changes, the relative control sizes specified by space quotas are preserved (see Figure 4-3).

Listing 4-3 shows you the corresponding QML.

Listing 4-3. main.qml

```qml
Page {
    Container {
        id: root
        topPadding: 20
        bottomPadding: 20
        leftPadding: 20
        rightPadding: 20
        Container {
            id: child1
            layout: StackLayout {
                orientation: LayoutOrientation.LeftToRight
            }
            Button {
                text: "button1"
                layoutProperties: StackLayoutProperties {
                    spaceQuota: 1
                }
            }
            Button {
                text: "button2"
                layoutProperties: StackLayoutProperties {
                    spaceQuota: 2
                }
            }
        }
        Button {
            horizontalAlignment: HorizontalAlignment.Fill
            text: "button3"
        }
        Container {
            id: child2
            layout: StackLayout {
                orientation: LayoutOrientation.RightToLeft
            }
            Button {
                text: "button4"
                layoutProperties: StackLayoutProperties {
                    spaceQuota: 4
                }
            }
            Button {
                text: "b5"
                layoutProperties: StackLayoutProperties {
                    spaceQuota: 1
                }
            }
            Button {
                text: "button6"
```

```
                    layoutProperties: StackLayoutProperties {
                        spaceQuota: 3
                    }

                }
            }
            TextArea {
                layoutProperties: StackLayoutProperties {
                    spaceQuota: 1
                }
            }
        }
    }
}
```

AbsoluteLayout

AbsoluteLayout allows you to precisely set the X and Y coordinates of controls within a container. In practice, unless you are designing your UI for a very specific screen resolution and orientation, you should not use an absolute layout. As mentioned, the main advantage of the absolute layout is that you have complete control on positioning the UI elements. However, the major downside is that your UI will not gracefully handle different screen resolutions and orientations (there are cases, however, where using an absolute layout makes sense; for example, when you are designing a custom control and need to position the UI elements precisely). Listing 4-4 shows you how to use an absolute layout for positioning a button on the screen.

Listing 4-4. Absolute Layout

```
Container {
    layout: AbsoluteLayout {}

    Button {
        text: "Button"
        layoutProperties: AbsoluteLayoutProperties {
            positionX: 100
            positionY: 100
        }
    }
}
```

DockLayout

You can use a DockLayout in order to dock child controls to a specific area of the parent container. The child control's docking area is specified by its horizontalAlignment and verticalAlignment properties, as illustrated in Listing 4-5 and Figure 4-4.

Listing 4-5. Dock layout

```
Page {
    Container {
        layout: DockLayout {}
```

```
    Button {
        text: "b1"
    }
    Button {
        text: "b2"
        verticalAlignment: VerticalAlignment.Center
    }
    Button {
        text: "b3"
        horizontalAlignment: HorizontalAlignment.Center
        verticalAlignment: VerticalAlignment.Bottom
    }
  }
}
```

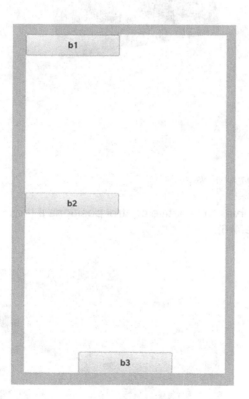

Figure 4-4. *Dock layout*

A DockLayout also has the following interesting characteristics:

- Controls can overlap (see Figure 4-5 and Figure 4-6). (The "z-order" determines which control is on top. Note that we used the overlapping property in the HelloCascades app from Chapter 1 in order to "hide" one image behind another.)

Figure 4-5. Dock layout with overlapping controls

■   A DockLayout preserves the relative control positions if the screen orientation
      changes (see Figure 4-6).

Figure 4-6. Dock layout with overlapping controls

Finally, Listing 4-6 shows the QML document corresponding to Figure 4-5 and Figure 4-6.

Listing 4-6. Dock layout with overlapping controls

```
import bb.cascades 1.2

Page{
    Container {
        leftPadding: 20
        rightPadding:20
        topPadding: 20
        bottomPadding: 20
        layout: DockLayout {}
        ImageView {
            horizontalAlignment: HorizontalAlignment.Right;
            imageSource:"asset:///swissalpsnight.png"
            preferredWidth: 600
        }
        ImageView {
            horizontalAlignment: HorizontalAlignment.Center;
            verticalAlignment: VerticalAlignment.Center;
            imageSource:"asset:///swissalpsday.png"
            preferredWidth: 600
            rotationZ: 10
        }
        TextField {
            verticalAlignment: VerticalAlignment.Bottom;
        }
    }
}
```

Text Controls

Text is probably the most ubiquitous control in any UI. Cascades therefore gives you lots of flexibility in handling text, as well as its appearance. You can customize the text styles by creating your own text style definitions. This section will review the three main text controls, which are Label, TextField, and TextArea, and show you how to customize their corresponding text style.

Text Styles

You can customize a text control's appearance by setting its textStyle.base property, which is an instance of the TextStyle object. In practice, you will use a TextStyleDefinition attached object to create a new TextStyle instance (in other words, the TextStyleDefinition object is a factory for TextStyle objects).Using a TextStyleDefinition, you can customize visual attributes such as font weight (light, normal, and bold), color, size, and alignment. When specifying a TextStyleDefinition, you will always start with a system default base, TextStyle, which gives you an initial set of attributes to work from. The SystemDefaults.TextStyles class gives you the following default text styles:

- SystemDefaults.TextStyles.BigText: The default text style for large text.

- SystemDefaults.TextStyles.BodyText: The default text style for body text.

- SystemDefaults.TextStyles.PrimaryText: The default text style for primary text.

- SystemDefaults.TextStyles.SmallText: The default text style for small text.

- SystemDefaults.TextStyles.SubtitleText: The default text style for subtitle text.

- SystemDefaults.TextStyles.TitleText: The default text style for title text.

Listing 4-7 shows you how you can use the default system text styles with a Label.

Listing 4-7. System Text Styles

```
import bb.cascades 1.2
Page {
    Container {
        Label {
            text: "This is big text"
            textStyle.base: SystemDefaults.TextStyles.BigText
        }
        Label {
            text: "This is title text"
            textStyle.base: SystemDefaults.TextStyles.TitleText
        }
        Label {
            text: "This is subtitle text"
            textStyle.base: SystemDefaults.TextStyles.SubtitleText
        }
         Label {
            text: "This is body text"
            textStyle.base: SystemDefaults.TextStyles.BodyText
        }
        Label{
            text: "This is primary text"
            textStyle.base: SystemDefaults.TextStyles.PrimaryText
        }
        Label{
            text: "This is small text"
            textStyle.base: SystemDefaults.TextStyles.SmallText
        }
    }
}
```

Listing 4-8 shows you how to customize a text style using a TextStyleDefintion.

Listing 4-8. Custom Text Style

```
import bb.cascades 1.2
Page {
    Container {
        attachedObjects: [
            TextStyleDefinition {
                id: myStyle
                base: SystemDefaults.TextStyles.BigText
                color: Color.DarkBlue
                fontWeight: FontWeight.Bold
            }
        ]
        Label {
            text: "Some bold text"
            textStyle.base: myStyle.style
        }
    }
}
```

The advantage of specifying a TextStyleDefinition object is that you will be able to reuse it throughout your UI without redefining text styles for each control.

Inline HTML and CSS

Besides using TextStyleDefinition objects for customizing text appearance, you can also resort to inline HTML and CSS. The supported HTML tags are: <a>, <b>, <br/>, <i>, <span>, <p>, <div>, <em>, and <strong>. Listing 4-9 shows you how to apply inline HTML text styling to a label.

Listing 4-9. Custom Text Style

```
import bb.cascades 1.2

Page {
    Label {
        text: "<html><b>Cascades</b> is <i>awesome!</i></html>"
    }
}
```

You can also embed a <style> tag inside <span> or <div> tags in order to apply CSS styling to your text, as shown in Listing 4-10.

Listing 4-10. CSS Styling

```
import bb.cascades 1.2

Page {
    Label {
        text: "<html><span style='text-decoration:underline'>Cascades</span> is"+
            "<span style='font-size:xx-large;font-style:italic;color:green'>awesome!</span>
</html>"
    }
}
```

Note that not all CSS attributes are supported in style definitions, but you can rely on the following ones (for additional details on how to use the attributes, refer to one of the numerous online CSS tutorials; a good starting point is www.w3schools.com/css/):   •

- `background-color`: Sets the text background color.

- `color`: Sets the text color (for example: red, green, gray, etc…).

- `direction`: Sets the text direction (for example: ltr which is left to right or rtl which is right to left)

- `font-family`: Specifies the text font family (for example: `font-family:"Courier New", Courier, monospace;`). The `font-family` property should hold several font names as a fallback system. You should always start with the font you want and end with a generic family.

- `font-size`: Specifies the font size (for example: `medium, large, x-large, xx-large`).

- `font-style`: Specifies the font style (`normal, italic, oblique`).

- `font-weight`: Specifies the font weight (`normal, bold, lighter, bolder, 100, 200, 300, 400, 500, 600, 700, 800, 900`). A normal font weight is 400 and bold is 700.

- `line-height`: Specifies the height of a line of text.

- `text-align`: Specifies the text's horizontal alignment (`left, right, center, justify`).

- `text-decoration`: Specifies whether the text should be underlined or strike-through (`none, underline, line-through`).

- `letter-spacing`: Adjusts the space between letters in the text (see www.w3schools.com/cssref/pr_text_letter-spacing.asp).

Label

You can use a label control to display a single or multiple lines of read-only text by setting its text property. You have already seen labels in action in the previous examples (see Listing 4-7 to Listing 4-9).

TextField

A `TextField` is a single-line control that accepts text input. A `TextField` has fixed height and variable width. Just like a label, you can control the text styling using a `TextStyleDefinition` object (in other words, all the techniques described in the previous sections apply to text fields). You can specify how the text field behaves in relation to its text input by specifying its `inputMode` property. The following are some common values:

- `TextFieldInputMode.Default`: This is the default input mode.

- `TextFieldInputMode.Text`: An input mode for a wide variety of text.

- `TextFieldInputMode.EmailAddress`: An input mode for e-mail addresses.

- TextFieldInputMode.Password: An input mode for passwords.

- TextFieldInputMode.NumericPassword: An input mode for numeric passwords.

- TextFieldInputMode.Url: An input mode for URLs.

- TextFieldInputMode.PhoneNumber: An input mode for phone numbers.

In fact, a TextFieldInputMode corresponds to default values for input and content flags. Input flags determine how the text that users type is parsed and interpreted by the text field. Content flags determine how the text that users type is displayed. In practice, using one of the default TextFieldInputMode types to preset the flags is more than adequate, and you should rarely need to set the input and content flags directly. The inputMode property value also determines the kind of virtual keyboard displayed to the user when entering text. For example, TextFieldInputMode.Text is the most flexible and suitable for a wide variety of text. This mode also includes word suggestions to help users type faster. The other input modes are optimized for specific tasks such as writing e-mails or entering numeric values. For example, Figures 4-7 and 4-8 illustrate the TextFieldInputMode. EmailAddress and TextFieldInputMode.NumericPassword respectively.

Figure 4-7. A virtual keyboard corresponding to an e-mail address input (image source: BlackBerry)

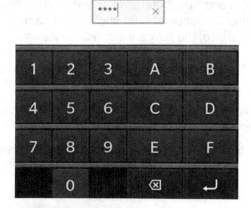

Figure 4-8. A virtual keyboard corresponding to numeric password input (image source: BlackBerry)

You can capture a TextField's input using its input grouped property, as illustrated in Listing 4-11.

Listing 4-11. Text Capture

```
import bb.cascades 1.2

Page {
    Container {
        TextField {
            id: myField
            inputMode: TextFieldInputMode.EmailAddress
            hintText: "Enter email address"
            input{
                submitKey: SubmitKey.Go
                onSubmitted: {
                    // handle input when submit key is pressed
                    // by extracting text from myField.text
                }
            }
        }
    }
}
```

The submitKey property controls the text that will appear on the virtual keyboard's Submit key (the Submit key is always located on the lower-right side of the virtual keyboard). The property can take one of the following values: SubmitKey.Go, SubmitKey.Join, SubmitKey.Next, SubmitKey.Search, SubmitKey.Send, SubmitKey.Submit, SubmitKey.Done, SubmitKey.Connect, SubmitKey.EnterKey, and SubmitKey.Replace.

You can also use a TextField's hintText property to suggest the purpose of the field to the user when there is no input (see Listing 4-11).

Validator

You can make sure that the user's input conforms to a certain set of rules by specifying a Validator class for the TextField using its validator property. For example, for a password field you could ensure that it is of a certain length and that it contains at least a digit. You can use the validator's mode property to specify when text validation should occur. For example, by setting the mode property to ValidationMode.Immediate, the user's input will be validated as the user types along, and by setting the property to ValidationMode.FocusLost, the user's input will be validated once the TextField has lost focus. During validation, you can update the validator's state by setting its state property, which can take one of the following values:

- ValidatationState.Unknown: Validation state is unknown. This state is used for cases where the validation process has not been initiated.

- ValidationState.InProgress: Validation is currently in progress.

- ValidationState.Valid: Validation has succeeded.

- ValidationState.Invalid: Validation has failed.

You should implement the actual validation in JavaScript by handling the validator's validate signal, as illustrated in Listing 4-12.

Listing 4-12. JavaScript Validation Using a Regular Expression

```
import bb.cascades 1.2

Page {
    Container {
        TextField {
            id: myField
            inputMode: TextFieldInputMode.NumbersAndPunctuation
            input {
                submitKey: SubmitKey.Go
                onSubmitted: {
                    // handle input when submit key is pressed
                    // by extracting value text from myField.text
                }
            }
            validator: Validator {
                mode: ValidationMode.Immediate
                errorMessage: "Invalid integer!"
                onValidate: {
                    // regexp for valid integer including optional sign
                    var regexp = /^\s*(\+|-)?\d+\s*$/;
                    var isValidInteger = regexp.test(myField.text);
                    if (regexp.test(myField.text))
                        state = ValidationState.Valid;
                    else
                        state = ValidationState.Invalid;
                }
            }
        }
    }
}
```

The regexp variable defines a valid integer (for example, 10, -99, and 0 are valid expressions, but 10.0 would be considered as invalid). The important point is that I am using the regexp variable to toggle the validator's validation state.

Finally, here a few best practices to consider:

■ Use a text field to let users input a single line of text, such as an e-mail address, a password, or a contact name.

■ Include hint texts in text fields (by doing so, you won't need to add a label describing the text field's purpose).

■ Don't use word prediction in e-mail, password, and contact name fields. Using word prediction in these cases will simply get in the user's way.

■ Provide clear error messages when using validators.

TextArea

A TextArea is very similar to a TextField and shares many of its properties (which they both inherit from AbstractTextControl). The main difference comes from the fact that a TextArea can handle multiple lines of text, whereas a TextField provides a single line. You can set the TextArea's inputMode using a TextAreaInputMode object (the possible values are TextAreaInputMode.Default, TextAreaInputMode.Text, TextAreaInputMode.Chat, TextAreaInputMode.Email, and TextAreaInputMode.Custom). Finally, you can also use the TextArea's editor object to track the current cursor position or the current selected text (see Listing 4-13).

Listing 4-13. TextArea Signal Handling

```
import bb.cascades 1.2
Page {
    Container {
        layout: DockLayout {

        }
        leftPadding: 20
        rightPadding: 20

        TextArea {
            id: myField
            inputMode: TextAreaInputMode.Chat
            hintText: "Enter some text"
            verticalAlignment: VerticalAlignment.Center
            preferredHeight: 500

            scrollMode: TextAreaScrollMode.Elastic
            onTextChanging: {
                console.log("text changing: "+text)
            }

            editor.onSelectionStartChanged: {
                console.log("selection start: "+selectionStart);
            }
            editor.onSelectionEndChanged: {
                console.log("selection end: "+selectionEnd);
            }
            editor.onSelectedTextChanged: {
                console.log("selectedTextChanged: " + selectedText)
            }
            editor.onCursorPositionChanged: {
                console.log("cursorPositionChanged: " + cursorPosition)
            }
        }
    }
}
```

Button

You can use buttons in order to capture touch events in your application. A Button can display some text, an image, or both. You can set the following properties on a Button:

- For sizing, you can set the preferredWidth, minWidth, and maxWidth properties. A button's height is fixed and you cannot change it. The button's width is increased automatically in order to fit text and images. A button will truncate its text if the text content is wider than the maxWidth property.

- The button's text property specifies the text that will be displayed on the Button.

- You can use the image or imageSource properties for specifying an image to be displayed on the Button. In most cases, you will use the imageSource property, which will usually correspond to the URL of an image located in a subfolder of your application's assets folder (you can also use the image property to specify a Image wrapped as a QVariant).

As explained in the previous chapters, the button will emit the clicked signal that you can handle in QML using the onClicked signal handler (see Listing 4-14).

Listing 4-14. Button Clicked Signal

```
Button{
    id: button
    text: "mybutton"
    onClicked: {
        console.log("I was clicked!")
    }
}
```

The following best practices apply to buttons:

- Set the button that users are most likely to tap as the default button. Also, don't make a button associated with a destructive action as the default button.

- Use single-word labels when possible.

- Use verbs that describe the associated action (for example: Login, Cancel, Delete, or Save).

Slider

A Slider is a control that allows the selection of a value from a range of values (see Figure 4-9). You can set the range using the fromValue and toValue properties. You can handle the value using the onImmediateValueChanged signal handler. In practice, you will have to round to the closest integer the immediateValue passed to the handler (see Listing 4-15).

Figure 4-9. Slider

Listing 4-15. Slider

```
import bb.cascades 1.0
Page {
    Container {
        TextField {
            id: texfield
        }
        Slider{
            id: slider
            fromValue: 0
            toValue: 100
            onImmediateValueChanged: {
                texfield.text = Math.round(immediateValue)
            }
        }
    }
}
```

Use a slider when a user needs to quickly set a value from a predetermined range of values.

ImageView

An ImageView is a visual control for displaying images (you used ImageView controls in Listing 4-3 and in the HelloCascades app from Chapter 1). You can either set the imageSource property, which is a URL specifying the location of the image, or set the image property, which is a Image wrapped as a QVariant (note that when you specify the imageSource property as an absolute path on the filesystem, you must prepend the path with "file://"). You can also set the ImageView's scalingMethod property, which specifies how the source image will be scaled within the control.

- ScalingMethod.AspectFit: Fit the image inside the area while preserving the correct aspect ratio.

- ScalingMethod.AspectFill: Stretch and crop the image to fill the entire assigned area while keeping the aspect ratio.

- ScalingMethod.Fill: Stretch the image to fill the assigned area.

- ScalingMethod.None: Content is either cropped or centered with no scaling.

Selection Controls

You can use a selection control to specify a criteria for refining the information displayed to the user. In practice, selection controls will display a list of options to the user so that he can perform a selection from the list. It is therefore not surprising that Cascades provides a wealth of controls organized around option selection. The purpose of this section is to pass the controls in review and illustrate their usage by starting with the essential building block, which is the Option control.

Option

The Option control represents the basic building block of a list of selectable items. You will therefore use an Option control combined with controls such as DropDown, RadioGroup, and SegmentedControl to display a selectable item in a list of items. You can set the Option's text, description, and imageSource properties to display the option on the screen and provide visual feedback. The Option's selected property indicates its state.

DropDown

A DropDown is a control that allows users to select an option from a list of options. As illustrated in Figure 4-11, a DropDown consists of a title bar and an expandable list of options. The list expands and collapses when you tap on the title bar. When the DropDown is expanded, each option displays a title with an optional description and/or image. When the user selects an option, the drop-down is collapsed and the selected option's title is displayed to the right on the title bar.

As illustrated in Listing 4-16, you can determine the user's selection by handling the drop-down's selectedIndexChanged signal and/or the option's selectedChanged signal (if an option is selected, selected=true will be passed to the signal).

Listing 4-16. DropDown

```
Page {
    DropDown {
        title: "Actors"
        enabled: true

        onSelectedIndexChanged: {
            console.log("SelectedIndex was changed to " + selectedIndex);
        }

        Option {
            id: clint
            text: "Clint Eastwood"
            description: "The Good, The Bad, The Ugly"
            value: "Blondie"

            onSelectedChanged: {
                if (selected == true) {
                    console.log(clint.value);
                }
            }
        }
        Option {
            id: robert
            text: "Robert De Niro"
            description: "Taxi Driver"
            value: "Travis Bickle"
            selected: true
```

```
        onSelectedChanged: {
            if (selected == true) {
                console.log(robert.value);
            }
        }
    }
    Option {
        id: jack
        text: "Jack Nicholson"
        // description omitted
        value: "J.J. Jake Gittes"
        onSelectedChanged: {
            if (selected == true) {
                console.log(jack.value);
            }
        }
    }

}
}
```

Figure 4-10 illustrates the corresponding UI.

Figure 4-10. DropDown

In practice, you should use a drop-down when you want your users to select a single option from a list of options. A drop-down also makes your UI more compact, thus saving you some screen real estate. You should not use drop-downs when you need to select multiple interconnected values (in this case, use a picker).

RadioGroup

A RadioGroup can be used to group a set of options together. However, only one option can be selected at a time. Options are displayed as radio buttons, with an optional text describing their purpose (see Figure 4-11).

Figure 4-11. *RadioGroup*

You can handle option selection by responding to the RadioGroup's selectedOptionChanged signal (or alternatively, you could also directly handle the Option's selectedChanged signal; see Listing 4-17).

Listing 4-17. *RadioGroup*

```
// Create a RadioGroup with three options
Page {
    RadioGroup {
        Option {
            id: option1
            text: "Easy"
            onSelectedChanged: {
                if (selected) {
                    console.log("Easy selected");
                }
            }
        }
        Option {
            id: option2
            text: "Hard"
            selected: true
            onSelectedChanged: {
                if (selected) {
                    console.log("Hard selected");
                }
            }
        }
        Option {
            id: option3
```

```
            text: "Very Hard"
            onSelectedChanged: {
                if (selected) {
                    console.log("Very hard selected");
                }
            }
        }
    }
  }
}
```

Use a `RadioButton` when users can choose between more than two mutually exclusive options.

SegmentedControl

A SegmentedControl displays a horizontal row of selectable options (in practice, you can display up to four visible options). A SegmentedControl is a great way of filtering content inside a view (for example, you will see in Chapter 5 how to use a SegmentedControl to dynamically switch QML components depending on the selected option). Listing 4-18 shows you how to create a SegmentedControl in QML.

Listing 4-18. SegmentedControl

```
Page {
    Container {
        SegmentedControl {
            id: segmented1
            Option {
                id: option1
                text: "Option 1"
                value: "option1"
                selected: true
            }
            Option {
                id: option2
                text: "Option 2"
                value: "option2"
            }
            Option {
                id: option3
                text: "Option 3"
                value: "option3"
            }
            onSelectedIndexChanged: {
                var value = segmented1.selectedValue
                console.debug("Selected value: " + value);
            }
        }
    }
}
```

And Figure 4-12 shows the corresponding UI.

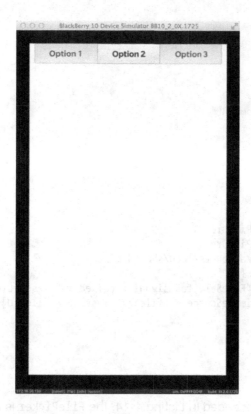

Figure 4-12. SegmentedControl

Pickers

A picker is a control for selecting items such as a picture, a file, or a date. I will describe in this section the FilePicker and the DataAndTimePicker, which come as standard controls with Cascades. (You can also create your own custom picker, but I won't cover this here. Custom pickers are nevertheless explained in the online BlackBerry 10 developer documentation.)

FilePicker

A FilePicker allows the user to either select a file from the file system (in picker mode) or specify a name and location for saving a file (in saver mode). For example, you can use a FilePicker to load an image from the device's photo folder in an ImageView (see Listing 4-19). (Note that in QML you must prefix the path returned by a FilePicker with "file://" before passing it to an ImageView.) You can also filter the file types by setting the FilePicker's type property. Finally, you can use the fileSelected signal to handle selection (the signal is emitted both in picker and saver modes).

Listing 4-19. FilePicker

```
import bb.cascades 1.0
import bb.cascades.pickers 1.0
```

```
Page {
    Container {
        ImageView{
            id: myImageView
        }
        Button {
            text: "FilePicker from QML"
            onClicked: {
                filePicker.open()
            }
        }
        attachedObjects: [
            FilePicker {
                id:filePicker
                type : FileType.Picture
                title : "Select Picture"
                directories : ["/accounts/1000/shared/misc"]
                onFileSelected : {
                    console.log("FileSelected signal received : " + selectedFiles);
                    myImageView.imageSource = "file://" + selectedFiles[0];
                }
            }
        ]
    }
}
```

Also note that in the example provided in Listing 4-14, the FilePicker is an attached object property of the Container (this enables you to selectively display the FilePicker when the button is pressed).

DateTimePicker

A DateTimePicker is a control for selecting a date and/or time. You can set the DateTimePicker's mode, which specifies how date and time are shown to the user (see Figure 4-13).

- DateTimePickerMode.Time: In this mode, the time is shown in two columns (hours and minutes).

- DateTimePickerMode.Date: This is the default mode. The date is shown in three columns (day, month, and year).

- DateTimePickerMode.DateTime: Shows the day and time in three columns (day, hours, and minutes).

- DateTimePickerMode.Timer: Shows the time in three columns, like a stopwatch (hours, minutes, and seconds).

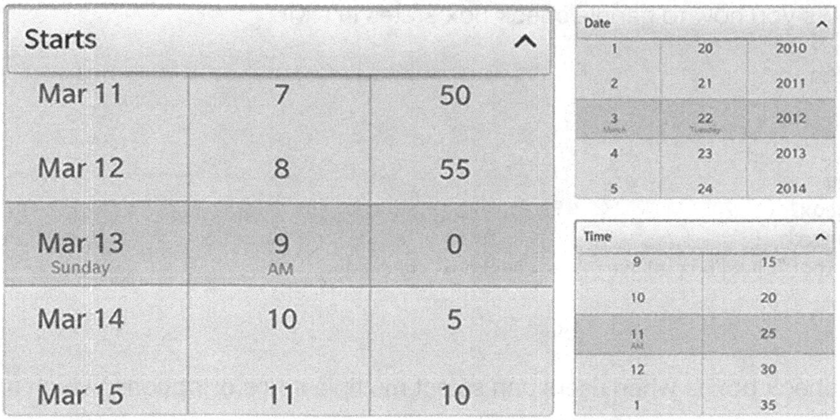

Figure 4-13. DateTimePiker (image source: BlackBerry web site)

Note that the internal representation of a date by the QDateTimePicker is a Qt QDateTime object, which is accessible with the QDateTimePicker.value property. In QML, there are several ways of setting this property: you can set the value property either by using a correctly formatted string or by using a JavaScript Date object. Finally, you can respond to the valueChanged signal to handle date changes.

CheckBox and ToggleButton

Check boxes and toggle buttons enable users to select options. Both controls inherit from AbstractToggleButton and share the following attributes:

- You can use the checked property to determine the state of the toggle control.
- You can handle the checkedChanged signal to capture state changes.

CheckBox

A CheckBox control has two states: checked or unchecked. You can also optionally display some text beside the check box explaining its purpose. If you include some text, it will always be left-aligned, and the check box will be right-aligned (see Figure 4-14).

Figure 4-14. CheckBox

Listing 4-20 shows you how to handle check box states in QML.

Listing 4-20. CheckBox

```
CheckBox {
    id: checkbox
    checked: true
    text: "Checkbox"
    onCheckedChanged: {
        console.log("checkbox state: " + checkbox.checked)
    }
}
```

In practice, use check boxes when users can select multiple items or options, which are not mutually exclusive.

ToggleButton

A toggle button is a kind of switch control, which can, for example, represent On/Off states (see Figure 4-15). Signal handling is identical to a check box.

Figure 4-15. CheckBox

You should use a toggle button when users can switch between two mutually exclusive options, such as On and Off.

ScrollView

A ScrollView is a container allowing the scrolling and zooming of its content. A ScrollView provides a viewport, which displays an area of the entire content. You can use a ScrollView when the content will not fit the UI entirely (for example, that would be the case if a container included many controls). Note that a ScrollView's content can also be an ImageView or a WebView (for example, you can use a ScrollView to zoom in or out of a picture). You can control the scrolling behavior by setting the ScrollView's scrollViewProperties property. Listing 4-21 shows you how to include a WebView in a ScrollView.

Listing 4-21. ScrollView

```
Page {
    ScrollView {
        WebView {
            url: "http://www.apress.com"
        }
```

```
        scrollViewProperties {
            scrollMode: ScrollMode.Vertical
            pinchToZoomEnabled: true
        }
    }
}
```

Use a ScrollView when

- A control's content does not fit the screen and you need to provide a viewport
  that you can navigate (by scrolling horizontally and/or vertically).

- You need to zoom in or out of content using a pinch gesture.

System Dialogs, Prompts, and Toasts

You can use the system dialog controls to pause your application flow and communicate important
information to the user. System dialogs can be used to ask the user to confirm an action, notify the
user of an event, or prompt the user for additional information.

SystemDialog

You can use a SystemDialog control to ask the user to confirm an action (see Listing 4-22). (Note that
you need to import the bb.system 1.2 library.)

Listing 4-22. SystemDialog with User Confirmation

```
import bb.cascades 1.2
import bb.system 1.2

Page {
    Container {
        layout: DockLayout {

        }
        Button {
            text: "Show Dialog!"
            verticalAlignment: VerticalAlignment.Center
            horizontalAlignment: HorizontalAlignment.Center
            onClicked: {
                myDialog.show();
            }
        }
        attachedObjects: [
            SystemDialog {
                title: "Save Changes"
                id: myDialog
                onFinished: {
                    switch (value) {
                        case (SystemUiResult.ConfirmButtonSelection):
```

```
                        console.log("save confirmed");
                        break;
                case (SystemUiResult.CancelButtonSelection):
                        console.log("save canceled");
                        break;
                default:
                        break;
                }
            }
        }
    ]

    }
}
```

To display the dialog, you need to call SystemDialog.show(). To determine the user's selection, you need to handle the SystemDialog.finished() signal. The SystemDialog's text property will be displayed on the dialog's title bar (see Figure 4-16).

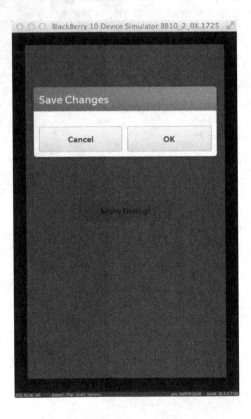

Figure 4-16. SystemDialog

SystemPrompt

You can use a SystemPrompt to ask for some input from the user before continuing with your application flow. The SystemPrompt will display two default buttons for accepting or rejecting the dialog box and an input field for user input. You can retrieve the user's input by calling SystemPrompt. inputFieldTextEntry() (see Listing 4-23).

Listing 4-23. SystemPrompt

```
import bb.cascades 1.2
import bb.system 1.2

Page {
    Container {
        layout: DockLayout {

        }
        Button {
            text: "Show Dialog!"
            verticalAlignment: VerticalAlignment.Center
            horizontalAlignment: HorizontalAlignment.Center
            onClicked: {
                myPrompt.show();
            }
        }
        attachedObjects: [
            SystemPrompt {
                title: "Enter a new file name"
                id: myPrompt
                onFinished: {
                    switch (value) {
                        case (SystemUiResult.ConfirmButtonSelection):
                            console.log("new file name is: "+myPrompt.inputFieldTextEntry())
                            break;
                        case (SystemUiResult.CancelButtonSelection):
                            console.log("new file canceled");
                            break;
                        default:
                            break;
                    }
                }
            }
        ]

    }
}
```

Figure 4-17 shows the SystemPrompt when displayed.

Figure 4-17. SystemPrompt

SystemToast

A toast is a simple pop-up message that is displayed for a predefined amount of time. The toast is for information purposes only and the user does not need to interact with it. Listing 4-24 shows you how to use a SystemToast to display a toast to the user.

Listing 4-24. SystemToast

```
import bb.cascades 1.2
import bb.system 1.2

Page {
    Container {
        layout: DockLayout {

        }
        Button {
            text: "Show Dialog!"
            verticalAlignment: VerticalAlignment.Center
            horizontalAlignment: HorizontalAlignment.Center
```

```
        onClicked: {
            myToast.show();
        }
    }
    attachedObjects: [
        SystemToast {
            id: myToast
            body: "Happy New Year!"
        }
    ]

    }
}
```

Summary

This chapter gave you a broad perspective of essential Cascades controls. You should now have a good understanding of the core controls and be able to use them in your own applications when designing single page UIs (the goal of the next chapter will be to show you how to add application navigation and structure using multiple pages).

Layout management is also an important topic covered in this chapter. The StackLayout was given a particular emphasis because it is the building block for creating device-independent and resizable UIs using space quotas. You also saw that in practice it is a good idea to use space quotas to define relative controls sizes instead of statically specifying a control's preferred size. Finally, you discovered how Cascades gives lots of flexibility in styling UI text by either using text style definition objects or by using inline HTML and CSS.

Chapter 5

Application Structure

An important step in designing your Cascades application is to plan how you will organize or structure the application's pages and navigation. In order to make sure that you will not face any design problems, you need to clearly understand your application flow by asking yourself the following questions:

- Is a single screen sufficient or should you use multiple screens? If your application requires multiple screens, how should you organize them (for example, should you use tabs in order to switch from one screen to another or should you build a navigation hierarchy)?

- Is your application data-centric? In that case, do you need to drill down through the data?

- What are the actions the user needs to perform?

The preceding list is certainly not exhaustive, but answering these questions at the very start will help you have a clear understanding of the structural elements of your application.

You will see in this chapter that Cascades provides you with all the necessary tools to help you design your application in order to provide the best possible user experience.

Application Templates

The Momentics IDE's New BlackBerry Project wizard is a great starting place for selecting your application scaffolding. You have the choice between four project templates, which basically cover most, if not all, of your needs in designing Cascades applications:

- *Standard empty project*: This is the template you have been using until now for designing your applications. It provides you a single Page where you can add your own Cascades controls.

- *List view*: Creates an application where the main UI element is a ListView displaying a list of items. The data for the list items is provided by an instance of a DataModel (we will study DataModel and ListView in detail in Chapter 6).

- *Tabbed pane*: Creates an application where the user can switch between Tabs. Each Tab contains an instance of an `AbstractPane` (in practice, you can only add a Page or a `NavigationPane` to the Tab).

- *Navigation pane*: Creates an application that uses a `NavigationPane` to display screens. Navigation is triggered when the user selects an action, which can be contextual or located on the Action bar (I will tell you more about actions and action bars in a moment).

Note that both the List view and the Navigation pane templates use navigation, which is a way to transition from one screen to another, in order to implement their functionality.

Let us now have a look at the `main.qml` files generated by each template (I am going to omit the standard empty project because you are already quite familiar with it).

Tabbed Pane Template

The `main.qml` file generated by the Tabbed Pane template is given in Listing 5-1.

Listing 5-1. Tabbed Pane Template, main.qml

```
import bb.cascades 1.0

TabbedPane {
    showTabsOnActionBar: true
    Tab { //First tab
        // Localized text with the dynamic translation and locale updates support
        title: qsTr("Tab 1") + Retranslate.onLocaleOrLanguageChanged
        Page {
            Container {
                Label {
                    text: qsTr("First tab") + Retranslate.onLocaleOrLanguageChanged
                }
            }
        }
    } //End of first tab
    Tab { //Second tab
        title: qsTr("Tab 2") + Retranslate.onLocaleOrLanguageChanged
        Page {
            Container {
                Label {
                    text: qsTr("Second tab") + Retranslate.onLocaleOrLanguageChanged
                }
            }
        }
    } //End of second tab
}
```

A tabbed pane is an extremely convenient way of organizing your application in multiples screens. Each Tab can contain an instance of an `AbstractPane` (in other words, you can use a `Page` or a `NavigationPane` as a child control). Figure 5-1 illustrates a resulting UI where the second tab has been selected.

Figure 5-1. *Tabs on Action bar with second Tab selected*

You can specify how a `TabbedPane` will appear on the Action bar by setting its `ShowTabsOnActionBar` property. If you change the property to false (or if you don't set it at all), the resulting layout will be identical to Figure 5-2.

Figure 5-2. Tabs in overflow menu

By touching the Tab1 icon, you will reveal the other tabs. Obviously, this layout is preferable if you have lots of tabs in your application.

Navigation Pane Template

Listing 5-2 gives the `main.qml` file generated by the Navigation pane template.

Listing 5-2. Navigation Pane Template, main.qml

```
import bb.cascades 1.0

NavigationPane {
    id: navigationPane

    Page {
        titleBar: TitleBar {
            // Localized text with the dynamic translation and locale updates support
            title: qsTr("Page 1") + Retranslate.onLocaleOrLanguageChanged
        }

        Container {
        }
```

```
        actions: ActionItem {
            title: qsTr("Second page") + Retranslate.onLocaleOrLanguageChanged
            ActionBar.placement: ActionBarPlacement.OnBar

            onTriggered: {
                // A second Page is created and pushed when this action is triggered.
                navigationPane.push(secondPageDefinition.createObject());
            }
        }
    }

    attachedObjects: [
        // Definition of the second Page, used to dynamically create the Page above.
        ComponentDefinition {
            id: secondPageDefinition
            source: "DetailsPage.qml"
        }
    ]

    onPopTransitionEnded: {
        // Destroy the popped Page once the back transition has ended.
        page.destroy();
    }
}
```

You can use the Navigation pane template to build drill-down applications. In Listing 5-2, a ComponentDefinition object is used to dynamically load a QML object defined in DetailsPage.qml (you will learn about ComponentDefinition in a moment). The root control is an instance of NavigationPane (this is a departure to a standard empty project, which contained a Page control as the root container). The NavigationPane provides the NavigationPane::push(bb::cascades::Page*) and bb::cascades::Page* NavigationPane::pop() methods in order to implement navigation. If a page is pushed on the navigation stack, it will be displayed to the user. The opposite effect is achieved by popping the page off the stack. In this case, the new page located at the top of the stack is displayed. An ActionItem triggers the actual navigation from one page to another.

List View Template

Listing 5-3 gives the main.qml generated by the List view template. (Listing 5-4 defines the page that is displayed when a ListView item is selected. Listing 5-5 defines the data to be loaded in the ListView.)

Listing 5-3. List View Template, main.qml

```
import bb.cascades 1.0
NavigationPane {
    id: nav
    Page {
        Container {
            ListView {
                dataModel: XmlDataModel {
                    source: "data.xml"
```

```
                }
            onTriggered: {

                if (indexPath.length > 1) {
                    var chosenItem = dataModel.data(indexPath);
                    var contentpage = itemPageDefinition.createObject();

                    contentpage.itemPageTitle = chosenItem.name
                    nav.push(contentpage);
                }
            }
        }

    }

    }
    attachedObjects: [
        ComponentDefinition {
            id: itemPageDefinition
            source: "ItemPage.qml"
        }
    ]
    onPopTransitionEnded: {
        page.destroy();
    }
}
```

Listing 5-4. List View Template, ItemPage.qml

```
import bb.cascades 1.0

Page {
    property alias itemPageTitle: titlebar.title
    titleBar: TitleBar {
        id: titlebar
    }
    Container {

    }
}
```

Listing 5-5. data.xml

```
<root>
    <header title="Header 1">
        <item  name="Item 1"/>
        <item  name="Item 2"/>
        <item  name="Item 3"/>
        <item  name="Item 4"/>
        <item  name="Item 5"/>
    </header>
```

```
    <header title="Header 2">
        <item  name="Item 1"/>
        <item  name="Item 2"/>
        <item  name="Item 3"/>
        <item  name="Item 4"/>
        <item  name="Item 5"/>
        <item  name="Item Gorilla"/>
    </header>
</root>
```

Here are the most important aspects of the code to consider:

- The root control is an instance of NavigationPane (again, this is a departure from the standard empty project that contained a Page control as the root container). The NavigationPane provides the NavigationPane::push(bb::cascades::Page*) and the bb::cascades::Page* NavigationPane::pop() methods in order to implement navigation. If a page is pushed on the navigation stack, it will be displayed to the user. The opposite effect is achieved by popping the page off the stack. In this case, the page located at the top of the stack is displayed. You should note that a List view template is essentially a special case of a Navigation pane template where navigation is triggered by selecting data items in a ListView.

- A ListView uses a DataModel in order to load its data. The ListView component has been designed around the MVC pattern. The DataModel implements the model part, the ListView plays the role of the controller, and a ListItemComponent handles the list view's visuals (you will see how the components interact in the next chapter).

- The navigation pane's attached object property includes a ComponentDefinition declaration, which is used to dynamically load a QML component (in this case, an instance of ItemPage, which is defined in ItemPage.qml, located in the same folder as main.qml). When you actually need to create the object, you will have to call ComponentDefinition.createObject().

- Notice how the indexPath array length is checked before navigating to ItemPage to ensure that the user has selected an item element and not a header. I will provide you with more details in the next chapter on how index paths are evaluated. For the moment, suffice to say that the array is used to uniquely locate a data element in the DataModel.

- The root element index path will be the empty array. The header elements will have a one-element index path array and the item elements will have an index path array containing two elements.

Figure 5-3 illustrates the resulting application and Figure 5-4 UI when Item 2 is selected from the list.

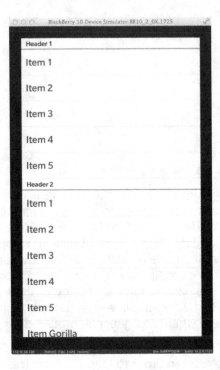

Figure 5-3. Master view

Figure 5-4. Details view

By touching the Back icon, you will pop the current page from the `NavigationPage`'s stack and display the `ListView`, which will once again be at the top of the stack.

Defining the Application Structure

In a very broad sense, application structure defines the way you organize your application to manage actions, menus, tabs, and, of course, navigation. You will see that BlackBerry 10 provides you lots of flexibility in the way the application flow and controls are visually organized and presented to the user. You are, however, encouraged to follow the BlackBerry 10 UI guidelines in order to guarantee the best user experience. You can also use the BlackBerry 10 wireframe design slides to plan your application screens and navigation. The previous chapter reviewed the essential controls for creating BlackBerry 10 UIs. This section reviews the additional controls used to create a supporting structure for your application out of those controls. If you consider a spoken language analogy, controls would be words and application structure would be the sentences built with those words (and hopefully "grammatically correct sentences" dictated by the BlackBerry 10 UI guidelines).

> You will find the UI Guidelines for BlackBerry 10 at `http://developer.blackberry.com/devzone/design/bb10/`.
>
> The wireframe design slides can be downloaded from `http://developer.blackberry.com/devzone/design/bb10/prototyping.html`.

Action Bar

Before looking at different application structures, I want to explain the action bar: the Action bar is located at the bottom of the screen and can contain actions, tabs, and menus. You can choose to display Tabs directly on the action bar as we did in Listing 5-1, or rather regroup them under a common Tab Menu, which will appear on the far left side of the Action bar. For example, in Figure 5-5, the Tabs are regrouped, and touching the Hub icon will reveal the remaining ones.

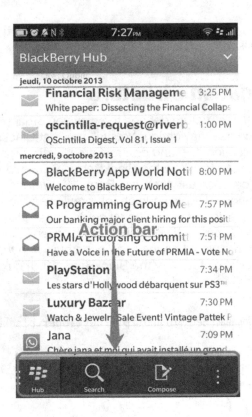

Figure 5-5. Action bar

The Action menu is located on the rightmost side of the Action bar. By pressing the icon with three vertical dots, the overflow menu is displayed with the corresponding Actions. Finally, Actions can appear directly on the action bar, which is the case of the Search and Compose Actions shown in Figure 5-5.

Single Page Applications

A single Page application is entirely built around a unique Page at the root of the scene graph. You have been essentially designing single Page applications until now. The biggest advantage of the single Page application structure is not only its simplicity, but also the capacity to provide the user a single screen where all content and Actions are presented in an extremely focused way during the entire application lifetime. You might think that building your application around a single Page might lack the flexibility required for more complex interactions. You will, however, see that you can provide a very enticing user experience based on the single Page design using the controls presented in the following sections (you will also be able to extend very naturally the concepts introduced for single Page applications to multiple Page or navigation-based apps).

Actions

I have informally mentioned Actions when I discussed the Action bar. This section will show you how to implement them in practice in your own applications. There are several places where you can define Actions:

■ You can add Actions to a Page by setting the Page's Actions property. You can also specify whether the Actions are displayed on the Action bar or in the Action overflow menu (by default, page Actions are located in the overflow menu and only the most used Actions should appear on the Action bar).

■ You can add context Actions to a UIControl, which will be displayed in a context menu when the user touches and holds the control in your app.

■ Finally, you can add Actions to a TitleBar.

ActionItem

An `ActionItem` object represents the actual Action. You can specify the following properties when declaring an `ActionItem`:

■ `ActionItem::title`: A text string that will be displayed with the Action (for example, on the Action bar or in a menu).

■ `ActionItem::imageSource`: A URL specifying the image set on the Action.

When the user triggers the Action, the `ActionItem::triggered()` signal is emitted. You can therefore use the `onTriggered:` handler in QML in order to react to user Actions.

Page Actions

Listing 5-6 illustrates how Actions are added to a Page control.

Listing 5-6. Actions

```
import bb.cascades 1.0
Page {
        actions: [
        ActionItem {
            id: action1
            title: "action1"
            onTriggered: {
                actionLabel.text = action1.title
            }
        },
        ActionItem {
            id: action2
            title: "action2"
            onTriggered: {
                actionLabel.text = action2.title
            }

    }
    ]
```

```
Container {
    Label {
        id: actionLabel
        text: "Hello Actions"
        textStyle.base: SystemDefaults.TextStyles.BigText
        horizontalAlignment: HorizontalAlignment.Center
    }
}
}
```

Figure 5-6 shows the action bar when all Actions are located in the overflow menu.

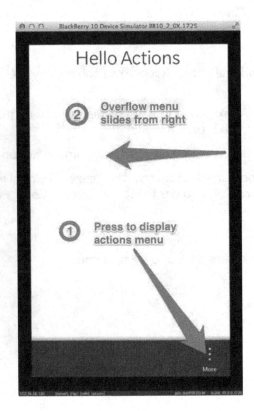

Figure 5-6. *Actions overflow menu*

And Figure 5-7 displays the expanded overflow menu.

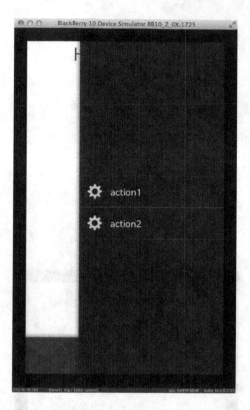

Figure 5-7. Expanded overflow menu

If you want to display actions directly on the Action bar, you need to set the ActionItem's
ActionBar.placement property to ActionBarPlacement.OnBar (see Listing 5-7 and Figure 5-8).

Listing 5-7. Actions on Action Bar

```
import bb.cascades 1.0

Page {
    actions: [
    ActionItem {
        id: action1
        title: "action1"
        ActionBar.placement: ActionBarPlacement.OnBar
        onTriggered: {
            actionLabel.text = action1.title
        }
    },
    ActionItem {
        id: action2
        title: "action2"
        ActionBar.placement: ActionBarPlacement.OnBar
```

```
            onTriggered: {
                actionLabel.text = action2.title
            }
        }
        ]
    Container {
        Label {
            id: actionLabel
            text: "Hello Actions"
            textStyle.base: SystemDefaults.TextStyles.BigText
            horizontalAlignment: HorizontalAlignment.Center
            contextActions:[
        }
    }
}
```

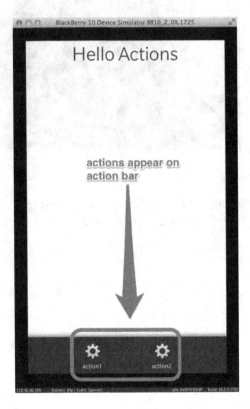

Figure 5-8. Actions on Action bar

Context Actions

You can also associate actions to a UIControl by setting the UIControl::contextActions property (see Listing 5-8).

Listing 5-8. Context Actions

```
import bb.cascades 1.0

Page {
    Container {
        Label {
            id: actionLabel
            text: "Hello Actions"
            textStyle.base: SystemDefaults.TextStyles.BigText
            horizontalAlignment: HorizontalAlignment.Center
            contextActions: [
                ActionSet {
                    Title:
                    ActionItem {
                        id: action1
                        title: "action1"
                        ActionBar.placement: ActionBarPlacement.OnBar
                        onTriggered: {
                            actionLabel.text = action1.title
                        }
                    }
                    ActionItem {
                        id: action2
                        title: "action2"
                        ActionBar.placement: ActionBarPlacement.OnBar
                        onTriggered: {
                            actionLabel.text = action2.title
                        }
                    }
                }
            ]
        }
    }
}
```

You need to touch and hold the Label in order to display the context Actions. Notice how the Actions are grouped in an Action set. (You can specify multiple Action sets, but at the moment, Cascades will take only the first one into account. This might change in future releases.)

MenuDefinition

You might have noticed that we mentioned menus in our discussion of Actions, but never actually had to define one. The reason is that Cascades will implicitly add Actions to predefined menus, depending on the Action's type. There are three predefined menus available in BlackBerry 10: the Actions menu appearing on the Action bar, the context menu displayed when you touch and hold a control, and the application-wide menu, which will be displayed when the user swipes down from the top of the screen (see Figure 5-9).

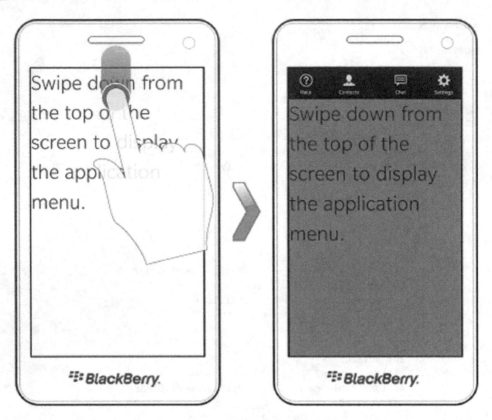

Figure 5-9. Displaying the Application menu (image source: BlackBerry web site)

The only case where you actually use a menu definition is when you need to add application-wide Actions, representing Actions that are not tied to a specific Page or control in your application. To build the application menu, you will use the MenuDefinition class, which lets you specify the following properties:

- MenuDefinition::helpAction: An instance of HelpActionItem that gives the user access to help functionality. You will have to display a help screen when this Action's triggered() signal is emitted.

- MenuDefinition::settingsAction: An instance of SettingsAction that gives the user access to application-wide settings. You will have to display a settings screen when this Action's triggered() signal is emitted.

- MenuDefinition::actions: A list of ActionItems to be displayed on the application menu.

The application menu will always display the HelpAction on the left most of the screen and the SettingsAction on the rightmost. The remaining Actions will appear in between. (However, a maximum of five Actions can appear on the menu. All of these items have also Internationalization enabled and are automatically translated.)

Listing 5-9 extends Listing 5-8 by adding Actions to the application menu.

Listing 5-9. Application Menu

```
import bb.cascades 1.0

Page {
    Menu.definition: MenuDefinition {
        settingsAction: SettingsActionItem {
            onTriggered: {
                actionLabel.text = "Settings selected!"
            }
        }
        helpAction: HelpActionItem {
            onTriggered: {
                actionLabel.text = "Help selected!"
            }
        }
        // Specify the actions that should be included in the menu
        actions: [
            ActionItem {
                title: "Action 1"
                onTriggered: {
                    actionLabel.text = "Action 1 selected!"
                }
            },
            ActionItem {
                title: "Action 2"
                onTriggered: {
                    actionLabel.text = "Action 2 selected!"
                }
            },
            ActionItem {
                title: "Action 3"
                onTriggered: {
                    actionLabel.text = "Action 3 selected!"
                }
            }
        ] // end of actions list
    } // end of MenuDefinition
    Container {
        Label {
            id: actionLabel
            text: "Hello Actions"
            textStyle.base: SystemDefaults.TextStyles.BigText
            horizontalAlignment: HorizontalAlignment.Center
            contextActions: [
                ActionSet {
                    title: "Label Actions"
                    ActionItem {
                        id: action1
                        title: "action1"
```

```
                    ActionBar.placement: ActionBarPlacement.OnBar
                    onTriggered: {
                        actionLabel.text = action1.title
                    }
                }
                ActionItem {
                    id: action2
                    title: "action2"
                    ActionBar.placement: ActionBarPlacement.OnBar
                    onTriggered: {
                        actionLabel.text = action2.title
                    }
                }
            }
        ]
    }
}
}
```

And the resulting menu is displayed in Figure 5-10.

Figure 5-10. Application menu

Because the application menu is application-wide, you should always specify the menu definition at the root of your scene graph, whether it is a page, navigation pane or a tabbed pane.

Segmented Control

A segmented control provides the user with a list of options, which are presented horizontally on the screen. You can use the option selection logic in order to dynamically modify the Page contents. Figures 5-11 and 5- 12 illustrate the process where Buttons are dynamically switched depending on the selected option (in a real-world scenario, you would switch entire containers of controls, but the concept stays the same).

Figure 5-11. Segmented control

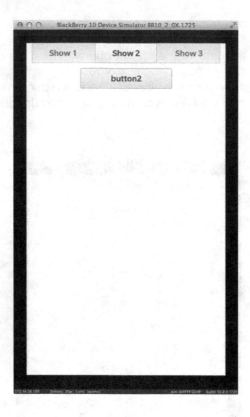

Figure 5-12. Segmented control

It is important to emphasize that the segmented control is not a container itself but rather enables you to respond to option selections. The corresponding code is shown in Listing 5-10.

Listing 5-10. Segmented Control

```
import bb.cascades 1.0
Page {
    Container {
        SegmentedControl {
            id: segmented
            Option {
                text: "Show 1"
                value: 1
            }
            Option {
                text: "Show 2"
                value: 2
            }
            Option {
                text: "Show 3"
                value: 3
            }
```

```
            onSelectedOptionChanged: {
                var value = segmented.selectedValue
                switch(value){
                        case 1:
                            container.replace(0, button1);
                            break;
                        case 2:
                            container.replace(0, button2);
                            break;
                        case 3:
                            container.replace(0, button2);
                            break;
                        default:
                            break;

                }

            }
            onCreationCompleted: {
                container.add(button1);
                segmented.selectedIndex = 0;
            }
            attachedObjects: [
                Button {
                    id: button1
                    text: "button1"
                },
                Button {
                    id: button2
                    text: "button2"
                },
                Button {
                    id: button3
                    text: "button3"
                }
            ]
        }
        Container {
            verticalAlignment: VerticalAlignment.Center
            horizontalAlignment: HorizontalAlignment.Center
            id: container
        }
    }
}
```

Title Bar

The Title bar is yet another way of extending your single Page application. If used judiciously, a TitleBar can really improve your application's user experience with minimal effort. The TitleBar really shines by giving you the ability to completely customize the controls that will appear on it.

For example, you have already seen a plain `TitleBar` in Figure 5-4, where the `ListView`'s selected item's "details" are displayed in the Navigation view. You can also include richer controls, as shown in Figure 5-13 (when you add controls to the `TitleBar`, the `TitleBar` can be expanded to display them).

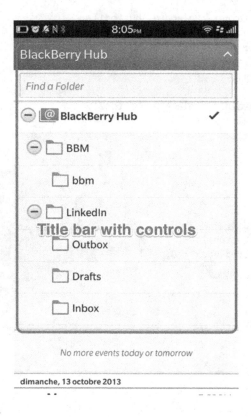

Figure 5-13. BlackBerry Hub TitleBar

In practice, you customize the `TitleBar` by setting its `Kind` property:

- `TitleBarKind.Default`: Allows "accept" and "dismiss" Action buttons to be displayed on the `TitleBar`.

- `TitleBarKind.Segmented`: Allows a `SegmentedControl` to appear on the `TitleBar`.

- `TitleBarKind.FreeForm`: Allows controls to be placed freely on the `TitleBar`.

Listing 5-11 shows how to add actions to the title bar.

Listing 5-11. TitleBar with Actions

```
Page {
    titleBar: TitleBar {
        title: "Create Task"
        kind: TitleBarKind.Default
        acceptAction: ActionItem {
            title: "OK"
```

```
        onTriggered: {
            // handle task creation here.
        }
    }
    dismissAction: ActionItem {
        title: "Cancel"
        onTriggered: {
            // handle task creation here
        }
    }
}

Container {
    //Todo: fill me with QML
    Label {
        horizontalAlignment: HorizontalAlignment.Center
        text: qsTr("Hello World") + Retranslate.onLocaleOrLanguageChanged
        textStyle.base: SystemDefaults.TextStyles.BigText
    }
}
}
```

The resulting UI is shown in Figure 5-14.

Figure 5-14. TitleBar with Actions

Using a segmented control is just as easy. I have rewritten the example provided in Listing 5-10 by setting the segmented control on the `TitleBar`, as shown in Listing 5-12.

Listing 5-12. TitleBar with Segmented Control

```
import bb.cascades 1.0
Page {
    titleBar: TitleBar {
        id: titlebar
        kind: TitleBarKind.Segmented
        options: [
            Option {
                text: "Show 1"
                value: 0
            },
            Option {
                text: "Show 2"
                value: 1
            },
            Option {
                text: "Show 3"
                value: 2
            }
        ]
        onSelectedOptionChanged: {
            var value = titlebar.selectedValue
            switch (value) {
                case 0:
                    container.replace(0, button1);
                    break;
                case 1:
                    container.replace(0, button2);
                    break;
                case 2:
                    container.replace(0, button3);
                    break;
                default:
                    break;
            }
        }
    }
    Container {
        topPadding: 50
        id: container
        onCreationCompleted: {
            container.add(button1);
            titlebar.selectedIndex = 0;
        }
        attachedObjects: [
            Button {
                horizontalAlignment: HorizontalAlignment.Center
                id: button1
```

```
                text: "button1"
            },
            Button {
                horizontalAlignment: HorizontalAlignment.Center

                id: button2
                text: "button2"
            },
            Button {
                horizontalAlignment: HorizontalAlignment.Center

                id: button3
                text: "button3"
            }
        ]
    }
}
```

The resulting UI is shown in Figure 5-15.

Figure 5-15. *TitleBar with segmented control*

Finally, you can customize the TitleBar so that it displays any set of controls on it. Listing 5-13 shows how to achieve this.

Listing 5-13. TitleBar with DateTimePicker

```
import bb.cascades 1.0
Page {
    titleBar: TitleBar {
        kind: TitleBarKind.FreeForm
        kindProperties: FreeFormTitleBarKindProperties {
            Container {
                layout: StackLayout {
                    orientation: LayoutOrientation.LeftToRight
                }
                leftPadding: 10
                rightPadding: 10
                Label {
                    text: "Hello title bar"
                    textStyle {
                        color: Color.White
                    }
                    verticalAlignment: VerticalAlignment.Center
                    layoutProperties: StackLayoutProperties {
                        spaceQuota: 1
                    }
                }
                TextField {
                    verticalAlignment: VerticalAlignment.Center
                    layoutProperties: StackLayoutProperties {
                        spaceQuota: 2
                    }
                }
            }
            expandableArea {
                content: DateTimePicker {
                    horizontalAlignment: HorizontalAlignment.Center
                    expanded: true
                }

            }
        }
    }

}
```

The resulting UI is shown in Figure 5-16.

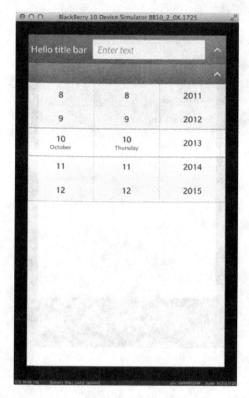

Figure 5-16. TitleBar with DateTimePicker

Sheet

A sheet provides the user an alternative flow in your application. Visually, it is displayed as a layer on top of the current screen. When the user completes the alternative flow, the sheet is closed and the main screen is displayed again. For example, in a task management application, the main screen could display the list of current tasks and you could use a sheet in order to create a new task (see Figures 5-17 and 5-18).

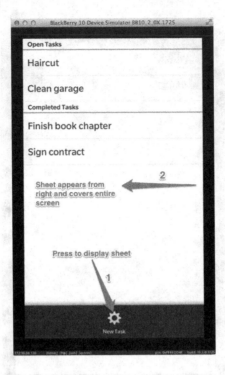

Figure 5-17. Sheet

Figure 5-18. Sheet, expanded

Listing 5-14 shows the QML document corresponding to Figure 5-17 and Figure 5-18.

Listing 5-14. Sheet

```
import bb.cascades 1.0
NavigationPane {
    id: nav
    Page {
        actions: ActionItem {
            title: "New Task"
            ActionBar.placement: ActionBarPlacement.OnBar
            onTriggered: {
                newTask.open();
            }
        }
        Container {
            ListView {
                dataModel: XmlDataModel {
                    source: "data.xml"
                }
            }
        }
    }
    attachedObjects: [
        Sheet {
            id: newTask
            Page {
                titleBar: TitleBar {
                    title: "Create Task"
                    kind: TitleBarKind.Default
                    acceptAction: ActionItem {
                        title: "OK"
                        onTriggered: {
                            // handle task creation here.
                            newTask.close();
                        }
                    }
                    dismissAction: ActionItem {
                        title: "Cancel"
                        onTriggered: {
                            // close sheet without creating new task
                            newTask.close();
                        }
                    }
                }
                Container {
                    topPadding: 10
                    leftPadding: 10
                    rightPadding: 10
                    Container {
                        layout: StackLayout {
                            orientation: LayoutOrientation.LeftToRight
                        }
```

```
                    Label{
                        text:"Name:"
                        verticalAlignment: VerticalAlignment.Center
                    }
                    TextField {
                        id: taskname
                        hintText: "Enter task name"
                    }
                }
            }
        }

        }
    ]
}
```

Attached Objects

All UIObjects have an attachedObjects property, which corresponds to a list of QObjects owned by the UIObject (formally, an attachedObjects property is defined as QDeclarativeListProperty<QObject> in C++). You will usually add to the list of attached objects business logic components that you need to access in the subnodes of the UIObject (you can also add visual controls as I did in Listing 5-12). The following are the most common usages of the attachedObjects property:

- Accessing QObject-derived classes (such as QTimer) from the QML layer. You can also use this approach to access your own custom C++ classes as long as they are derived from QObject (see Chapter 3).

- Declare component definitions using the ComponentDefinition class (see Listing 5-2).

- Define a FilePicker, SystemPrompt or SystemDialog that you can selectively hide or show.

Dynamic QML Components

There are several reasons why you would want to dynamically create QML components:

- *Modularity and reusability*: Using a single QML document is fine when you design relatively simple UIs. As your applications evolve and the UIs become more complex, you will realize that managing a large monolithic QML document can quickly become untractable. QML is an extensible component-based language (see Chapter 2). You can therefore construct your UI by assembling modular and reusable components that you can load dynamically.

- *Improving application start-up*: Loading a large QML document can take a long time during application start-up. In order to accelerate the process, you can initially load the essential UI elements (for example, the main screen) and then dynamically load the rest of the UI during the application lifetime.

■ *Effective memory management*: A large QML document can consume memory unnecessarily. Therefore, being able to dynamically create and destroy QML objects can optimize memory and resource management (you have actually already seen this in action in Listing 5-4, where the ItemPage component is dynamically created and destroyed). For example, in the case of an application with many tabs, it would make sense to only load a tab's contents when it is selected by the user, and unload the contents when the user switches to another tab.

If you have decided to dynamically manage your UI, you actually need a method to instantiate QML objects. In this case, you can use instances of ComponentDefinition or ControlDelegate as QML objects factories. Both objects fulfill the same role: a ComponentDefinition is the imperative instantiation method (using JavaScript); a ControlDelegate and a Delegate are the declarative way. (In particular, you can use a Delegate to dynamically load a tab's content. I will illustrate this in the section about Delegate objects.)

ComponentDefinition

A ComponentDefinition class is used to define QML Components so that they can be dynamically created. You can define components "inline" or by loading content from a QML file identified by an URL. You have actually seen the latter used in Listings 5-2 and 5-3 to switch pages during navigation.

You can define both visual and nonvisual objects using a ComponentDefinition. A definition can also be provided inline in the QML document using the ComponentDefintion's content property, or reference another QML file using the ComponentDefintion's source property.

ControlDelegate

A ControlDelegate is the declarative way of dynamically loading QML objects. A ControlDelegate plays the role of a placeholder in your main QML document scene graph. The ControlDelegate will then load in-place its QML content as soon as you set the ControlDelegate.delegateActive property to true. Listing 5-15 illustrates how to use control delegates in practice (the example is based on the segmented control described in Listing 5-10; but this time, the controls are dynamically loaded).

Listing 5-15. ControlDelegate

```
import bb.cascades 1.0
Page {
    Container {
        SegmentedControl {
            id: segmented
            Option {
                text: "Show 1"
                value: 1
            }
            Option {
                text: "Show 2"
```

```
                value: 2
            }
            Option {
                text: "Show 3"
                value: 3
            }
            onSelectedOptionChanged: {
                var value = segmented.selectedValue
                switch (value) {
                    case 1:
                        // probable QML engine bug. If braces are not included, only the
                        // first statement is executed and the others ignored.
                        {
                            controlDelegate.source = "Control1.qml"
                            var control = controlDelegate.control;
                            if (control != undefined) {
                                control.message.connect(textfield.handleMessage);
                            }
                        }
                        break;
                    case 2:
                        controlDelegate.source = "Control2.qml"
                        break;
                    case 3:
                        controlDelegate.source = "Control3.qml"
                        break;
                    default:
                        break;
                }
            }
            onCreationCompleted: {
                segmented.selectedIndex = 0;
                controlDelegate.source = "Control1.qml"
                var control = controlDelegate.control;
                if (control != undefined) {
                    control.message.connect(textfield.handleMessage);
                }
            }
        }
    }
    ControlDelegate {
        id: controlDelegate
        horizontalAlignment: HorizontalAlignment.Center
        delegateActive: true
        onError: {
            console.log("Error while loading the delegate: " + errorMessage)
        }
    }
```

```
TextField {
    id: textfield
    // A custom JavaScript function to handle the
    // message signal emitted by Control1
    function handleMessage(message) {
        textfield.text = message;
    }
}
    }
  }
}
```

Depending on the selected option in the segmented control, the corresponding QML control will be dynamically loaded by the ControlDelegate.

The running application is shown in Figures 5-19 and 5-20.

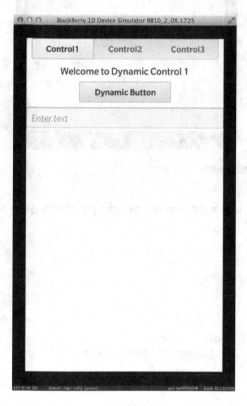

Figure 5-19. Control1 loaded ControlDelegate

Figure 5-20. Control2 loaded by ControlDelegate

The corresponding control implementations are given by Listings 5-16 and 5-17.

Listing 5-16. Control1.qml

```
import bb.cascades 1.0
Container {
    id: root
    signal message(string s);
        Label{
            text: "Welcome to Dynamic Control 1"
            horizontalAlignment: HorizontalAlignment.Center
        }
        Button{
            id: button
            text: "Dynamic Button"
            onClicked:{
                root.message(button.text);
            }
        }
}
```

Listing 5-17.   Control2.qml

```
import bb.cascades 1.0
Container {
    Label {
        text: "Welcome to Dynamic Control 2"
        horizontalAlignment: HorizontalAlignment.Center
    }
    DateTimePicker {
        horizontalAlignment: HorizontalAlignment.Center

    }
}
```

Delegate

A Delegate is used to dynamically create or delete an object from QML. The Delegate exposes an active property, which specifies whether the source QML component should be loaded (active: true) or unloaded (active:false). The Delegate's source property defines the source QML component. For example, Listing 5-18 shows you how to dynamically load a Tab in a TabbedPane using a Delegate.

Listing 5-18.   Dynamic Tab

```
TabbedPane {
    Tab {
        id: tab1
        delegate: Delegate {
            id: tabDelegate
            source: "sourcetab1.qml" // tab1 contents is loaded from sourcetab1.qml
        }
        delegateActivationPolicy: TabDelegateActivationPolicy.Default
    }
}
```

The TabDelegateActivationPolicy enumeration can take one of the following values:

■ TabDelegateActivationPolicy.Default: Cascades chooses the activation policy (typically, the source object is loaded when a tab is selected).

■ TabDelegateActivationPolicy.None: You control when the source object is created or deleted.

■ TabDelegateActivationPolicy.ActivatedWhileSelected: The tab content is loaded when it is selected, and deleted when it's no longer selected (this improves application start time, but can slow down tab switches).

■ TabDelegateActivationPolicy.ActivatedWhenSelected: The tab content is loaded when selected and never deleted during the lifetime of the tab.

■ TabDelegateActivationPolicy.ActiveImmediately: The tab content is loaded as soon as the source property is set. The content is unloaded when the source property is cleared.

Multiple Page Applications

Pages are essentially the building blocks for more complex application structures. For example, navigation-based and tabbed-based applications are essentially an aggregation of Pages. In other words, you can reuse the concepts introduced for single Page applications in the broader context of navigation-based or tabbed-based applications.

Navigation-Based Application

You can build a navigation-based application by using a NavigationPane as the root control in your scene graph. This class represents a set of pages—arranged in a stack—that users can navigate. In order to display a page, you need to push it on the NavigationPane's stack. The NavigationPane will always display the page on the top of the stack.

You will notice that the stack metaphor is particularly well-suited for implementing drill-down or "master-detail" views. When you need to navigate back from the detail view to the master view, you simply pop the pages from the NavigationPane's stack (see Figure 5-21).

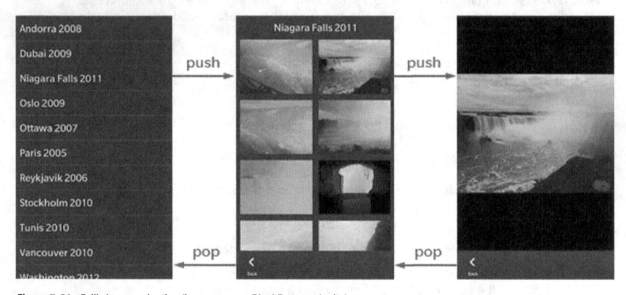

Figure 5-21. *Drill-down navigation (image source: BlackBerry web site)*

You can use the following NavigationPane methods to implement navigation:

- NavigationPane.push(child): Pushes a Page on the stack of this NavigationPane.

- Page NavigationPane.pop(): Pops the top of the stack from this NavigationPane. The NavigationPane keeps the ownership of the Page.

- List NavigationPane.navigateTo(targetPage): Navigates to targetPage if it is present in the stack of this NavigationPane. Any pages above the one navigated to in the stack will be removed from the stack.

When a page is popped from the NavigationPane's stack, the NavigationPane::popTransitionEnde
d(Page* page) signal is emitted. The NavigationPane still keeps ownership of the Page, but you can
delete it if it's no longer needed (see Listing 5-2).

Tab-Based Application

A tab-based application's UI is designed around tabs, which can either contain a Page or a
NavigationPane. The user taps a tab to display the associated screen. Tabs either appear directly on the
action bar or are located in the tab menu on the leftmost side of the action bar. In practice, the possibility
to add a Page or a NavigationPane to tabs enables you to design complex navigation structures.

The root control of a tab-based application is the TabbedPane. You will usually use the following
properties and methods in order to manage the TabbedPane:

■ TabbedPane.activePane: The AbstractPane (a Page or a NavigationPane), which
is currently shown by the TabbedPane.

■ TabbedPane.showTabsOnActionBar: If true, tabs will be placed on the Action bar;
otherwise, tabs will be placed in the Tab Menu on the left of the Action bar.

■ TabbedPane.tabs: The list of tabs added to the TabbedPane.

■ TabbedPane.activeTab: The tab that is currently active in the TabbedPane.

■ TabbePane.add(tab): Adds a Tab to the TabbedPane.

Note that in order to add your Page or NavigationPane to the TabbedPane, you first need to add the
Page or NavigationPane to a Tab and then add the Tab to the TabbedPane.

■ Tab.setContent(content): Sets the content of this Tab, which has to a
NavigationPane or Page. Ownership of the content is transferred to this Tab.
If this Tab already has content, the old content is still owned by this Tab.

Summary

This chapter explained how to use the templates available in the New BlackBerry Project wizard as a
starting point for your own applications. The Page control was introduced as a fundamental building
block for customizing application screens with Actions and Menus. Techniques such as dynamic
loading of QML components using ControlDelegates, ComponentDefinitions, and Delegates
showed you how to not only optimize your application performance but also introduced additional
possibilities for providing an enticing and rich user experience.

A ControlDelegate plays the role of a placeholder in your QML document for a control that you
can dynamically load using a ComponentDefinition (a ComponentDefinition can also be used from
JavaScript to dynamically load a component using its load method). A Delegate object can be used
to dynamically load a Tab object in a TabbedPane.

Finally, application structure was defined as your app's supporting elements—such
as menus, actions, and navigation—used for enhancing your app's user experience.
Application structure is also governed by the BlackBerry 10 UI guidelines, which can be found at
http://developer.blackberry.com/design/bb10/.

Chapter 6

ListView and DataModel

A `ListView` is a fundamental Cascades control because it gives you an efficient way of displaying to the user hierarchical data on a screen where the real estate is relatively limited. List views are therefore one of the most flexible controls available in the Cascades framework and provide you lots of options for specifying how your data will be rendered as list items. Another important aspect of list views is their ability to clearly separate your data from its visual appearance by using the model-view-controller pattern. As illustrated in Figure 6-1, the `ListView` plays the role of a controller, which handles—among other things—user interactions; the `DataModel` represents your data; and, finally, a `ListItemComponent` is a QML template defining visual controls for rendering your data. You can also define multiple `ListItemComponents` for different data item types (I will tell more about types in the "Data Models" section. For the moment, simply keep in mind that a data model can define a type, which is used by the ListView to render a data item.).

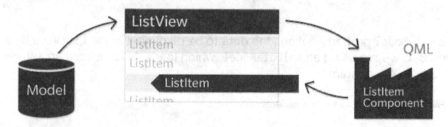

Figure 6-1. *ListView MVC architecture (image source: BlackBerry)*

Also, as briefly mentioned in the previous chapter, you can use a `ListView` as your main UI control for data-centric apps.

This chapter will initially concentrate on the visual and user interaction aspects of a list view, and at a later stage, will explore how data models are implemented. You cannot completely separate both concepts, but it is useful not to initially focus too much on the intricacies of data models.

After having read this chapter, you will have a good understanding of

- How to use list views in your own applications to display hierarchical data to the user.

- Create navigation-based apps using a ListView as the main UI control.

- Use the standard data models provided by Cascades to display data in a ListView.

- Implement your own "custom" data models for data types or sources not supported out of the box by Cascades.

List Views

A ListView aggregates a data model and its visual representation. This section will mostly focus on the visual aspects and touch interactions of the ListView, and the next section will give you a more detailed description of data models. Listing 6-1 illustrates a minimal ListView control added to a Page control.

Listing 6-1. ListView

```
import bb.cascades 1.2
Page {
    ListView {
        id: listview
        dataModel: XmlDataModel {
            id: people
            source: "people.xml"
        }
    }
}
```

The ListView's dataModel property defines the data to be displayed in the ListView (in the example shown in Listing 6-1, we are using an XmlDataModel, which loads its data from an XML file; Listing 6-2 gives you the sample XML content).

Listing 6-2. XML File Representing Actors and Presidents

```
<people>
    <category value="Actors">
        <person name="John Wayne"/>
        <person name="Kirk Douglas"/>
        <person name="Clint Eastwood"/>
        <person name="Spencer Tracy"/>
        <person name="Lee Van Cleef"/>
    </category>
    <category value="US Presidents">
        <person name="John F. Kennedy"/>
        <person name="Bill Clinton"/>
        <person name="George Bush"/>
        <person name="Barack Obama"/>
    </category>
</people>
```

And Figure 6-2 illustrates the resulting `ListView`.

Figure 6-2. Flat list of items

As illustrated in Figure 6-2, the list view's items have been successfully loaded from the XML document; however, the hierarchical structure of the XML document has been "flattened," which is not what we want (the Actors and US Presidents categories should, in fact, appear as header items, with actors and presidents displayed under the corresponding headers).

ListItemComponent Definition

A `ListItemComponent` is a kind of factory, which contains a QML component definition. The actual component is a visual control (or simply a visual) responsible for rendering data items of a given type. In other words, a `ListView` uses a `ListItemComponent` to create a visual representation of its data items. The following properties are used in the component definition:

- `QString ListItemComponent::type()`: The data item type that this component definition should be used for.

- `QDeclarativeComponent* ListItemComponent::content()`: The QML component definition used for creating the visuals responsible for rendering the data item whose type is `ListItemComponent::type()`. (Note that a `QDeclarativeComponent` is very similar in nature to a `ComponentDefinition`, which is used to define QML components for dynamic creation, see Chapter 5). `content` is also `ListItemComponent`'s default property (see Chapter 2 for an explanation of default properties).

Listing 6-3 shows you how to use a `ListItemComponent` in practice.

Listing 6-3. ListItemComponent Definition with Container As a Root Visual

```
import bb.cascades 1.2
Page {
    ListView {
        id: listview
        dataModel: XmlDataModel {
            id: people
            source: "people.xml"
        }
        listItemComponents:[
            ListItemComponent {
                type: "category"
                Container{
                    id: container
                    Label {
                        id: myLabel
                        text: container.ListItem.data.value // equivalent to ListItemData.value
                    }
                }
            }
        ] // ListItemComponents
    } // ListView
}
```

As illustrated in Listing 6-3, you can add a `ListItemComponent` to the `ListView`'s `listItemComponents` property (in a moment, you will see that you can define multiple `ListItemComponents` corresponding to different data item types in the data model). At runtime, the `ListView` uses the component definition to instantiate the visuals for rendering its data items (therefore, in the previous code, the visuals created at runtime are the `Container`, which is the root visual, and the `Label`). The `ListView` also dynamically attaches the `ListItem` *attached property* to the root visual, which is the `Container`. (An attached property is a mechanism for dynamically adding a property, which was not part of a control's initial definition.) Finally, the `Label` uses the `Container`'s `ListItem` property to access the data item.

There is still one point that needs to be clarified in Listing 6-3: How is the current data node type determined by the `ListView` to select the correct `ListItemComponent` component definition? In the "Data Models" section, you will see that the data model provides the type information. For example, in the specific case of an `XmlDataModel`, the returned type corresponds to the name of the tag in the XML document. Therefore, the `XmlDataModel` will return the `category` type for the corresponding XML tag shown in Listing 6-2.

The root visual's `ListItem` property also defines the following properties, which you can use in your component definition (note that you have already used the data property in Listing 6-3 to access the data item):

- `ListItem.initialized`: States whether the root visual is initialized or not. The `initialized` property is `true` when the initialization of the root visual is finished (in other words, all properties have been updated to reflect the current item). Otherwise, the property is `false`. For performance reasons, `ListViews` « recycle » `ListItems`. The data model should therefore only be updated when the ListItem is initialized. For example, if a CheckBox is used for updating a corresponding item status in the data model, the onCheckChanged() slot should check the ListItem's initialized property before propagating the change to the data model. If the ListItem is not initialized, you could potentially corrupt the data model's state.

- ListItem.data: The data item returned by DataModel::data(). Common values are QString, QVariantMap, and QObject*. Note that in QML you can use the mapname.keyname and objectname.propertyname syntax to access individual data items exposed by a map or an object, respectively. Also, as mentioned previously, the ListItem property is only defined on the root visual. You will therefore have to use the <rootId>.ListItem.data notation to access the data property from any visual located further down the tree. As a convenience, the ListView also provides the ListItemData alias, which is a context property accessible from anywhere in the visual tree (equivalently, instead of setting the Label's text property using container.ListItem.data.value, you could have used ListItemData.value).

- ListItem.indexPath: The index path identifying this item in the data model.

- ListItem.view: The ListView in which this item is visible.

- ListItem.component: The ListItemComponent from which this visual has been created.

- ListItem.active: true if the visual is active (in other words, the user is pressing on it).

- ListItem.selected: true if this visual is selected. An item is typically selected if the user intends to perform an action on the item or access details for the item (the "Detecting Selection" section will give you more information about handling selection).

Note The visuals created from a ListItemComponent definition do not share the same document context as main.qml, where the ListView has been declared. This means that only the properties defined in the ListItem attached property are visible to the root visual at runtime. In other words, you can't access by id as you would usually do for any of the controls declared in main.qml. You will see how to circumvent this problem in the "Context Actions" section.

Header Definition

Cascades provides standard controls that you can use for rendering list items. For example, you could use a standard Header control instead of a Label in order to render items of type category. A Header control has title and subtitle properties that you can set using the ListItemData property (see Listing 6-4; note that only the Header's title is set).

Listing 6-4. Header Visual

```
import bb.cascades 1.2
Page {
    ListView {
        id: listview
        dataModel: XmlDataModel {
            id: people
            source: "people.xml"
        }
        listItemComponents:[
            ListItemComponent {
                type: "category"
                Header {
                    title: ListItemData.value
                }
            }
        ] // listItemComponents
    } // ListView
} // Page
```

Figure 6-3 illustrates the resulting UI.

Figure 6-3. List of people with header items

StandardListItem Definition

Let's now modify the XML document shown in Listing 6-2 to include additional information such as the person's date of birth, a picture, and name of spouse (see Listing 6-5).

Listing 6-5. Updated XML Data Source

```
<people>
    <category value="Actors">
        <person name="John Wayne" born="May 26, 1907" spouse="Pilar Pallete" pic="wayne.jpg"/>
        <person name="Kirk Douglas" born="December 9, 1916" spouse="Anne Buydens"
            pic="douglas.jpg"/>
        <person name="Clint Eastwood" born="May 31, 1930" spouse="Dina Eastwood"
            pic="eastwood.jpg"/>
        <person name="Spencer Tracy" born="April 5, 1900" spouse="Louise Treadwell"
            pic="tracy.jpg"/>
        <person name="Lee Van Cleef" born="January 9, 1925" spouse="Barbara Havelone"
            pic="vancleef.jpg"/>
    </category>
    <category value="US Presidents">
        <person name="John F. Kennedy" born="May 29, 1917" spouse="Jacqueline Kennedy"
            pic="kennedy.jpg"/>
        <person name="Bill Clinton" born="August 19, 1946" spouse="Hillary Rodham Clinton"
            pic="clinton.jpg"/>
        <person name="George Bush" born="July 6, 1946" spouse="Laura Bush" pic="bush.jpg"/>
        <person name="Barack Obama" born="August 4, 1961" spouse="Michelle Obama"
            pic="obama.jpg"/>
    </category>
</people>
```

If you try to display the updated XML document given by Listing 6-5, the resulting UI will be similar to Figure 6-4, which is not what you want (only the person's date of birth is displayed).

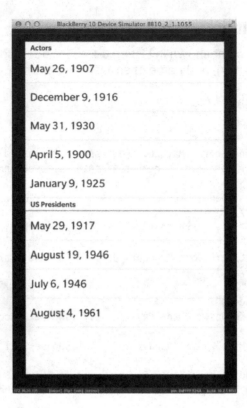

Figure 6-4. List of people displayed incorrectly

In fact, just as with `Header` items, you need a way to tell the `ListView` how to render items of type `person`. You can achieve this in several ways, but I will first show you how to use the `StandardListItem` visual (see Listing 6-6).

Listing 6-6. StandardListItem Visual

```
import bb.cascades 1.2
Page {
    ListView {
        id: listview
        dataModel: XmlDataModel {
            id: people
            source: "people.xml"
        }
        onTriggered: {
        }
        listItemComponents:[
            ListItemComponent {
                type: "category"
                Header {
                    title: ListItemData.value
                }
            },
```

```
        ListItemComponent {
            type: "person"
            StandardListItem {
                title: ListItemData.name
                description: ListItemData.born
                status: ListItemData.spouse
                imageSource: "asset:///pics/"+ListItemData.pic
            }
        }
    ] // ListItemComponents
} // ListView
}
```

A StandarListItem is a control with a standard list of properties to be displayed in a ListView. The
properties are title (displayed in bold text), description, status, and imageSource (all properties
are optional). For example, the code in Listing 6-6 uses a StandardListItem control to render an item
of person type by using the corresponding XML attributes provided by the data model. Figure 6-5
illustrates the resulting UI (note that the person's picture is loaded from the application's assets folder).

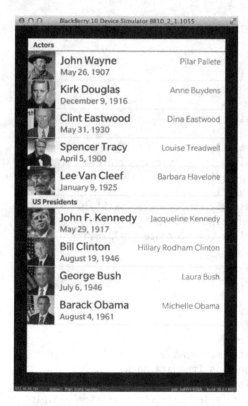

Figure 6-5. Updated list with each person's details

CustomListItem Definition

You can even further customize the list item rendering by using a CustomListItem visual. The CustomListItem defines a highlight, a divider, and a user-specified control for rendering a data item. The highlight, which is defined by the highlightAppearance property, determines what the list item looks like when it is selected. The divider, which is defined by the dividerVisible property, determines if a divider should be shown in order to separate the list item from adjacent items. Finally, the content property used for rendering the list item can be any Cascades control you decide to use (note that if you use a Container, you will be able to aggregate several controls). To illustrate how to use a CustomListItem in practice, Listing 6-7 shows you how to customize the list's headers with a CustomListItem.

Listing 6-7. CustomListItem Visual

```
import bb.cascades 1.2
Page {
    ListView {
        id: listview
        dataModel: XmlDataModel {
            id: people
            source: "people.xml"
        }
        listItemComponents:[
            ListItemComponent {
                type:"category"
                CustomListItem {
                    dividerVisible: true
                    Label {
                        text: ListItemData.value
                        // Apply a text style to create a large, bold font with
                        // a specific color
                        textStyle {
                            base: SystemDefaults.TextStyles.BigText
                            fontWeight: FontWeight.Bold
                            color: Color.create ("#7a184a")
                        }
                    } // Label
                } // CustomListItem
            },
            ListItemComponent {
                type: "person"
                StandardListItem {
                    title: ListItemData.name
                    description: ListItemData.born
                    status: ListItemData.spouse
                    imageSource: "asset:///pics/"+ListItemData.pic
                }
            }
        ] // listItemComponents
    }
}
```

The `CustomListItem` illustrated in Listing 6-7 uses a `Label` control to apply text styling to the header element (see Figure 6-6 for the resulting UI).

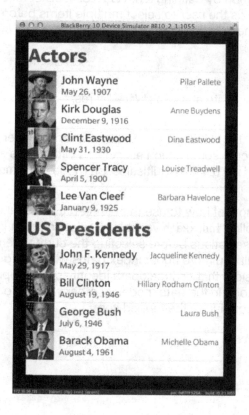

Figure 6-6. Custom headers

There is no obligation to use the predefined controls mentioned earlier as the `content` property of a `ListItemComponent`. As a matter of fact, you can simply use any Cascades control to display the data item to the user. For example, in the case of a rich data model, you could add multiple Cascades controls—such as a `CheckBox`, a `Label`, and an `ImageView`—to a `Container` playing the role of the root visual (the main advantage of leveraging the stock `Header`, `StandardListItem`, and `CustomListItem` controls is to provide a smooth Cascades look and feel across your applications).

Detecting Selection

Displaying an item and customizing its visual is one aspect of `ListView` programming. However, you will also need to detect item selection so that your users can interact with the `ListView`. The following topics will be discussed in this section:

- Detecting the selected item when the user performs a single tap in the `ListView`.
- Using item selection to navigate from a master view to a details view.

- Handling context actions when the user performs a long press on an item.

- Handling multiselection by defining a `MultipleSelectActionItem` control. Multiselection enables the user to select multiple items before triggering a context action on the selected items.

Single Tap

You can handle a single tap on an item in a `ListView` by responding to the `ListView`'s `triggered()` signal:

- `triggered(QVariantList indexPath)`: Emitted when the user taps an item with the intention to execute some action associated with it. The signal will not be emitted when the `ListView` is in multiselection mode. The `indexPath` parameter identifies the tapped item.

Listing 6-8 gives you an example of how to use the `triggered()` signal in practice: the `ListView`'s `onTriggered` slot uses the implicit `indexPath` variable to select an item in the `ListView` (note that the code clears any previous selections before selecting the current item). In QML, an index path is an array of integers. I will tell you more about index paths when we discuss data models. For the moment, you can simply consider that an index path identifies the tapped item. An index path is also a kind of pointer to the data node in the data model. In other words, you can use the index path to access the data node corresponding to the tapped item.

Listing 6-8. ListView, onTriggered() Slot

```
ListView {
    id: listview
    dataModel: XmlDataModel {
        id: people
        source: "people.xml"
    }
    onTriggered: {
        listview.clearSelection();
        select(indexPath);
    }
    listItemComponents: [// ... code omitted]
}
```

Note that when the item is selected (either programmatically or in multiselection mode), the `ListView` emits the `selectionChanged()` signal:

- `selectionChanged(QVariantList indexPath, bool selected)`: Emitted when the selection state has changed for an item (in other words, the item has been either selected or deselected). You can use the `selected` parameter to determine if the item is selected (`true`) or not (`false`).

Referencing an Item in an Action

A user-triggered action can use the index path of the currently selected item to get to the corresponding data node (see Listing 6-9).

Listing 6-9. Using Selected Item in Action

```
Page {
    actions: [
        ActionItem {
            ActionBar.placement: ActionBarPlacement.OnBar
            title: "Share"
            onTriggered: {
                if(listview.selected().length > 1){
                    var dataItem = listview.dataModel.data(listview.selected());
                    // share data item.
                }
            } // onTriggered
        }
    ]
    ListView {
        id: listview
        dataModel: XmlDataModel {
            id: people
            source: "people.xml"
        }
        onTriggered: {
            listview.clearSelection();
            toggleSelection(indexPath);
        }
        listItemComponents: [// ... code omitted]
    } // ListView
} // Page
```

The code shown in Listing 6-9 uses the "Share" action's `triggered()` signal to retrieve the data node corresponding to the current selected item in the `ListView`. See Figure 6-7. Because we are only interested in `person` type data items, the code checks whether the item's index path size is bigger than 1 before accessing the data node. (The index path of the root node in the data hierarchy is an empty array; header items, which correspond to the `category` type, have an index path of size 1, and "leaf" items, which correspond to the `person` type, have an index path of size 2.) Also, if you need to define multiple actions on an item, it is usually better to use context actions (see the following section for more information on context actions).

Figure 6-7. Share action on selected item

Navigating a Master-Details View

You can use a single tap on an item to implement master-details navigation. To illustrate this, let's "retrofit" the ListView in a navigation pane (see Listing 6-10).

Listing 6-10. ListView Navigation

```
import bb.cascades 1.2
NavigationPane {
    id: nav
    attachedObjects: [
        ComponentDefinition {
            id: itemPageDefinition
            source: "PersonDetails.qml"
        }
    ]
    onPopTransitionEnded: {
        page.destroy();
    }
    Page {
        ListView {
            id: listview
```

```
        dataModel: XmlDataModel {
            id: people
            source: "people.xml"
        }
        onTriggered: {
            if (indexPath.length > 1) {
                var person = people.data(indexPath);
                var personDetails = itemPageDefinition.createObject();
                personDetails.person = person
                nav.push(personDetails);
            }
        }
        listItemComponents: [
            // ...code omitted
        ]
    } // ListView
  }// Page
} // NavigationPane
```

If you look at Listing 6-10 carefully, you will notice that it is very similar to the code generated by the list view template introduced in Chapter 5 (see Listing 5-3). In other words, by simply rearranging the QML document, and by adding a NavigationPane, you have managed to create a navigation-based application using a ListView as the main UI element. The navigation from the ListView to the details page is initiated by the ListView's triggered() signal. The details page is defined by the PersonDetails control, which I will explain shortly. Note that before pushing a new PersonDetails page on the NavigationPane's stack, you need to initialize the PersonDetails's person property with the selected data node (because the data node will be used by PersonDetails to initialize its controls).

The PersonDetails page definition is shown in Listing 6-11.

Listing 6-11. PersonDetails.qml

```
import bb.cascades 1.0
Page {
    property variant person;
    Container {
        verticalAlignment: VerticalAlignment.Center
        horizontalAlignment: HorizontalAlignment.Center
        topPadding: 50
        ImageView {
            horizontalAlignment: HorizontalAlignment.Center
            imageSource: "asset:///pics/"+person.pic
            preferredWidth: 400
            preferredHeight: 400
        }
        Label {
            textStyle.base: SystemDefaults.TextStyles.BigText
            horizontalAlignment: HorizontalAlignment.Center
                text: person.name
        }
```

```
        Label {
            textStyle.base: SystemDefaults.TextStyles.SubtitleText
            horizontalAlignment: HorizontalAlignment.Center
            text: "date of birth: "+person.born
        }
    } // Container
} // Page
```

As mentioned previously, the person property corresponds to the selected node in the data model and is used to initialize the controls located on the page (the data node is a map and you can use its keys to retrieve the underlying data). To navigate back to the ListView, the user can use the Back button on the action bar. Figure 6-8 illustrates the corresponding UI when the details view is shown.

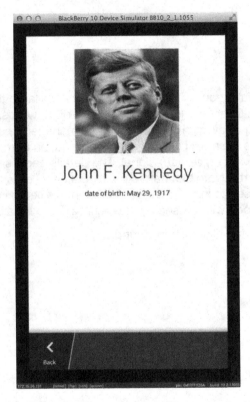

Figure 6-8. Details view showing JFK (Back button will return to list view)

Context Actions

You can define context actions on the root visual located in a ListItemComponent definition. The actions will then appear in a context menu when the user performs a long press on an item (see Listing 6-12).

Listing 6-12. Context Actions

```
ListItemComponent {
    type: "person"
    StandardListItem {
        id: standardListItem
        title: ListItemData.name
        description: ListItemData.born
        status: ListItemData.spouse
        imageSource: "asset:///pics/" + ListItemData.pic
        contextActions: [
            ActionSet {
                DeleteActionItem {
                    onTriggered: {
                        var myview = standardListItem.ListItem.view;
                        var dataModel = myview.dataModel;
                        var indexPath = myview.selected();
                        // data model must support item deletion.
                        dataModel.removeItem(indexPath);
                    }
                }// DeleteActionItem
            }// ActionSet
        ] // ContextActions
    } // StandardListItem
} // ListItemComponent
```

Actions are covered in full detail in Chapter 5. You can therefore refer to that chapter if the code in Listing 6-12 does not seem clear to you. Also, looking at the DeleteActionItem's onTriggered() slot, you will notice that the code is accessing the ListView using the root visual's ListItem property (typically, you would use the ListView's id directly). Once again, this would not work because the ListView's id has been defined in a different document context and is not visible to the DeleteActionItem. Instead, you must use the StandardListItem's ListItem attached property to get to the view.

Accessing the Application Delegate

If you review ListItem's properties, you will notice that ListItem does not provide a property to reference the application delegate (or, as a matter of fact, any other object added to main.qml's document context). As mentioned in Chapter 3, document contexts are hierarchical in nature. Therefore, if you set a property in the root context created by the QML declarative engine, it will be visible to all document contexts (because the root context is inherited by all document contexts). This is very similar to a global variable, which will be visible anywhere in your code. As illustrated in Listing 6-13, the standard way of setting the application delegate was to use the main.qml document context (see Chapter 3 for more details about document contexts).

Listing 6-13. Application Delegate Set on main.qml Document Context

```
// Create scene document from main.qml asset, the parent is set
// to ensure the document gets destroyed properly at shut down.
QmlDocument *qml = QmlDocument::create("asset:///main.qml").parent(this);
qml->documentContext()->setContextProperty("_app", this);
```

Therefore, to make sure that the app delegate is visible from all contexts, you will need to use the root document context instead of `main.qml`'s document context (see Listing 6-14).

Listing 6-14. Application Delegate Set on the Root Context

```
QDeclarativeEngine* engine = QmlDocument::defaultDeclarativeEngine();
QDeclarativeContext* rootContext = engine->rootContext();
rootContext->setContextProperty("_app", this);
```

Finally, if you need to access a specific control defined in `main.qml`, you will have to declare a property alias referencing the original property in the `ListView` (see Listing 6-15).

Listing 6-15. ListView Property Alias

```
TextField{
    id: myfield
}

ListView {
    id: listview
    property alias text: myfield.text; // accessible as ListItem.view.text
}
```

Multiple Selection Mode

In multiple selection mode, the user can quickly select multiple items in the `ListView` and then use a context action to process those items (note that the action will appear in a special overflow context menu and will only be visible when multiple selection mode is active). Listing 6-16 shows you how to implement multiple selection mode.

Listing 6-16. Multi-Selection Mode

```
Page {
    actions: [
        MultiSelectActionItem {
            multiSelectHandler: listview.multiSelectHandler
        }
    ]
    ListView {
        id: listview
        dataModel: XmlDataModel {
            id: people
            source: "people.xml"
        }
        multiSelectHandler {
            status: "0 items selected"
            actions: [
                ActionItem {
                    title: "Share"
                    onTriggered:{
                        // handle share items}
                    }
```

```
                } // ActionItem
            ] // actions
        } // multiSelectHandler
        onSelectionChanged: {
            listview.multiSelectHandler.status =
                listview.selectionList().length + " items selected";
        }
        onTriggered:{
            // code omitted
        }
        listItemComponents:[
            // code omitted
        ]
    } // ListView
} // Page
```

The previous code first defines a MultiSelectActionItem using the Page's actions property (this will effectively create a "Select items" action in the overflow menu; see Figure 6-9). Then the Page's MultiSelectActionItem has to reference a MultiSelectHandler, which is defined using the ListView's multiSelectHandler property. In other words, the MultiSelectActionItem is a special type of ActionItem that references a MultiSelectHandler, which actually defines ActionItems (the ActionItems will be displayed only when multiselection mode is active). Also note that in multiselection mode, the ListView's triggered() signal is not emitted when an item is selected. Instead, if you need to determine which item has been selected, you will need to use the ListView's selectionChanged() signal. Finally, a MultiSelectHandler can also display a status and a cancel button (see Listing 6-16 and Figure 6-10).

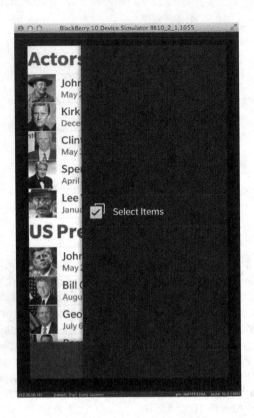

Figure 6-9. Multiselection (step 1)

Figure 6-10. Multiselection (step 2)

Figure 6-9 and Figure 6-10 illustrate the steps involved in multiple selection mode.

You can also define a `MultiSelectActionItem` directly in the `ListView` (Listing 6-17) by setting the `ListView`'s `multiSelectAction` property (in this case, the multiple selection mode will be available as a context action; in other words, it will appear after a long press on a `ListView` item).

Listing 6-17. multiSelectionHandler in ListView

```
Page{
    ListView {
        id: listview
        dataModel: XmlDataModel {
            id: people
            source: "people.xml"
        }
        multiSelectAction: MultiSelectActionItem {
            multiSelectHandler: listview.multiSelectHandler
        }
        multiSelectHandler {
            // same as before
        }
    }
}
```

Layout

In all the examples provided until now, you have used the ListView's default layout, which is a StackListLayout. You can, however, customize the layout by using a GridListLayout, which will display the list items in a grid. I am not going to get into specifics of the GridListLayout, but I will mention that you can use it to display list items as image thumbnails. For example, Listing 6-18 shows you how to use an ImageView to display image thumbnails.

Listing 6-18. GridListLayout

```
import bb.cascades 1.2
import bb.data 1.0

Page {
    Container {
        ListView {
            id: listview
            layout: GridListLayout {
            }
            dataModel: XmlDataModel {
                id: datamodel
                source: "people.xml"
            }
            listItemComponents: [
                ListItemComponent {
                    type: "person"
                    ImageView {
                        imageSource: "asset:///pics/" + ListItemData.pic
                        scalingMethod: ScalingMethod.AspectFill
                    }
                } // LisitItemComponent
            ]
        } // ListView
    } // Container
} // Page
```

Figure 6-11 illustrates the resulting UI.

Figure 6-11. Image thumbnails

Note that for the thumbnails to be displayed correctly in the ListView, the data model has to be flat (see Listing 6-19).

Listing 6-19. Flat XML Model

```
<people>
    <person name="John Wayne" pic="wayne.jpg"/>
    <person name="Kirk Douglas" pic="douglas.jpg"/>
    <person name="Clint Eastwood" pic="eastwood.jpg"/>
    <person name="Spencer Tracy" pic="tracy.jpg"/>
    <person name="Lee Van Cleef" pic="vancleef.jpg"/>
    <person name="John F. Kennedy" pic="kennedy.jpg"/>
    <person name="Bill Clinton" pic="clinton.jpg"/>
    <person name="George Bush" pic="bush.jpg"/>
    <person name="Barack Obama" pic="obama.jpg"/>
</people>
```

Creating Visuals in C++

Before getting into the details of data models in the next section, I want to quickly mention that you can create visuals in C++ using the `ListItemProvider` class. Note that a recurring theme in this book has always been to use the declarative power of QML to create your UI, and that C++ should be exclusively used for your app's business logic. Therefore, `ListItemProvider` is mentioned here for the sake of completeness without getting into the implementation details (the techniques shown in the previous sections based on `ListItemComponent` objects should be preferred in most cases in practice).

`ListItemProvider` is essentially a factory interface for creating visuals in C++. For your own `ListItemProvider` subclass, you must implement the following pure virtual functions:

- `VisualNode* ListItemProvider::createItem(ListView* listview, const QString& type)`: A factory method for creating a VisualNode. Returns a visual for the listview for an item of the given type. Note that the `ListView` will take ownership of the `VisualNode` instance.

- `void ListItemProvider::updateItem(ListView* listView, VisualNode* visual, const QString& type, const QVariantList& indexPath, const QVariant& data)`: Updates the specified list item based on the provided item type, index path, and data.

A `VisualNode` is the parent class of all Cascades controls, including custom controls. You can therefore create your own custom control in C++ and return it from `ListItemProvider::createItem()` (or alternatively, you could use a Cascades `Container` as the root visual).

Note that `VisualNode`s are kept in an internal cache and « recycled » by the `ListView` to improve performance. You should therefore be aware that you can't store a data model's state in a `VisualNode` and access it at a later time. You must always make sure that an item's state is updated and stored in the data model directly (I will tell you more about recycling in the following section).

Finally, the visual node returned by the `ListItemProvider` instance can optionally implement the `ListItemListener` interface, which is called by the `ListView` to handle focus and item states:

- `ListItemListener::select(bool    select)`: Called by the `ListView` when an already visible item becomes selected. `select` is `true` when the item is selected; it is `false` otherwise.

- `ListItemListener::activate(bool activate)`: Called by the `ListView` when an already visible item is active. An item is active while a user is pressing the item.

- `ListItemListener::reset(bool selected, bool activated)`: Called by the `ListView` when an item is about to be shown. If `selected` is `true`, the item should appear selected. If `activated` is `true`, the item should appear active.

> **Note**   For examples of how the previous classes can be used in practice, you can refer to the cascadescookbookcpp project, which can be found on GitHub at `https://github.com/blackberry/Cascades-Samples/tree/master/cascadescookbookcpp`. Look in the project's `src` folder for the `RecipeItemFactory` and `RecipeItem` classes, which respectively provide implementations for `ListItemProvider` and `ListItemListener` classes.

Data Models

Now that you have a good overview of the UI aspects of a ListView, it is time to consider what happens behind the scenes in a data model. A data model not only encapsulates data but also specifies how it will be mapped to the contents of a list view. The data model can be an arbitrarily complex tree structure, but the list view will always display at most a two-level deep hierarchy. You can, however, set any node in the list view as the root of the hierarchy. It is also important to emphasize that the data model does not care about any visual adornments of the data. In other words, a data model is all about data description (the actual data presentation and formatting is taken care of by the visuals described in the "List Views" section). Finally, the Cascades framework comes out of the box with several standard data models than you can readily plug into your own applications.

Before actually delving into the details of a data model's implementation, you need to understand how data nodes are located in the data model using index paths (which is the topic of the next section).

Index Paths

An index path is simply an array of integers identifying an item in the DataModel. The root node of a data model always has an empty index path. The items immediately under the root node have an index path of size 1. The items two levels down have an index path of size 2, and so on. For example, Figure 6-12 illustrates a hypothetical data model for fruits and vegetables.

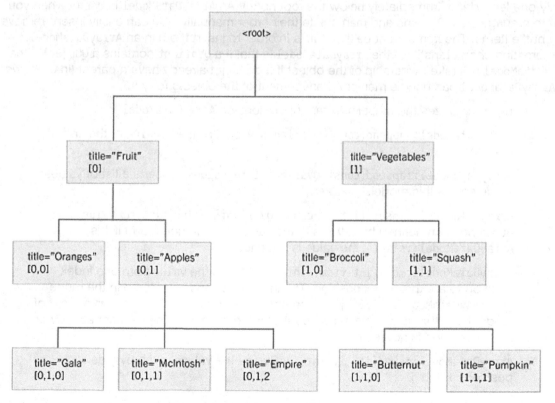

Figure 6-12. Visual representation of index paths (image source: BlackBerry)

As illustrated in Figure 6-12, an index path is an ordered list of integers. The last integer in the list always represents the ordering of the item relative to its siblings, starting at 0 (the preceding integers point to the item's parent). For example, "Empire" is the third child item of "Apples," and therefore the last integer's value will be 2 (the preceding values will be [0,1], which point to "Empire's" parent, "Apples"). In QML, you can access the individual index values of an index path using a JavaScript array (in C++ an index path is defined as a QVariantList of integers).

Standard Data Models

Cascades comes out of the box with a few standard data models that you can immediately use in your own applications. You have already used the XmlDataModel, which is a great drop-in model for prototyping the visual aspects of your ListView. However, XmlDataModel has its own set of limitations: for example, you can't update the data by adding or removing items. Therefore, in practice, you will have to use one of the other standard data models or take the extra step of implementing your own DataModel instance from scratch. You can also broadly categorize data models as sorted and unsorted models (a sorted data model will use a key for sorting its data items). In this section, I concentrate on the ArrayDataModel and GroupDataModel.

ArrayDataModel

An ArrayDataModel is an unsorted *flat* DataModel (in others words, the ArrayDataModel's hierarchy is only one level deep, immediately below the root node). An ArrayDataModel is useful when you want to manage a list of items and manipulate their order manually. You can easily insert, remove, and shuffle items. The items must be QVariants in order to insert them in an ArrayDataModel. An interesting characteristic of the ArrayDataModel is that if a QVariant contains a QObject*, the ArrayDataModel will take ownership of the object if it does not already have a parent (in other words, the ArrayDataModel can handle memory management of the objects for you).

The following summarizes the most important operations on ArrayDataModel:

- ArrayDataModel::append(const QVariant& value): Inserts value at the end of this model.

- ArrayDataModel::append(const QVariantList& values): Inserts a list of values at the end of this model.

- ArrayDataModel::insert(int i, const QVariant& value): Inserts value at the position defined by i. If i is 0, the value is preprended, and if i is ArrayDataModel::size(), the value is appended.

- ArrayDataModel::move(int from, int to): Moves the value from one index position to another index position. The index positions have to be in the range [0,ArrayDataModel::size()]. This method has no effect if the indexes are out of range. Note that this is practically equivalent to an insert. The element already at the to position is not removed.

- ArrayDataModel::swap(int i, int j): Swaps the values given by index positions i and j.

- `ArrayDataModel::removeAt(int i)`: Removes the value at index position i. If the value is a QObject* owned by the `ArrayDataModel`, it will also be deleted.

- `ArrayDataModel::replace(int i, const QVariant& value)`: Replaces the item at specified index position i with value. If the previous value at position i is owned by the `ArrayDataModel`, it will be deleted.

Note that these descriptions have essentially provided you with a C++ perspective of the `ArrayDataModel`. You can nevertheless call the previous functions from QML because they are all marked as `Q_INVOKABLE` in C++ (for example, Listing 6-20 shows you how to use an `ArrayDataModel` in QML).

Listing 6-20. ArrayDataModel

```
import bb.cascades 1.2
Page {
    Container {
        ListView {
            id: listview
            dataModel: ArrayDataModel {
                id: arrayDataModel
            }
            listItemComponents: [
                ListItemComponent {
                    type: ""
                    StandardListItem {
                        title: ListItemData
                        description: "Fruit"
                        status: "Good for you!"
                    }
                }
            ]
            onTriggered: {
                listview.clearSelection();
                listview.toggleSelection(indexPath);
            }
        } // ListView
        onCreationCompleted: {
            var values = ["apple", "banana", "peach", "tangerine"]
            arrayDataModel.append(values);
            arrayDataModel.append("mango");
        }
    } // Container
} // Page
```

By default, an `ArrayDataModel` will always return an empty string for the `type` property. You will therefore have to also define an empty string for `ListItemComponent`'s type property in the previous example so that the ListView matches the `ListItemComponent` to the `ArrayDataModel`'s items.

Finally, the StandardListItem's title property is bound to ListItemData, which directly corresponds to a data node in the ArrayDataModel (unlike some of the previous examples in this chapter, where the returned data node was a map and you had to use ListItemData.<keyname> to access the actual data value).

Let's now consider the case where the list of fruits is stored in a JSON file, rather than creating them in the onCreationCompleted() slot (see Listing 6-21). In that case, you will have to use a DataSource to load the JSON content and append the values to the ArrayDataModel (a DataSource loads data from a local source such as a JSON or XML file or an SQL database). (You can also use the DataSource's query property to specify an SQL query statement or an XML path. Finally, the DataSource's source property specifies a local file or a remote URL from which the data is loaded.)

Listing 6-21. fruits.json

```
[
    {
        "name" : "apple",
        "description" : "fruit"
    },
    {
        "name" : "banana",
        "description" : "fruit"
    },
    {
        "name" : "peach",
        "description" : "fruit"
    },
    {
        "name" : "tangerine",
        "description" : "fruit"
    },
    {
        "name" : "mango",
        "description" : "fruit"
    }
]
```

Listing 6-22 shows you how to use a DataSource to load the JSON document shown in Listing 6-21 in an ArrayDataModel.

Listing 6-22. DataSource

```
import bb.cascades 1.2
import bb.data 1.0
Page {
    Container {
        ListView {
            id: listview
            dataModel: ArrayDataModel {
                id: arrayDataModel
            }
```

```
        listItemComponents: [
            ListItemComponent {
                type: ""
                StandardListItem {
                    title: ListItemData.name
                    description: ListItemData.description
                    status: "Good for you!"
                }
            }
        ]
        onTriggered: {
            listview.clearSelection();
            listview.toggleSelection(indexPath);
        }
    } // ListView
    attachedObjects: [
        DataSource {
            id: dataSource
            source: "asset:///fruits.json"
            onDataLoaded: {
                for (var i = 0; i < data.length; i ++) {
                    arrayDataModel.append(data[i]);
                }
            }
        }
    ]
    onCreationCompleted: {
        dataSource.load();
    }
    } // Container
} // Page
```

As illustrated in Listing 6-22, you need to add the import bb.data 1.0 statement before using the DataSource control in QML. Also, as shown in the code, the ListView's onCreationCompleted slot loads the data in the DataSource. As soon as the loading process has completed, the DataSource triggers the dataLoaded() signal, which is used to populate the ArrayDataModel (the signal passes an implicit data parameter, which is either an array if the root element in the JSON document is an array, or a map if the root element is an object).

GroupDataModel

GroupDataModel is a sorted data model where you can specify keys to sort the model's items. Data items can be QVariantMap objects and/or QObject* pointers (you might recall from Chapter 3 that a QVariantMap is a typedef QMap<QString, QVariant>). If the data item is a QVariantMap, a GroupDataModel will try to sort it by matching its own keys with corresponding keys in the QVariantMap. If the item is a QObject*, it will try to match the keys with object properties. Obviously, to sort an item correctly, it must contain a corresponding key or property. You can also specify multiple keys for the GroupDataModel. In that case, the items will be sorted by applying the sorting criteria in the order the keys have been defined.

Items can also be automatically grouped by setting the GroupDataModel::grouping property. When grouping is enabled, a two-level hierarchy is automatically created for you and passed to the list view for display. The first level (with an index path of size 1) corresponds to the grouping headers and is generated by a GroupDataModel. The second level (with an index path of size 2) corresponds to the data items. Finally, a GroupDataModel's type property will return "header" for header items and "item" for all other items).

The following summarizes the most important operations on GroupDataModel:

- GroupDataModel::GroupDataModel(const QStringList& keys, QObject* parent=0): Constructs a new GroupDataModel with the specified sorting keys.

- GroupDataModel::insert(QObject* object): Inserts the QObject* in the GroupDataModel. If the object has no parent, the GroupDataModel will take ownership of the object.

- GroupDataModel::insert(const QVariantMap& item): Inserts the QVariantMap in this GroupDataModel.

- GroupDataModel::insertList(const QVariantList& items): Inserts the QVariantList in this GroupDataModel. The items can be either instances of QVariantMap or QObject*.

- GroupDataModel::setGrouping(bb::cascades::ItemGrouping::Type itemGrouping): Sets the grouping logic for this GroupDataModel. ItemGrouping::Type can be ItemGrouping::None (items are not grouped), ItemGrouping::ByFirstChar (items will be grouped by first character), and ItemGrouping::ByFullValue (items are grouped using entire strings).

- GroupDataModel::setSortAscending(bool ascending): If true, items are sorted in ascending order; otherwise, items are sorted in descending order.

Once again, these methods are all accessible from QML (see Listing 6-23 for an example showing how to use a GroupDataModel in QML; note how the sorting keys are defined in the onCreationCompleted() slot).

Listing 6-23. GroupDataModel

```
import bb.cascades 1.2
import bb.data 1.0
Page {
    Container {
        ListView {
            id: listview
            dataModel: GroupDataModel {
                id: groupDataModel
            }
            listItemComponents: [
                ListItemComponent {
                    type: "item"
```

```
                    StandardListItem {
                        title: ListItemData.name
                        description: ListItemData.description
                        status: "Good for you!"
                    }
                }
            ]
        onTriggered: {
            listview.clearSelection();
            listview.toggleSelection(indexPath);
        }
    } // ListView
    attachedObjects: [
        DataSource {
            id: dataSource
            source: "asset:///fruitsandvegetables.json"
            onDataLoaded: {
                for (var i = 0; i < data.length; i ++) {
                    groupDataModel.insert(data[i]);
                }
            }
        }
    ]
    onCreationCompleted: {
        dataSource.load();
        groupDataModel.sortingKeys = ["name", "description"];
    }
    } // Container
} // Page
```

Finally, Figure 6-13 shows you a ListView with an updated version of the JSON, which includes
vegetables. This mainly illustrates how items are clustered and sorted by the GroupDataModel
(once again, keep in mind that the GroupDataModel automatically generates the header items).

Figure 6-13. Sorted GroupDataModel

Mapping Item Types

The ListView essentially uses a DataModel's item type to select the corresponding visual for rendering the item. You can further refine the way data items are mapped to types by using one of the following techniques:

- In QML, you can define a JavaScript « mapping » function in the ListView. The function will have to return a string specifying the type of a given data item and an index path.

- You can choose to override a DataModel::itemType(const QVarianList & indexPath) in C++ so that it returns a meaningful type (for example, you could define a MyArrayDataModel class, which inherits from ArrayDataModel and overrides the ArrayDataModel::itemType(const QVarianList & indexPath) method to return something other than the empty string).

- You can implement the ListItemTypeMapper interface in C++ and then assign it to the ListView using ListView::setListItemTypeMapper(ListItemTypeMapper* mapper).

Defining a JavaScript Mapping Function

In QML, you can define a JavaScript "mapping function" in the ListView's body declaration, which will « override » the DataModel::itemType(const QVariantList& indexPath) method provided by the DataModel. For example, Listing 6-24 shows you how to override the default « item » and « header » types returned by a GroupDataModel using a JavaScript.

Listing 6-24. JavaScript Mapping Function

```
import bb.cascades 1.2
import bb.data 1.0
Page {
    Container {
        ListView {
            id: listview
            dataModel: GroupDataModel {
                id: groupDataModel
            }
            function itemType(data, indexPath) {
                return (indexPath.length == 1 ? "myheader" : "myitem");
            }
            listItemComponents: [
                ListItemComponent {
                    type: "myheader"
                    CustomListItem {
                        dividerVisible: true
                        Label {
                            text: ListItemData
                            textStyle {
                                base: SystemDefaults.TextStyles.BigText
                                fontWeight: FontWeight.Bold
                                color: Color.create("#7a184a")
                            }
                        }
                    }
                },
                ListItemComponent {
                    type: "myitem"
                    StandardListItem {
                        id: standardListItem
                        title: ListItemData.name
                        description: ListItemData.description
                        status: "Good for you!"

                    }
                }
            ]
        } // ListView
```

```
        attachedObjects: [
            DataSource {
                id: dataSource
                source: "asset:///fruitsandvegetables.json"
                onDataLoaded: {
                    for (var i = 0; i < data.length; i ++) {
                        groupDataModel.insert(data[i]);
                    }
                }
            }
        ]
        onCreationCompleted: {
            dataSource.load();
            groupDataModel.sortingKeys = [ "name", "description" ];
        }
    } // Container
} // Page
```

The code shown in Listing 6-24 is very similar to Listing 6-23, except that a JavaScript mapping function has been introduced. The rendering has also been customized so that items of type « myheader » are rendered in bold (see Figure 6-14).

Figure 6-14. Sorted GroupDataModel with custom headers

Implementing ListItemTypeMapper

The `ListItemTypeMapper` interface can be used in C++ to map a data item to an item type. Here again, the main disadvantage of using a `ListItemTypeMapper` is that you will have to reference the `ListView` from C++, which is something you should try to avoid in practice because it adds tight coupling between your QML UI and C++ business logic (note that to access the `ListView` from C++, you will also have to set its `objectName` in QML). On the other hand, A `ListItemTypeMapper` cleanly separates the type mapping logic from the actual data model implementation. In other words, by implementing a `ListItemTypeMapper` class, you can save yourself the necessity of extending one of the standard data model classes to override `DataModel::itemType()`.

Listing 6-25 shows you how to set a `ListView`'s `ListItemTypeMapper` in C++ (for illustration purposes, `MyListItemTypeMapper`'s methods have been defined inline).

Listing 6-25. ListItemTypeMapper

```
#include <bb/cascades/Application>
#include <bb/cascades/QmlDocument>
#include <bb/cascades/AbstractPane>
#include <bb/cascades/ListItemTypeMapper>
#include <bb/cascades/ListView>

using namespace bb::cascades;

class MyListItemTypeMapper : public ListItemTypeMapper, QObject{
public:
    MyListItemTypeMapper(QObject* parent) : QObject(parent){};
    ~MyListItemTypeMapper(){};
    QString itemType(const QVariant& data, const QVariantList& indexPath){
        return (indexPath.length() == 1 ? "myheader" : "myitem");
    }
};

ApplicationUI::ApplicationUI(bb::cascades::Application *app) :
    QObject(app)
{

    QmlDocument *qml = QmlDocument::create("asset:///main.qml").parent(this);

    // Create root object for the UI
    AbstractPane *root = qml->createRootObject<AbstractPane>();
    ListView* listView = root->findChild<ListView*>("listview");
    MyListItemTypeMapper* mapper = new MyListItemTypeMapper(listView);
    listView->setListItemTypeMapper(mapper);

    // Set created root object as the application scene
    app->setScene(root);
}
```

Implementing a Custom Data Model

You might need to implement your own data model if you are trying to access a complicated data structure, which is not easily readable with one of the data models discussed previously. In this case, you can opt for extending the abstract `DataModel` class (see Listing 6-26).

Listing 6-26. DataModel Interface

```
class DataModel : public QObject {
    Q_OBJECT

public:
    Q_INVOKABLE virtual int childCount(const QVariantList &indexPath) = 0;
    Q_INVOKABLE virtual bool hasChildren(const QVariantList &indexPath) = 0;
    Q_INVOKABLE virtual QVariant data(const QVariantList &indexPath) = 0;
    Q_INVOKABLE virtual QString itemType(const QVariantList &indexPath);

signals:
    void itemAdded(QVarianList indexPath);
    void itemRemoved(QVariantList indexPath);
    void itemUpdated(QVariantList indexPath);
    // itemChanged() omitted
};
```

As shown in Listing 6-26, DataModel defines the following methods for which you will have to provide an implementation:

- ■ int DataModel::hasChildren(const QVariantList& indexPath): Returns true if the data item identified by indexPath has children; it is false otherwise. This is a pure virtual function.

- ■ int DataModel::childCount(const QVariantList& indexPath): Returns the number of children of the data item specified by indexPath.

- ■ QVariant DataModel::data(const QVariantList& indexPath): Returns the data item that is associated with indexPath wrapped as a QVariant.

You will also need to override the DataModel::itemType() function that is used by the ListView to match the corresponding ListItemComponent for creating the item visuals (or alternatively, provide a ListItemTypeMapper implementation to the ListView, as illustrated in the previous section):

- ■ QString DataModel::itemType(const QVariantList& indexPath): Returns the type of the data item identified by the indexPath. By default, the method returns an empty string.

DataModel also defines the following signals that you can use to notify the ListView when the DataModel's state changes:

- ■ void DataModel::itemAdded(QVariantList indexPath): Emitted when a new item has been added to this DataModel. indexPath gives the index path of the new item.

- ■ void DataModel::itemRemoved(QVariantList indexPath): Emitted when an item has been removed from this DataModel. indexPath is the index path of the removed item.

- ■ void DataModel::itemUpdated(QVariantList indexPath): Emitted when an item has been updated. indexPath is the index path of the updated item.

A fourth signal, `DataModel::itemChanged()`, is not covered here, but it can be used for notifying bulk operations such as multiple additions and removals (the signal can be used in practice to optimize notifications, rather than emitting multiple-times more granular signals, such as `DataModel::itemAdded()` and `DataModel::itemRemoved()`).

Finally, you should keep in mind that your `DataModel` can return to the `ListView` any kind of data that can be contained in a `QVariant` (however, the typical data types packaged as `QVariants` are `QString`, `QVariantMap`, and `QObject*`).

To illustrate a `DataModel` implementation in practice, let's replace the `XmlDataModel` used in Listing 6-6 with our own custom model. Also, let's switch the data source format from XML to JSON. Listing 6-27 gives you an equivalent JSON representation of the XML document provided in Listing 6-5 (note that unlike the XML document, the JSON format is nonhierarchical. However, a new job attribute has been introduced to differentiate an Actor from a President).

Listing 6-27. people.json

```
[
    {
        "name" : "John F. Kennedy",
        "born" : "May 29, 1917",
        "spouse" : "Jacqueline Kennedy",
        "pic" : "kennedy.jpg",
        "job" : "president"
    },
    {
        "name" : "Bill Clinton",
        "born" : "August 19, 1946",
        "spouse" : "Hillary Rodham Clinton",
        "pic" : "clinton.jpg",
        "job" : "president"
    },
    {
        "name" : "John Wayne",
        "born" : "May 26, 1907",
        "spouse" : "Pilar Pallete",
        "pic" : "wayne.jpg",
        "job" : "actor"
    },
    // more presidents and actors in no particular order.
]
```

The data model class definition is in Listing 6-28.

Listing 6-28. MyDataModel.h

```
#ifndef MYDATAMODEL_H_
#define MYDATAMODEL_H_

#include <QObject>
#include <bb/cascades/DataModel>
#include <bb/data/JsonDataAccess>
```

```
class MyDataModel: public bb::cascades::DataModel {
Q_OBJECT

Q_PROPERTY(QString source READ source WRITE setSource NOTIFY sourceChanged);
public:

    MyDataModel(QObject* parent = 0);
    virtual ~MyDataModel();

    Q_INVOKABLE int childCount(const QVariantList& indexPath);
    Q_INVOKABLE QVariant data(const QVariantList& indexPath);
    Q_INVOKABLE bool hasChildren(const QVariantList& indexPath);
    Q_INVOKABLE QString itemType(const QVariantList& indexPath);
    Q_INVOKABLE void removeItem(const QVariantList& indexPath);

signals:
    void sourceChanged();

private:
    QString source();
    void setSource(QString source);
    void load(QString filename);

    QString m_source;
    QVariantList m_presidents;
    QVariantList m_actors;
};

#endif /* MYDATAMODEL_H_ */
```

The MyDataModel class definition declares a source property, which can be set in QML to identify the source file containing the JSON data. The m_presidents and m_actors member variables are used to store the data items loaded from the JSON file. Finally, all virtual functions declared in the DataModel interface are overridden (the function definitions are discussed next).

The setSource() method is called when MyDataModel's source property is set in QML (Listing 6-29). The method updates the corresponding m_source member variable and then calls the load() function, which is responsible for loading the JSON data from the file system.

Listing 6-29. MyDataModel::setSource()

```
void MyDataModel::setSource(QString source) {
    if (m_source == source)
        return;
    m_source = source;
    this->load(source);
    emit sourceChanged();
}
```

The load() function given in Listing 6-30 uses a JsonDataAccess object to load the contents of the JSON file (note that the function assumes that the file is located in the application's assets folder). Because the root object in the JSON file is an array, we try to "cast" the QVariant returned by the JsonDataAccess.load() method into a QVariantList object. Finally, the function uses the job attribute for each data entry to determine the appropriate member container to update (either m_actors or m_presidents).

Listing 6-30. MyDataModel::load()

```
void MyDataModel::load(QString source) {
    bb::data::JsonDataAccess json;
    QVariantList entries =
        json.load(QDir::currentPath() + "/app/native/assets/" + source).toList();
    if (!json.hasError()) {
        for (int i = 0; i < entries.length(); i++) {
            QVariantMap entry = entries[i].toMap();
            if (entry["job"] == "actor") {
                m_actors.append(entry);
            }
            else {
        m_presidents.append(entry);
            }
        }
    }
}
```

Let's now concentrate on the functions declared in the DataModel interface.

The hasChildren() method shown in Listing 6-31 returns true for the root and header nodes, and false otherwise (the root node's index path size is 0; the header node's index path size is 1).

Listing 6-31. MyDataModel::hasChildren()

```
bool MyDataModel::hasChildren(const QVariantList &indexPath) {
    if ((indexPath.size() == 0) || (indexPath.size() == 1))
        return true;
    else
        return false;
}
```

The childCount method shown in Listing 6-32 returns the children of a given data node. Since we want to keep the same hierarchical structure as the one defined in the original XML structure, the childCount() method will return 2 for the root item (this corresponds to the header items "Actors" and "US Presidents". Also note that the header items do not actually exist in the JSON file; the data model will dynamically create them). For items two levels deep in the data hierarchy with an index path of size 1, we return the number of elements in the m_actors and m_presidents list, respectively.

Listing 6-32. MyDataModel::childCount()

```
int MyDataModel::childCount(const QVariantList &indexPath) {
    if (indexPath.size() == 0) {
        return 2; // for headers "Actors" and "US Presidents"
    } else {
        if (indexPath.size() == 1) {
            if (indexPath.at(0).toInt() == 0) {
                return m_actors.size();
            } else if (indexPath.at(0).toInt() == 1) {
                return m_presidents.size();
            }
        } else {
            return 0;
        }
    }
}
```

The data node given by an index path is returned by the data() method (see Listing 6-33). The data nodes corresponding to header items—with an index path of size 1—are dynamically created. The data nodes—with an index path of size 2—are returned from the m_actors and m_presidents member variables (also, we keep the same structure as the original XML document by returning the Actors' values before the US Presidents values).

Listing 6-33. MyDataModel::data()

```
QVariant MyDataModel::data(const QVariantList &indexPath) {
    if (indexPath.size() == 1) {
        if (indexPath.at(0).toInt() == 0) {
            QVariantMap actorsHeader;
            actorsHeader["value"] = "Actors";
                return actorsHeader;
            } else {
                QVariantMap presidentsHeader;
                presidentsHeader["value"] = "US Presidents";
                return presidentsHeader;
            }
        } else if (indexPath.size() == 2) {
            if (indexPath.at(0) == 0) {
                return m_actors.at(indexPath.at(1).toInt());
            } else {
                return m_presidents.at(indexPath.at(1).toInt());
            }
        }
    }
    QVariant v;
    return v;
}
```

Finally, the itemType() method shown in Listing 6-34 returns the data type of the node given by an index path.

Listing 6-34. MyDataModel::itemType()

```
QString MyDataModel::itemType(const QVariantList &indexPath) {
    if (indexPath.size() == 1)
        return "category";
    if (indexPath.size() == 2)
        return "person";
    return "";
}
```

We can also add methods to our data model implementation to update its items. For example, a MyDataModel::removeItem(const QVariantList& indexPath) method can be associated with a DeleteActionItem to remove an item (see Listing 6-35).

Listing 6-35. MyDataModel::removeItem()

```
void MyDataModel::removeItem(const QVariantList& indexPath){
    if(indexPath.size() == 2){
        if(indexPath.at(0) == 0){
            m_actors.removeAt(indexPath.at(1).toInt());
        }else{
            m_presidents.removeAt(indexPath.at(1).toInt());
        }
        emit itemRemoved(indexPath);
    }
}
```

Note how the itemRemoved() signal is emitted in Listing 6-35 for notifying the ListView that the data model has changed (if you omit the signal, the ListView's visual appearance would not be updated). In a similar way, you could implement methods for adding and updating items.

Before actually using the MyDataModel in QML, you will need to register it with the QML type system in main.cpp (see Listing 6-36).

Listing 6-36. main.cpp

```
#include <MyDataModel.h>

Q_DECL_EXPORT int main(int argc, char **argv)
{
    qmlRegisterType<MyDataModel>("ludin.datamodels", 1, 0, "MyDataModel");

    Application app(argc, argv);

    // Create the Application UI object, this is where the main.qml file
    // is loaded and the application scene is set.
    new ApplicationUI(&app);

    // Enter the application main event loop.
    return Application::exec();
}
```

Finally, you can replace XmlDataModel with MyDataModel in main.qml (see Listing 6-37).

Listing 6-37. main.qml

```
import bb.cascades 1.2
import ludin.datamodels 1.0

Page {
    id: page
    Container {
        ListView {
            id: listview
            dataModel: MyDataModel {
                source: "people.json"
            }
            listItemComponents: [
                ListItemComponent {
                    type: "category"
                    CustomListItem {
                        id: customListItem
                        dividerVisible: true
                        Label {
                            text: ListItemData.value
                            // Apply a text style to create a large, bold font with
                            // a specific color
                            textStyle {
                                base: SystemDefaults.TextStyles.BigText
                                fontWeight: FontWeight.Bold
                                color: Color.create("#7a184a")
                            }
                        } // Label
                    } // CustomListItem
                },
                ListItemComponent {
                    type: "person"
                    StandardListItem {
                        id: standardListItem
                        title: ListItemData.name
                        description: ListItemData.born
                        status: ListItemData.spouse
                        imageSource: "asset:///pics/" + ListItemData.pic
                        contextActions: [
                            ActionSet {
                                DeleteActionItem {
                                    onTriggered: {
                                        var myview = standardListItem.ListItem.view;
                                        var datamodel = myview.dataModel;
                                        var indexPath = myview.selected();
                                        datamodel.removeItem(indexPath);
                                    }
                                } // DeleteActionItem
                            } // ActionSet
```

```
                ] // ContextActions
              } // StandardListItem
          } // ListItemComponent
        ] // ListItemComponents
      } // ListView
   } // Container
} // Page
```

Asynchronous Data Models

A ListView must be responsive and be able to display its items as fast as possible. You must therefore ensure that the data model's methods covered in the previous section are very fast and nonblocking. In practice, a method could block because you are trying to load a very large or a remote data set. As an immediate consequence, the Cascades UI will also freeze or behave extremely sluggishly. Therefore, to avoid any of these negative impacts on your Cascades UI, you will have to use asynchronous data model methods combined with signals such as DataModel::itemAdded()to update the ListView.

I will not show you how to create an asynchronous data model in this chapter because it is a relatively advanced concept. The subject is covered in the online documentation, however (and it is important to keep in mind that there are techniques for handling very large data sets). The following are pointers to the developer's documentation, which also provide a complete asynchronous data model example:

- Asynchronous data processing is covered by the document found at http://developer.blackberry.com/native/documentation/cascades/ui/lists/asynch_data.html.

- Managing very large data sets is covered by the document found at http://developer.blackberry.com/native/documentation/cascades/device_platform/data_access/data_manager.html.

Persistence

By default, none of the standard data models have methods for loading data nodes from the file system or saving them back to the file system (XmlDataModel is an exception: you can load an XML document by specifying the XmlDataModel's source property, but you cannot save the document). Again this is not a limitation because you can easily subclass a data model to add persistence.

Updating Data Items with Cascades Controls

Items in a data model can be updated by using Cascades controls. For example, let's suppose that we have extended the JSON document given in Listing 6-21 to include the availability of a given fruit or vegetable (see Listing 6-38).

Listing 6-38. fruitsandvegetables.json

```json
[
    {
        "name" : "apple",
        "description" : "fruit",
        "available" : "false"
    },
    {
            "name" : "ananas",
        "description" : "fruit",
        "available" : "true"
    },
    {
            "name" : "avocado",
        "description" : "fruit",
        "available" : "false"
    },
    {

        "name" : "banana",
        "description" : "fruit",
        "available" : "false"
    },
    {
            "name" : "broccoli",
        "description": "vegetable",
        "available" : "true"
    },
    // more fruits and vegetables
]
```

In your QML UI, you can also include a check box to update the availability of a given fruit. In that case, you will have to also handle the checkChanged() signal emitted by the check box and update the data model accordingly (see Listing 6-39).

Listing 6-39. main.qml

```qml
import bb.cascades 1.2
import bb.data 1.0

Page {
    Container {
        ListView {
            id: listview
            objectName: "listview"
            dataModel: GroupDataModel {
                id: groupDataModel
            }
            listItemComponents: [
                ListItemComponent {
                    type: "myheader"
```

```
                    CustomListItem {
                        dividerVisible: true
                        Label {
                            text: ListItemData
                            textStyle {
                                base: SystemDefaults.TextStyles.BigText
                                fontWeight: FontWeight.Bold
                                color: Color.create("#7a184a")
                            }
                        }
                    }
                }
            },
            ListItemComponent {
                type: "myitem"
                CustomListItem {
                    id: customItem
                    Container {
                        verticalAlignment: VerticalAlignment.Center
                        layout: StackLayout {
                            orientation: LayoutOrientation.LeftToRight
                        }
                        CheckBox {
                            id: checkBox
                            checked: ListItemData.available

                            onCheckedChanged: {
                                if (customItem.ListItem.initialized) {
                                    var index = customItem.ListItem.indexPath;
                                    console.log("Changing " + index);
                                    var dataModel = customItem.ListItem.view.dataModel;
                                    var val = dataModel.data(index);
                                    val.available = checked;
                                    dataModel.updateItem(index, val);
                                    console.log("after update: "
                                            +dataModel.data(index).name+
                                            ", available: "
                                            +dataModel.data(index).available);
                                }
                            } // onCheckedChanged
                        }
                        Label {
                            text: ListItemData.name
                        }
                    } // Container
                } // CustomListItem
            } // ListItemComponent
        ] // ListItemComponents
    } // ListView
    attachedObjects: [
        DataSource {
            id: dataSource
            source: "asset:///fruitsandvegetables.json"
```

```
        onDataLoaded: {
            for (var i = 0; i < data.length; i ++) {
                groupDataModel.insert(data[i]);
            }
        }
    }
]
onCreationCompleted: {
    dataSource.load();
    groupDataModel.sortingKeys = [ "name", "description" ];
}
    }
}
```

As shown in Listing 6-39, you need to make sure that the ListItem is initialized before handling the state update (otherwise, the ListView might be in the process of recycling the visual and the check box might be in a transient state). If the ListItem is effectively initialized, you can proceed by updating the data model. You can achieve this by first getting a copy of the data item, then updating the copy, and finally, replacing the original item with the copy in the data model (data items are returned as QVariants by the data model, and therefore you can only get a copy the original data item, as opposed to a reference to the original data).

Figure 6-15 illustrates the resulting UI.

Figure 6-15. Sorted GroupDataModel with CheckBox

Summary

This chapter introduced the ListView, which is one of Cascades' most flexible controls. You can use a ListView to display arbitrarily complex hierarchical information as a succinct list of items. ListViews conveniently separate data from presentation using the MVC pattern. The ListView plays the role of a controller. A DataModel handles application data, and ListItemComponents define the visuals in charge of rendering a data item. Cascades also gives you standard visuals, such as StandardListItem and Header, to ensure a consistent look and feel across Cascades applications.

A ListView communicates with its DataModel using a tree abstraction, where each node in the tree is identified by an index path. The root node's index path is an empty array. The ListView will, at most, render two sublevels of your data under the root node. You can, however, set the root node anywhere in your data model, giving you effectively deeper than two levels of interaction.

Chapter 7

HTTP Networking

HTTP networking is ubiquitous on mobile devices. This book would certainly not be complete if it did not include a chapter explaining how to use the BlackBerry 10 networking services. In this chapter, I am going to exclusively concentrate on HTTP networking, which covers about 90 percent of the cases you will face during application development. Also, BlackBerry 10 leverages the underlying QtNetwork module, which makes HTTP programming amazingly simple. The goal of this chapter is to show you how the different networking classes work together to access HTTP servers from a BlackBerry 10 mobile device.

An immediate application of networking is obviously to build a "rich thin client" where you use Cascades to build your application's native user interface and remotely access business logic implemented as rest services. By now you must have realized that Cascades and QML make user interface design a snap. Adding networking to the mix just opens a completely new dimension of connected applications. For example, exposing enterprise services securely to your workforce—something that BlackBerry has always been at the forefront with—is an obvious practical application.

After having read this chapter, you will have a good understanding of

- The Qt networking classes.
- How to use the networking classes to build connected Cascades applications.
- How to design responsive UIs by handling network requests and replies asynchronously.

Another important goal of this chapter is to illustrate all the concepts introduced so far by writing a slightly more complex app than the ones demonstrated so far. The application will take the form of a Cascades client app for a remote weather REST service and will emphasize the separation of UI logic from the core business logic written in C++. The application will also show you how to breakdown your C++ code in classes with delimited responsibilities.

Qt Networking Classes

HTTP networking using Qt mostly involves the following classes:

- QNetworkAccessManager: This class allows you to send network requests and receive replies. The QNetworkAccessManager's API is entirely asynchronous, thus guaranteeing that the user interface thread is not blocked during an HTTP request.

- QNetworkRequest: This class encapsulates all the required information for an HTTP request. Typically, you will be using QNetworkRequest's url property to access an HTTP URL.

- QNetworkReply: This is QNetworkRequest's counterpart; it encapsulates the data received from the server.

QNetworkAccessManager

QNetworkAccessManager is the grand dispatcher of all the network interactions in your application. You will generally use a single instance of this class to handle all the networking logic of your app. The QNetworkAccessManager object holds the common configuration and settings for the requests it sends. It should be noted that all functions in this class are *reentrant*. This means that you can call the class methods multiple times, even if a given network request has not yet completed (this is also possible because the class methods are asynchronous, or in other words, nonblocking). If necessary, the QtNetworkAccessManager internally queues the requests it receives, but has the capability to process multiple requests concurrently. The following is a review of QNetworkAccessManager's most important methods:

- QNetworkReply* QNetworkAccessManager::get(const QNetworkRequest& request): Posts a request to obtain the contents of the target specified by request. For the HTTP protocol, the request corresponds to the HTTP GET request. Returns a pointer to a QNetworkReply object, opened for reading, which can be used to retrieve data as soon as it is available.

- QNetworkReply* QNetworkAccessManager::post(const QNetworkRequest& request, const QByteArray& data): Sends an HTTP POST request to the destination specified by request and returns a pointer to a QNetworkReply object opened for reading. QNetworkReply contains the server's response. The QByteArray instance contains the data to be uploaded to the server.

- QNetworkReply* QNetworkAccessManager::post(const QNetworkRequest& request, QIODevice* data): Similar to the previous method, but this time the posted data is passed as a pointer to a QIODevice object. In other words, you can use this method to post the contents of a file by passing a QFile object as the second method parameter (this is possible because QFile inherits from QIODevice).

- QNetworkReply* QNetworkAccessManager::post(const QNetworkRequest& request, QHttpMultipart* multipart): Posts the content of a multipart message to the destination identified by request.

- `QNetworkReply* QNetworkAccessManager::put(const QNetworkRequest& request, const QByteArray& data)`: Sends an HTTP PUT request to the destination specified by request and returns a pointer to a QNetworkReply object opened for reading. This method makes sense in the context of a REST service, where PUT is used for creating a resource and POST for updating or modifying one. The QNetworkReply object contains the optional server response. The QByteArray instance contains the data to be uploaded to the server. Just as with an HTTP POST request, the method is overloaded and can also take a QIODevice* and QHttpMultipart* as a second parameter.

- `QNetworkConfiguration QNetworkAccessManager::configuration()`: Returns the network configuration that will be used to create the network session.

- `void QNetworkAccessManager::setConfiguration(const QNetworkConfiguration& config)`: Sets the network configuration that will be used to create the network session.

- `QNetworkCookieJar QNetworkAccessManager::cookieJar()`: Returns an instance of QNetworkCookieJar used to store cookies obtained from the network, as well as cookies about to be sent.

- `void QNetworkAccessManager::setCookieJar(QNetworkCookieJar* cookieJar)`: Sets the manager's cookie jar. The cookie jar will be used by all requests dispatched by the network manager.

- `void QNetworkAccessManager::setCache(QAbstractNetworkCache* cache)`: Sets the network manager's cache. The cache is used for all requests dispatched by the manager. You can use this function to specify an object that implements additional features, such as saving cookies to permanent storage or caching JavaScript and CSS files. Note that, by default, the network manager does not cache data. QAbstractNetworkCache provides the interface for cache implementation. As implied by its name, QAbstractNetworkCache is an abstract base class that cannot be instantiated. Instead, you can use a QNetworkDiskCache, which provides a concrete implementation. You can also control cache configuration with the QNetworkRequest request object (this will be explained in the next section).

Note As mentioned previously, you should always reuse the same QNetworkAccessManager instance. Note that you can conveniently access the default declarative engine's QNetworkAccessManager instance by using the QMLDocument::defaultDeclarativeEngine()->networkAccessManager() method call (because QMLDocument::defaultDeclarativeEngine() is a static method, you can always access the associated default declarative engine from anywhere in your code).

QNetworkRequest

A QNetworkRequest object holds a URL to be requested by a QNetworkAccessManager. You can specify the target URL using one of the following methods:

- QNetworkRequest::QNetworkRequest(const QUrl& url = QUrl()): Constructs a new network request with url as the URL to be requested.

- QNetworkRequest::setURL(const QUrl& url): Sets the URL this network request is referring to.

You can also provide additional information to further customize the request (for example, by setting header values, request priorities, and cache configurations). In the specific case of caching, you can specify the cache behavior by setting a QNetworkRequest's CacheLoadControlAttribute attribute, as follows:

- QNetworkRequest::setAttribute(QNetworkRequest::CacheLoadControlAttribute, const QVariant& value): Sets the cache behavior. The following are the possible values:

  - QNetworkRequest::AlwaysNetwork: Always load from the network and do not check if the cache has a valid entry.

  - QNetworkRequest::PreferNetwork: This is the default behavior; load from the network if the cache entry is older.

  - QNetworkRequest::PreferCache: Load from the cache first; otherwise, load from the network. Note that you risk loading stale data in this case.

  - QNetworkRequest::AlwaysCache: Always try to load from the cache. In other words, this option corresponds to an offline mode. Note that you can use QNetworkRequest::PreferCache for specific file types, such as CSS and JavaScript, where you are certain that they will not change during the application's lifetime.

Because you can specify the cache behavior on a *per request* basis, this can be very convenient if you have multiple requests of different kinds. However, for the biggest majority of network requests, you can simply set the target URL and pass the request to the QNetworkAccessManager.

QNetworkReply

QNetworkReply encapsulates the server's response and provides all the necessary functionality for retrieving the received data. The class inherits from QIODevice, which is the abstract base class for devices supporting reading and writing blocks of data. You will generally use the QByteArray QIODevice::read(qint64 maxSize) and QByteArray QIODevice::readAll() methods to retrieve the data. The former method reads, at most, maxSize bytes from the device. The latter reads all available data from the device. Both methods return the data as a QByteArray.

The following summarizes QNetworkReply's most important methods:

- bool QNetworkReply::isRunning() const: Returns true if the corresponding request is still being processed.

- QByteArray QNetworkReply::read(qint64 maxSize): Inherited from QIODevice; see description given at the start of this section.

- `QByteArray QNetworkReply::readAll()`: Inherited from `QIODevice`; see description given at the start of this section.

- `QNetworkRequest QNetworkReply::request()`: Returns the request that was posted for this reply.

- `QUrl QNetworkReply::url()`: Returns the URL of the content downloaded or uploaded. Note that the URL may be different from the one specified in the original request.

- `NetworkError QNetworkReply::error()`: Returns the error that was found during the processing of this request. Returns `QNetworkReply::NoError` if the request was processed successfully. Check the API documentation for all the possible values taken by the `QNetworkReply::NetworkError` enumeration.

- `QVariant QNetworkReply::attribute(Attribute code, const QVariant& defaultValue = QVariant())`: Returns the attribute associated with code. If code has not been set, returns defaultValue. Attributes are metadata that are used to pass additional information from the reply back to the application. As you will see in the examples section, you will use this property to detect HTTP redirects.

- `QNetworkReply::abort()`: Aborts the operation immediately and closes any network connections still open.

QNetworkReply can also emit the following signals:

- `QNetworkReply::finished()`: This signal is emitted when the reply has finished processing. The data can be retrieved by calls to `QNetworkReply::read()` or `QNetworkReply::readAll()`.

- `QNetworkReply::downloadProgress(qint64 bytesReceived, qint64 bytesTotal)`: This signal is emitted to indicate the data download's progress for a given network request. The download is finished when bytesReceived is equal to bytesTotal. Note that you should handle this signal when large amounts of data are being downloaded to convey some feedback to the user (for example, by displaying a Cascades ProgressIndicator). (You can also opt to process the data in chunks, as it becomes available.) The bytesReceived parameter indicates the number of bytes received, whereas bytesTotal indicates the total number of bytes expected to be downloaded. Note that if the total number of bytes to be downloaded is unknown, bytesTotal will be −1, but when the download has completed bytesReceived will always be equal to bytesTotal.

- `QNetworkReply::uploadProgress(qint64 bytesSent, qint64 bytesTotal)`: This signal is emitted to indicate the upload progress of a network request. The upload is finished when bytesSent is equal to bytesTotal.

- `QNetworkReply::sslErrors(const QList<QSslError>& errors)`: This signal is emitted if the SSL/TLS session encountered errors during the setup, including certificate verification errors. The list of errors is provided by the errors parameter.

> **Note**   You should always warn the user if `ssl` errors occur and give him the option to cancel the request.

HTTP Networking Examples

The examples provided in this section illustrate typical usage scenarios of the networking classes.

HTTP GET

Let's start with a simple GET request to access a REST service. The data in the response will be returned in JSON format. To parse the object, you will have to use an instance of the Cascades JsonDataAccess class and handle the JSON structure in-memory. The Qt object constructed from JSON by the JsonDataAccess instance will always be a QVariant that either contains a QVariantList (if an array of JSON objects is returned by the service) or a QVariantMap (if a single object is returned). The mapping between JSON types and Qt types is summarized as follows:

- int: Mapped to a QVariant(Int64). To access the contained int use QVariant::toInt().

- uint: Mapped to a QVariant(Uint64). To access the contained uint use QVariant::toUInt().

- real: Mapped to a QVariant(double). To access the contained real use QVariant::toReal().

- string: Mapped to a QVariant(const char*). To access the contained string use QVariant::toString().

- boolean: Mapped to a QVariant(bool). To access the contained boolean use QVariant::toBool().

- array: Mapped to a QVariant(QVariantList). To access the contained array use Qvariant::toList().

- object: mapped to a QVariant(QVariantMap). To access the contained object, use QVariant::toMap().

The requested URL corresponds to the list of categories defined in my WordPress blog and is given at http://aludin.com?json=get_category_index. Listing 7-1 shows you an example of the returned JSON object.

Listing 7-1. JSON Response

```
{
    "status": "ok",
    "count": 2,
    "categories": [
        {
            "id": 2,
            "slug": "lifeinit",
```

```
            "title": "Life in IT, Anti-Patterns of Efficiency",
            "description": "",
            "parent": 0,
            "post_count": 2
        },
        {
            "id": 3,
            "slug": "mobile-computing",
            "title": "Mobile Computing",
            "description": "",
            "parent": 0,
            "post_count": 1
        }
    ]
}
```

Listing 7-2 shows you how to perform the HTTP GET request to retrieve the JSON document displayed in Listing 7-1.

Listing 7-2. ApplicationUI::getCategories()

```
ApplicationUI::getCategories(){
    QString url("http://aludin.com?json=get_category_index");
    QNetworkRequest request(url);

    QNetworkReply* reply = this->m_networkManager->get(request);
    bool result = connect(reply, SIGNAL(finished()), this,
                    SLOT(onCategoriesFinished()));
    Q_ASSERT(result);
}
```

It is not shown in the previous code, but you can safely assume that ApplicationUI::my_networkManager has been initialized with the default declarative engine's QNetworkAccessManager.

And Listing 7-3 illustrates how to perform the actual JSON response parsing once it has been returned by the service.

Listing 7-3. ApplicationUI::onCategoriesFinished()

```
void ApplicationUI::onCategoriesFinished() {
    QNetworkReply* reply = static_cast<QNetworkReply*>(QObject::sender());
    if (!reply->error()) {
        JsonDataAccess jda;
        QVariant response = jda.load(reply);
        QVariantMap map = response.toMap(); // get root JSON object
        QString statusValue = map["status"].toString();
        QVariantList categories = map["categories"].toList(); // get categories array.
        for(int i=0; i<categories.size(); i++){
            QString title = categories[i].toMap()["title"].toString();
        }
    }
    reply->deleteLater();
}
```

You will see later that you can conveniently chain the QVariant method calls to navigate the JSON object structure. Note that as a convenience and for clarity, I am using strings literals directly in the code, but ideally you should use string constants to avoid sprinkling your code with literals.

Finally, if your request takes additional parameters, you should use URL encoding to make sure that the parameters do not contain reserved HTTP characters (see Listing 7-4).

Listing 7-4. URL Percent-Encoding

```
QString date("50-2010/05/11 22:45:19 +0000");
QString encodedDate = QString(QUrl::toPercentEncoding(date));
QString getUrl = QString("http://www.aservice.com");
getUrl.append("?date=");
getUrl.append(encodedDate);
```

HTTP POST

Posting data is just as simple as performing HTTP GET requests. You will have to specify the data parameters by adding them to a QByteArray. You also need to make sure that you separate each parameter-value pair with an ampersand, as shown in Listing 7-5.

Listing 7-5. Post Example

```
void ApplicationUI::doPost(){
    // Setup the webservice url
    QUrl postUrl = QUrl("http://www.aservice.com");
    QByteArray postData;

    postData.append("param1=value1&").append("param2=value2&").append("param3=value3");

    // Call the webservice
    QNetworkReply* reply = this->m_networkManager->post(QNetworkRequest(postUrl), postData);
    bool result = connect(reply, SIGNAL(finished()), this,
                          SLOT(onPostFinished()));
    Q_ASSERT(result);
}
```

Once again, in practice you should use percent-encoding for the parameters you pass to the POST request. Also, in the onPostFinished() slot, don't forget to release the QNetworkReply instance using QNetworkReply::deleteLater().

Handling an HTTP Redirect

At certain times, you will have to process an HTTP redirect. A redirect is not an error and simply indicates that a resource has moved. Listing 7-6 shows you how to handle the situation.

Listing 7-6. Redirect Check Example

```
void ApplicationUI::onRequestFinished(QNetworkReply* reply){
    if(reply->error() == QNetworkReply::NoError){
        QVariant redirect =
        reply->attribute(QNetworkRequest::RedirectionTargetAttribute);
        if(!redirect.isNull()){
            QUrl originalUrl = reply->request().url();
            QUrl newUrl = originalUrl.resolved(redirect.toUrl());
            // send new network request using newUrl
        }else{
            // process data
        }
    }else{
        // handle error in response
    }
    reply->deleteLater();
}
```

In practice, you should always be ready to handle HTTP redirects.

Handling Authentication

Certain HTTP services will require authentication before providing you access to their resources. In those cases, you can use the QNetworkAccessManager::authenticationRequired(QNetworkReply* reply, QAuthenticator* authenticator) signal to handle the authentication request. Listings 7-7 and 7-8 illustrate how to implement authentication in your own code.

Listing 7-7. ApplicationUI.hpp

```
ApplicationUI::ApplicationUI(bb::cascades::Application *app) :
    QObject(app),
    m_networkManager(QMLDocument::defaultDeclarativeEngine->networkAccessManager())
{
    bool result = connect(m_networkManager,
                    SIGNAL(authenticationRequired(QNetworkReply*, QAuthenticator*)), this,
                    SLOT(onAuthenticationRequired(QNetworkReply*, QAuthenticator*)));
    Q_ASSERT(result);
}
```

Listing 7-8. ApplicationUI.cpp Authentication Handler

```
void ApplicationUI::onAuthenticationRequired(QNetworkReply* reply,
                                             QAuthenticator* authenticator)
{
    SystemCredentialsPrompt prompt = new SystemCredentialsPrompt;
    prompt->exec();
    authenticator->setUser(prompt->usernameEntry());
    authenticator->setPassword(prompt->passwordEntry());
    prompt->deleteLater();
}
```

The QNetworkAccessManager::authenticationRequired(QNetworkReply*, QAuthenticator*) signal is connected to the corresponding slot in the application delegate's constructor. Therefore, whenever a server request needs to be authenticated, the slot will be called. As shown in Listing 7-8, you can use a SystemCredentialsPrompt object to display a modal dialog requesting the user's credentials (see Figure 7-1). Note that the majority of Cascades controls methods are nonblocking (in other words, they return immediately and processing continues). However, in this specific case, we want to be able to call a blocking method until the user has provided his credentials. To achieve this behavior, you should call SystemCredentialsPrompt::exec() instead of SystemCredentialPrompt::show(), which is the nonblocking version. (Internally, SystemCredentialsPrompt::exec() creates a nested event loop to provide the blocking functionality. When the nested event loop is exited, control is returned to the main event loop). Note that once you have finished with the prompt object, you must call QObject::deleteLater() instead of deleting the object immediately.

Figure 7-1. Credentials prompt

Finally, the authenticator should be updated with the user's credentials, which are sent back to the server.

Weather2

I promised you in Chapter 2 that we would build a weather app relying on the REST service introduced at the time. In essence, I want to illustrate how you can design an enticing Cascades UI on top of raw data (which would be the JSON document returned by the weather service). You will also learn how to combine multiple services together (such as Google Maps) to further enrich your application. Finally, you will see how the networking classes are used in practice to perform asynchronous requests. The application we are about to design is called, quite appropriately, Weather2 (the default Weather app is bundled with BlackBerry 10). The finished application's UI is shown in Figures 7-2, 7-3, and 7-4. The application has two tabs. On the first tab, you can perform a query by country, state, or city using a text field. If your query returns multiple results, the application will ask you to select a city from a list of values displayed in a SystemListDialog (see Figure 7-2).

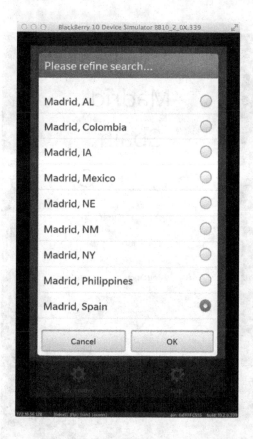

Figure 7-2. *City selection*

As soon as you have selected a city, the weather conditions are displayed, including the city's latitude and longitude (see Figure 7-3).

Figure 7-3. City view

If you select the second tab, a map will be displayed, with the city location highlighted by a small icon representing the weather conditions (see Figure 7-4).

Figure 7-4. Map view

Application Design

Before actually looking at the app implementation, let's summarize once again the most important BlackBerry 10 design principles and recommendations (you can refer to Chapter 3 for a more detailed discussion of these points):

■ Separate UI logic from business logic. Although it is possible to directly access Cascades controls from C++, the preferable way to build BlackBerry 10 apps is by clearly decoupling the UI logic from the rest of the application's logic written in C++. As stated in Chapter 3, one of the major strengths of QML and C++ integration is the ability to implement the QML UI separately from C++. The C++ business logic can therefore be blissfully unaware of the QML layer (in other words, using QObject::findChildren()to access Cascades controls by object name from C++ is considered a bad practice because it adds tight coupling between UI and business logic).

- Prefer signals for communicating between QML and C++.

- Prefer properties and QML bindings to synch data between QML and C++ (you will also notice that at times I pass data as signal parameters). A QML component can have its properties bound to a C++ class' properties. If a C++ property is updated, a signal has to be emitted from C++ in order notify the QML declarative engine, which then updates the corresponding QML bound property. Note that bindings can be defined both ways: the declarative engine will also automatically update the C++ bound property when the corresponding QML property changes.

- Break down your UI in multiple QML components instead of designing it as a single monolithic bloc. This will save you major headaches when you need to selectively update UI parts. Indeed, the ability to extend QML with your own custom components is a major advantage that you should leverage as much as possible.

Having emphasized these points, let's start with the UI design.

Note   The source code for the Weather2 application can be found in this book's repository on GitHub at https://github.com/aludin/BB10Apress.

Creating the UI

Weather2's UI is split between four QML components:

- `main.qml`: The QML document initially loaded by the application delegate. It defines a tabbed pane containing two tabs (see Listing 7-9).

- `WeatherDetails.qml`: The control responsible for handling user input for weather requests. The control also manages various system prompts for notifying or requesting additional information from the user, when necessary (you will see that the prompts are defined as attached objects).

- `City.qml`: The control responsible for displaying the weather data for a given city. Note that this control is referenced in `WeatherDetails.qml` (see Listing 7-10).

- `WeatherMap.qml`: The control responsible for displaying a map with the weather conditions for the selected city (see Listing 7-11).

Listing 7-9. main.qml

```
import bb.cascades 1.2
TabbedPane {
    id: tabbedPane
    showTabsOnActionBar: true
```

```
        Tab {
            title: "City weather"
            Page {
                WeatherDetails {
                    // control loaded from WeatherDetails.qml
                }
            }
        }
        Tab {
            title: "Map"
            Page {
                WeatherMap {
                    // control loaded from WeatherMap.qml
                }
            }
        }
    }
}
```

As you can see in Listing 7-9, the WeatherDetails and WeatherMap controls are used as content properties for page controls. The QML engine will therefore automatically load the controls from the corresponding files located in the assets folder of your application project (note that WeatherDetails.qml and WeatherMap.qml are located in the same folder as main.qml).

Let us now have a look at the WeatherDetails control implementation (see Listing 7-10).

Listing 7-10. WeatherDetails.qml

```
import bb.cascades 1.2
import bb.system 1.2
Container {
    id: main
    background: back.imagePaint
    function onError(message) {
        errorPrompt.title = message;
        errorPrompt.show();
    }

    function onMultipleCitiesFound(cities) {
        citiesDialog.clearList();
        for (var i = 0; i < cities.length; i ++) {
            citiesDialog.appendItem(cities[i]);
        }
        citiesDialog.show();
    }

    function onFinished() {
        progress.cancel();
    }
```

```
onCreationCompleted: {
    _app.weather.multipleCitiesFound.connect(main.onMultipleCitiesFound);
    _app.weather.error.connect(main.onError);
    _app.weather.finished.connect(main.onFinished);
    progress.cancelButton.label = "Cancel";
    progress.confirmButton.label = "";
}

attachedObjects: [
    ImagePaintDefinition {
        id: back
        repeatPattern: RepeatPattern.XY
        imageSource: "asset:///images/background.jpg"
    },
    SystemListDialog {
        id: citiesDialog
        onFinished: {
            if (value == SystemUiResult.ConfirmButtonSelection) {
                _app.weather.cityWeather(citiesDialog.selectedIndices[0]);
                progress.show();
            }
        }
    },
    SystemPrompt {
        id: errorPrompt
        onFinished: {
            _app.weather.cityWeather(errorPrompt.inputFieldTextEntry());
            progress.show();
        }
    },
    SystemProgressDialog {
        id: progress
        title: "Retrieving city"
        onFinished: {
            if (value == SystemUiResult.CancelButtonSelection) {
                _app.weather.cancel();
            }
        }
    }
]
layout: StackLayout {
    orientation: LayoutOrientation.BottomToTop
}
TextField {
    id: location
    inputMode: TextFieldInputMode.Default
    textStyle.textAlign: TextAlign.Center
    input {
        submitKey: SubmitKey.Go
        submitKeyFocusBehavior: SubmitKeyFocusBehavior.Lose
```

```
            onSubmitted: {
                _app.weather.cityWeather(location.text);
                progress.show();
            }
        }
        hintText: "Enter city or country name"
    }
    City{
        // control loaded from City.qml
    }
}
```

As you can see, WeatherDetails.qml mostly contains some JavaScript code responsible for signal handling. Also, an important point to consider is the way the emitted signals from C++ are connected to the JavaScript functions in the main container's onCreationCompleted slot (in other words, the onError(), onMultipleCitiesFound(), and onFinished() JavaScript functions or slots for signals emitted by the _app.weather C++ object). Also note how the location text field's onSubmitted slot is used for calling the _app.weather.cityWeather() slot, which is defined in C++. If the user's initial query returns multiple cities, a SystemListDialog is displayed, asking him to further refine the query. In the same manner, if an error occurs because the user's query is incorrect, a SystemPrompt is displayed, asking him to correct the query. In both cases, _app.weather.cityWeather() is called with the user's updated query.

The City control is mostly a visual control for displaying the results of a weather request: the control uses labels and an image view for displaying the weather conditions for a given city. All QML properties defined in the control are bound to corresponding C++ properties (for example, Listing 7-11 gives you the binding for the current temperature).

Listing 7-11. City Control, Binding Example

```
Label {
    id: temperature
    text: _app.weather.cityinfo.temperature
    horizontalAlignment: HorizontalAlignment.Center
    textStyle {
        fontWeight: FontWeight.W100
        color: Color.Black
        fontSize: FontSize.PercentageValue
        fontSizeValue: 250
    }
}
```

In the example provided in Listing 7-11, the label's text property is bound to the _app.weather.cityinfo.temperature property, which is defined in C++ (as you will see in a moment). Therefore, when the _app.weather.cityinfo.temperature property is updated in C++, the QML declarative engine automatically updates the label's text property.

The final QML component to consider is the WeatherMap component, which appears on the second tab. Listing 7-12 gives you component definition.

Listing 7-12. WeatherMap Control

```
import bb.cascades 1.2
import ludin.utils 1.0
Container {
    layout: DockLayout {
    }
    onCreationCompleted: {
        _app.weather.cityinfo.coordinatesChanged.connect(mapclient.setCoordinates);
        scrollview.zoomToPoint(320, 220, 2, ScrollAnimation.Smooth);
    }
    attachedObjects: [
        GoogleMapClient {
            id: mapclient
        }
    ]
    ScrollView {
        id: scrollview
        horizontalAlignment: HorizontalAlignment.Fill
        verticalAlignment: VerticalAlignment.Fill
        scrollViewProperties {
            scrollMode: ScrollMode.Both
            pinchToZoomEnabled: true
        }
        ImageView {
            id: citymap
            image: mapclient.image
        }
    }
}
```

Here again, the control is relatively simple. It mainly consists of an image view responsible for displaying a map of the current weather conditions for a given location. The GoogleMapClient attached object provides the actual weather image. Once again, QML bindings are used to synch the image view and the image map generated by the GoogleMapClient attached object. Finally, the current map coordinates are provided to the GoogleMapClient attached object by the _app.weather.cityinfo.coordinatesChanged() signal (the signal to the slot connection is done in the main container's onCreationCompleted slot).

Adding the C++ Implementation

Let us now turn our attention to the C++ implementation. The most important factor to consider is how to organize your code so that you can define classes with specific responsibilities:

- WeatherClient: Responsible for performing the REST requests to the Weather Underground service (www.wunderground.com/weather/api). The class also handles the parsing of the JSON response.

- CityInfo: Encapsulates the weather data once it has been returned by the Weather Underground service. Note that the QML City control has its properties bound to CityInfo's properties.

- GoogleMapClient: A client for generating static maps using the Google Maps service. An instance of this class is defined as an attached object property of the WeatherMap control.

- ApplicationUI: The standard application delegate reachable from the QML layer of your application through the QML document context.

The class relationships are also quite simple: the ApplicationUI object has a WeatherClient weather property, which in turn has a CityInfo property. The properties are accessible from QML as _app.weather and _app.weather.cityinfo, respectively.

WeatherClient

The WeatherClient class definition is given in Listing 7-13.

Listing 7-13. WeatherClient Class Definition

```
#ifndef WEATHERCLIENT_H_
#define WEATHERCLIENT_H_

#include <QObject>

#include <QNetworkAccessManager>
#include <QNetworkReply>

#include "CityInfo.h"
#include "GoogleMapClient.h"

class WeatherClient : public QObject {
    Q_OBJECT
    Q_PROPERTY(CityInfo* cityinfo READ city CONSTANT)
public:
    WeatherClient(QObject* parent=0);
    virtual ~WeatherClient();

signals:
    void multipleCitiesFound(QStringList cities);
    void keyError(const QString& message);
    void error(const QString& message);
    void finished();

public slots:
    void cityWeather(QString city);
    void cityWeather(int selectedIndex);
    void cancel();

private slots:
    void onCityRequestFinished();
    void onCategoriesFinished();
private:
    CityInfo* city() const;
```

```
    void updateCityInfo(const QVariantMap& map);

    QString m_apiKey;
    QNetworkAccessManager* m_networkManager;
    QList<QNetworkReply*> m_networkReplies;
    CityInfo* m_cityInfo;
    QStringList m_cities;

    // static char* constant tags omitted
};

#endif /* WEATHERCLIENT_H_ */
```

The class definition declares multiple slots and signals. To perform an initial weather request, the WeatherClient::cityWeather(QString city) slot has to be called from QML (you might recall from Chapter 3 that C++ slots and functions marked as Q_INVOKABLE can be called from QML). Also note that the signals are the same as those handled in JavaScript by the WeatherDetails control (see Listing 7-10). The multipleCitiesFound signal is emitted when a user query corresponds to multiple cities. (The cities are stored in a QStringList and passed as a parameter to the signal. As soon as the user selects a specific city, the WeatherClient::cityWeather(int selectedIndex) slot is called from QML and a new request is sent to the weather service.) The error signal is emitted when the Weather Underground service returns an error (the error is passed as a QString parameter to the signal), and, finally, the finished signal is emitted when a network request has completed.

Let us now turn our attention to the WeatherClient member function definitions.

Constructor

Listing 7-14 gives you the WeatherClient constructor.

Listing 7-14. WeatherClient Constructor

```
WeatherClient::WeatherClient(QObject* parent) :
    QObject(parent),
    m_networkManager(QmlDocument::defaultDeclarativeEngine()->networkAccessManager()),
    m_cityInfo(new CityInfo(this))
{
    JsonDataAccess jda;
    QVariant keyMap = jda.load(
    QDir::currentPath() + WeatherClient::m_apiKeyPath);

    if (jda.hasError()) {
        emit keyError("Error, could not read api key");
    } else {
        m_apiKey = keyMap.toMap()[WeatherClient::m_keyTag].toString();
    }
}
```

The constructor proceeds by initializing the class members using a member initialization list. The constructor body then tries to load the Weather Underground API key, which is required for each service request. The API key is stored in a JSON file located in a subfolder of your application's assets folder. If the constructor fails to load the key, a signal is emitted so that the UI layer can display an error message to the user. WeatherClient::m_apiKeyPath and Weather::m_keyTag are string constants that respectively identify the full path to the key file and the corresponding JSON tag.

> **Note**   You will need an API key for the Weather Underground service. You will therefore have to create a developer account at www.wunderground.com/weather/api. You will then be able to generate a new key that you can set in the wunderground.json file located in your project's assets/apikey folder.

REST Service Request

A service request is handled by the WeatherClient::cityWeather(QString city) member function (see Listing 7-15).

Listing 7-15.   WeatherClient::cityWeather(QString city)

```
void WeatherClient::cityWeather(QString city) {
        QString urlString("http://api.wunderground.com/api/");
        urlString.append(WeatherClient::m_apiKey);
        urlString.append("/conditions/q/");

        urlString.append(city);
        urlString.append(".json");

        QNetworkRequest request;
        request.setUrl(QUrl(urlString));

        QNetworkReply* reply = this->m_networkManager->get(request);
        bool result = connect(reply, SIGNAL(finished()), this,
                        SLOT(onCityRequestFinished()));
        Q_ASSERT(result);
        this->m_networkReplies.append(reply);
}
```

The WeatherClient::cityWeather(QString city) function dynamically creates a GET request URL by concatenating the city parameter and the API key previously loaded in the class constructor (the constructed URL will have the following structure: http://api.wunderground.com/api/ <api key>/conditions/q/<city>.json). As soon as the GET request has been submitted, you will have to connect the QNetworkReply's finished() signal to the WeatherClient's onCityRequestFinished() slot. Finally, when the request has completed, WeatherClient::onCityRequestFinished() will be called (see Listing 7-16).

Working with the Returned JSON

Before actually looking at how the returned JSON document is parsed by the
`WeatherClient::onCityRequestFinished()` slot, let us quickly study the structure of the document
returned by the Weather Underground service. As a matter of fact, you can conveniently use your
browser to perform HTTP requests and study the responses returned by the service. For example,
you can use the following URL to retrieve the weather conditions for Los Angeles:
`http://api.wunderground.com/api/<key_value>/conditions/q/Los Angeles, CA.json`.

The corresponding JSON structure is shown in Listing 7-16 (note that in order to save some page
space, I have removed the JSON elements that we will not need to parse or use in our code).

Listing 7-16. Wunderground JSON Response, Single City

```
{
    "response": {
        "version": "0.1",
        "termsofService": "http://www.wunderground.com/weather/api/d/terms.html",
        "features": {
            "conditions": 1
        }
    },
    "current_observation": {
        "display_location": {
            "full":"Los Angeles, CA",
            "city":"Los Angeles",
            "state":"CA",
            "state_name":"California",
            "country":"US",
            "latitude":"33.97457886",
            "longitude":"-118.24745941",
        },
        "observation_time":"Last Updated on October 7, 3:58 AM PDT",
        "weather":"Clear",
        "temperature_string":"63.1 F (17.3 C)",
        "icon_url":"http://icons-ak.wxug.com/i/c/k/nt_clear.gif"
    }
}
```

Remembering what I previously told you about parsing JSON documents with a JsonDataAccess
object, you can see the following:

- From the structure of the document shown in Listing 7-11, the root object is a
  `QVariantMap`. Supposing that `result` is the `QVariant` variable obtained with the
  call to `JsonDataAccess::load()`, the root object is therefore obtained with a call
  to `result.toMap()`.

- One level down, the `current_observation` object contained in the root object is
  retrieved using `result.toMap()["current_observation"].toMap()`.

- Similarly, the latitude attribute is retrieved by chaining method calls as follows:
  `result.toMap()["current_observation"].toMap()["display_location"].`
  `toMap()["latitude"].toString()`.

Once you get the hang of chaining the method calls, you will see that you can parse arbitrarily complex JSON structures.

There will be cases where the JSON response will return a list of cities instead of a single observation (this will happen when the city request matches multiple values). For example, if your request URL is http://api.wunderground.com/api/<key_value>/conditions/q/Los Angeles.json (note the missing state specification), the returned JSON document will be given in Listing 7-17.

Listing 7-17. *Wunderground JSON Response, Multiple Results*

```json
{
    "response": {
        "version": "0.1",
        "termsofService": "http://www.wunderground.com/weather/api/d/terms.html",
        "features": {
          "conditions": 1
        },
        "results": [
        {
            "name": "Los Angeles",
            "city": "Los Angeles",
            "state": "CA",
            "country": "US",
            "country_iso3166":"US",
            "country_name":"USA",
            "zmw": "90001.1.99999",
            "l": "/q/zmw:90001.1.99999"
        },
        {
            "name": "Los Angeles",
            "city": "Los Angeles",
            "state": "",
            "country": "CH",
            "country_iso3166":"CL",
            "country_name":"Chile",
            "zmw": "00000.10.85703",
            "l": "/q/zmw:00000.10.85703"
        },
        {
            "name": "Los Angeles",
            "city": "Los Angeles",
            "state": "",
            "cojuntry": "PH",
            "country_iso3166":"PH",
            "country_name":"Philippines",
            "zmw": "00000.31.98752",
                    "l": "/q/zmw:00000.31.98752"
        }
        ]
    }
}
```

Here again, it is quite easy to retrieve the list of cities using the following call chain:

```
result.toMap()["response"].toMap()["results"].toList()
```

And finally, if the request contains an error, the returned JSON document will be similar to Listing 7-18.

Listing 7-18. JSON Response with Error

```
{
  "response": {
      "version":"0.1",
      "termsofService":"http://www.wunderground.com/weather/api/d/terms.html",
      "features": {
      },
      "error": {
          "type": "keynotfound",
          "description": "this key does not exist"
      }
  }
}
```

In other words, you can check for the presence of an error object inside the response in order to make sure that your request was handled correctly by the service (the presence of the error object would be given by the following call chain: `result.toMap()["response"].toMap()contains("error")`).

Now that you have a basic understanding of the JSON document structure, you can see how the service response is parsed in the `WeatherClient::OnCityRequestFinished()` slot (see Listing 7-19).

Listing 7-19. WeatherClient::onCityRequestFinished()

```
void WeatherClient::onCityRequestFinished() {
    QNetworkReply* reply = static_cast<QNetworkReply*>(QObject::sender());
    if (!reply->error()) {
        JsonDataAccess jda;
        QVariant response = jda.load(reply);
        QVariantMap map = response.toMap();
        if (map.contains(WeatherClient::m_currentObservationTag)) {
            this->updateCityInfo(map);
        } else { // else 1
            if (map[WeatherClient::m_responseTag].toMap().contains(
            WeatherClient::m_errorTag)) {
                emit error(map[WeatherClient::m_responseTag]
                        .toMap()[WeatherClient::m_errorTag]
                        .toMap()[WeatherClient::m_descriptionTag].toString());
            } else { // else 2
                m_cities.clear();
                QVariantList results = map[WeatherClient::m_responseTag]
                                    .toMap()[WeatherClient::m_resultsTag].toList();
                for (int i = 0; i < results.length(); i++) {
                    QVariantMap city = results[i].toMap();
```

```
                    if (city[WeatherClient::m_countryTag].toString()
                        == WeatherClient::m_USATag) {
                            m_cities.append(city[WeatherClient::m_nameTag].toString()
                            + ", "+ city[WeatherClient::m_stateTag].toString());
                    } else { // else 3
                        m_cities.append(city[WeatherClient::m_nameTag].toString() + ", "
                        + city[WeatherClient::m_countryNameTag].toString());
                    } // else 3
                } // for
                    emit multipleCitiesFound(m_cities);
            } // else 2
        } // else 1
    }
    m_networkReplies.removeOne(reply);
    reply->deleteLater();
    emit finished();
}
```

Here is a quick description of the code:

1. You will need to handle three cases in the response: a response can either contain the current weather conditions for a city, a list of cities, or an error object. Before even handling the response, we first need to check that the request was handled correctly and that there are no errors in the QNetworkReply object.

2. We then proceed by parsing the JSON response.

3. If the JSON result contains a current_observation object, we handle it immediately with a call to WeatherClient::updateCityInfo(const QVariantMap& map).

4. Otherwise, we check if a service error has occurred. If this is the case, we emit the error signal with the corresponding error message.

5. If there are no errors, then multiples cities have been returned by the request. In this case, we populate the m_citiesList QStringList and emit the multipleCitiesFound(m_citiesList) signal, which will be handled in QML.

6. Finally, we schedule the QNetworkReply object for deletion and emit the finished() signal.

The WeatherService::updateCityInfo(const QVariantMap& map) method (used in Listing 7-20) is straightforward and is used for updating the m_cityInfo member variable (which is accessible as the cityinfo property from QML).

Listing 7-20. WeatherClient::updateCityInfo()

```
void WeatherClient::updateCityInfo(const QVariantMap& data) {
    QVariantMap currentObservation =
    data[WeatherClient::m_currentObservationTag].toMap();
    m_cityInfo->setCity(currentObservation[WeatherClient::m_displayLocationTag]
                        .toMap()[WeatherClient::m_cityTag].toString());
    m_cityInfo->setState(currentObservation[WeatherClient::m_displayLocationTag]
                        .toMap()[WeatherClient::m_stateNameTag].toString());

    m_cityInfo->setWeather(currentObservation[WeatherClient::m_weatherTag].toString());

    m_cityInfo->setTemperature(currentObservation[WeatherClient::m_temperatureTag]
                            .toString());

    m_cityInfo->setCoordinates(currentObservation[WeatherClient::m_displayLocationTag]
                            .toMap()[WeatherClient::m_latitudeTag].toString(),
                            currentObservation[WeatherClient::m_displayLocationTag]
                            .toMap()[WeatherClient::m_longitudeTag].toString(),
                            currentObservation[WeatherClient::m_iconUrlTag].toString());

    m_cityInfo->setLastObservation(currentObservation[WeatherClient::m_observationTimeTag]
                            .toString());
}
```

CityInfo

Listing 7-21 gives you the CityInfo class definition.

Listing 7-21. CityInfo Class Definition

```
#ifndef CITY_H_
#define CITY_H_
#include <QObject>
#include <bb/cascades/Image>
#include <QNetworkAccessManager>

class CityInfo : public QObject {
    Q_OBJECT
    Q_PROPERTY(QString city READ city NOTIFY cityChanged)
    Q_PROPERTY(QString state READ state NOTIFY stateChanged)
    Q_PROPERTY(QString latitude READ latitude NOTIFY latitudeChanged)
    Q_PROPERTY(QString longitude READ longitude NOTIFY longitudeChanged)
    Q_PROPERTY(QString weather READ weather NOTIFY weatherChanged)
    Q_PROPERTY(QVariant weatherIcon READ weatherIcon NOTIFY weatherIconChanged)
    Q_PROPERTY(QString temperature READ temperature NOTIFY temperatureChanged)
    Q_PROPERTY(QString lastObservation READ lastObservation NOTIFY lastObservationChanged)

public:
    CityInfo(QObject* parent = 0);
    virtual ~CityInfo();
```

```cpp
        void setCoordinates(const QString& latitude, const QString& longitude,
                            const QString& weatherIconUrl);

        // accessors.
    void setCity(const QString& city);
    QString city() const;

    void setState(const QString& state);
    QString state() const;

    void setLatitude(const QString& latitude);
    QString latitude() const;

    void setLongitude(const QString& longitude);
    QString longitude() const;

    void setWeather(const QString& weather);
    QString weather() const;

    void setTemperature(const QString& temperature);
    QString temperature() const;

    void setLastObservation(const QString& lastUpdated);
    QString lastObservation() const;

signals:
    void cityChanged();
    void stateChanged();
    void latitudeChanged();
    void longitudeChanged();
    void coordinatesChanged(const QString& latitude, const QString& longitude,
                                const  QString& markerUrl);
    void weatherChanged();
    void weatherIconChanged();
    void temperatureChanged();
    void lastObservationChanged();

private slots:
        void onWeatherIconRequestFinished();

private:
    QVariant weatherIcon()const;

    void setWeatherIconUrl(const QString& iconUrl);
    void downloadWeatherIcon(const QString& iconUrl);

    QNetworkAccessManager* m_networkManager;
    QString m_city;
    QString m_state;
    QString m_latitude;
    QString m_longitude;
    QString m_temperature;
```

```
    QString m_lastObservation;
    QString m_weather;
    QString m_weatherIconUrl;
    bb::cascades::Image m_weatherIcon;
};
```

Note that the properties declared in the class definition are the ones used by the QML City control bindings (see Listing 7-11). Also, the Notify signals are required for updating the QML bindings when the C++ properties change.

If you look at Figure 7-3, you will notice that a small icon is used for representing the current weather conditions. The Weather Underground service provides a URL pointing to a downloadable image representing the current conditions (see the icon_url element in the JSON response in Listing 7-16). The CityInfo class therefore uses the URL to download the icon and display it in QML as an ImageView. Listings 7-22 and 7-23 provide the code for downloading the image.

Listing 7-22. CityInfo::downloadWeatherIcon

```
void CityInfo::downloadWeatherIcon(const QString& iconUrl) {
    QNetworkRequest request;
    request.setUrl(QUrl(iconUrl));

    QNetworkReply* reply = this->m_networkManager->get(request);
    bool result = connect(reply, SIGNAL(finished()), this,
                          SLOT(onWeatherIconRequestFinished()));
    Q_ASSERT(result);
}
```

You should be quite familiar by now with the code shown in Listing 7-22. An HTTP request for downloading the image is created and submitted to the network access manager. The interesting part of the code is located in Listing 7-23, which handles the HTTP response.

Listing 7-23. CityInfo::onWeatherIconRequestFinished

```
void CityInfo::onWeatherIconRequestFinished() {
    QNetworkReply* reply = static_cast<QNetworkReply*>(QObject::sender());
    if (reply) {
        if (reply->error() == QNetworkReply::NoError) {
            QByteArray data = reply->readAll();
            m_weatherIcon = bb::cascades::Image(bb::utility::ImageConverter::decode(data));
            emit weatherIconChanged();
        }
        reply->deleteLater();
    }
}
```

The code essentially builds a bb::cascades::Image from the returned data using a bb::utility::ImageConverter class, and updates the m_weatherIcon member variable. Note that we also need to emit the weatherIconChanged signal, which will in turn notify the declarative engine to update the QML binding for the City.weatherImage property.

The last piece of the puzzle is to access the Image object as a QVariant from QML using the weatherIcon property (see Listing 7-24).

Listing 7-24. CityInfo::onWeatherIcon()

```
QVariant CityInfo::weatherIcon() const {
    return QVariant::fromValue(m_weatherIcon);
}
```

GoogleMapClient

The GoogleMapClient class generates a static map using the coordinates returned by the Weather Underground service. Here again, the class encapsulates the map generation functionality and exclusively uses properties and signals to communicate with the QML layer. When the GoogleMapClient::setCoordinates() slot is called, a new request to the Google Maps service is sent. If you look at the WeatherMap control's onCreationCompleted slot, you will notice that the CityInfo::coordinatesChanged() signal is connected to the GoogleMapClient::setCoordinates() slot (see Listing 7-12) (in other words, the GoogleMapClient()::setCoordinates() slot will be called each time the CityInfo object's coordinates are updated).

Listing 7-25 shows you the GoogleMapClient::setCoordinates() slot implementation.

Listing 7-25. CityInfo::setCoordinates()

```
void GoogleMapClient::setCoordinates(const QString& latitude,
    const QString& longitude, const QString& markerUrl) {
    if((m_latitude == latitude) &&
        (m_longitude == longitude) &&
        (m_markerUrl == markerUrl)) return;
    m_latitude = latitude;
    m_longitude = longitude;
    m_markerUrl = markerUrl;
    this->createMap();
}
```

Finally, the GoogleMapClient::setCoordinates() method internally calls the GoogleMapClient::createMap() method, which is responsible for building the network request to the Google Maps service (see Listing 7-26).

Listing 7-26. GoogleMapClient::createMap()

```
void GoogleMapClient::createMap() {
    QNetworkRequest request;
    request.setUrl(QUrl(this->buildUrlString()));
    QNetworkReply* reply = this->m_networkManager->get(request);
    bool result = connect(reply, SIGNAL(finished()), this, SLOT(onMapReady()));
    Q_ASSERT(result);
}
```

I am going to omit the code for handling the HTTP response, which is done in `GoogleMapClient::onMapReady()`, because it is very similar to `WeatherClient::onWeatherIconReques Finished()` (shown in Listing 7-23). (In retrospect, we could have designed a common base class implementing the image download logic. This is something you could try to refactor.)

The request URL is built with a call to `GoogleMapClient::buildUrlString()` (see Listing 7-27).

Listing 7-27. GoogleMapClient::buildUrlString()

```
QString GoogleMapClient::buildUrlString() {
    QString cityMapUrl("http://maps.googleapis.com/maps/api/staticmap?center=");
    cityMapUrl.append(m_latitude);
    cityMapUrl.append(",");
    cityMapUrl.append(m_longitude);
    cityMapUrl.append("&");
    cityMapUrl.append("zoom=7&size=640x640&sensor=false&");
    cityMapUrl.append("maptype=hybrid&");
    cityMapUrl.append("markers=");
    cityMapUrl.append("icon:");
    cityMapUrl.append(m_markerUrl);
    cityMapUrl.append("|");
    cityMapUrl.append(m_latitude);
    cityMapUrl.append(",");
    cityMapUrl.append(m_longitude);
    cityMapUrl.append("|");
    cityMapUrl.append("scale=2");
    return cityMapUrl;
}
```

The code shown in Listing 7-27 essentially creates a new request for a map centered on the `m_latitude` and `m_longitude` coordinates. The marker parameter for indicating the coordinates is defined as the URL of the icon returned by the Weather Underground service. (If you specify an image URL as a marker, Google Maps will add it as a marker on your map. By default, when no markers are specified, Google will use its own for the coordinates). This illustrates how you can combine, in practice, multiple services in your own app (we could say that we have built a mashable app).

If you are interested in finding out more about the Google static maps API, you can refer to the following URL: `https://developers.google.com/maps/documentation/staticmaps`.

ApplicationUI

As usual for Cascades applications, the application delegate ties everything together and provides you the access point for the `WeatherClient` and `CityInfo` instances (note that the delegate itself is set as a QML document context property; see Listings 7-28 and 7-29).

Listing 7-28. ApplicationUI Definition

```
class ApplicationUI : public QObject
{
    Q_OBJECT
    Q_PROPERTY(WeatherClient* weather READ weatherClient CONSTANT)
```

```
public:
    ApplicationUI(bb::cascades::Application *app);
    virtual ~ApplicationUI() { }

private:
    WeatherClient* weatherClient();
    WeatherClient* m_weatherClient;
};
```

Listing 7-29. ApplicationUI Constructor

```
ApplicationUI::ApplicationUI(bb::cascades::Application *app) :
                QObject(app), m_weatherClient(new WeatherClient(this)) {

        // Create scene document from main.qml asset, the parent is set
        // to ensure the document gets destroyed properly at shut down.
        QmlDocument *qml = QmlDocument::create("asset:///main.qml").parent(this);
        qml->documentContext()->setContextProperty("_app", this);

        // Create root object for the UI
        AbstractPane *root = qml->createRootObject<AbstractPane>();

        // Set created root object as the application scene
        app->setScene(root);
}
```

Finally, to make the WeatherClient, CityInfo and GoogleMapClient classes available as new QML
types, you need to register them with the QML type system. This is done in the application's main
function (see Listing 7-30).

Listing 7-30. main.cpp

```
Q_DECL_EXPORT int main(int argc, char **argv)
{
    qmlRegisterType<CityInfo>("ludin.utils", 1, 0, "CityInfo");
    qmlRegisterType<WeatherClient>("ludin.utils", 1, 0, "WeatherClient");
    qmlRegisterType<GoogleMapClient>("ludin.utils", 1, 0, "GoogleMapClient");

    Application app(argc, argv);

    // Create the Application UI object, this is where the main.qml file
    // is loaded and the application scene is set.
    new ApplicationUI(&app);

    // Enter the application main event loop.
    return Application::exec();
}
```

The first two calls to qmlRegisterType() are required because you are using CityInfo and WeatherClient as properties accessible from QML. The last call is required so that you can define the GoogleMapClient class as an attached object in the WeatherMap control. (You also need to add the import ludin.utils 1.0 statement at the start of your QML document; see the WeatherMap control in Listing 7-12.)

Summary

This chapter provided an overview of the BlackBerry 10 networking classes based on the QtNetwork module. The networking classes are completely generic, but this chapter showed you how to use them for the HTTP protocol. QNetworkManager plays the role of the grand dispatcher to submit network requests and handle responses. The class supports the usual HTTP verbs (GET, PUT, and POST), which makes it a breeze to use with restful services. An HTTP request is encapsulated by a QNetworkRequest instance and the response can be handled using a corresponding QNetworkReply instance. Networking is completely asynchronous, thus ensuring that UI thread is not blocked during an HTTP request. Finally, it should be emphasized that the networking classes are reentrant, meaning that you can call them multiple times from a single thread without corrupting their state.

Chapter 8

Personal Information Management APIs

As you start developing Cascades business and productivity apps, you will realize the necessity for leveraging core services such as searching contacts, sending messages, and managing calendar entries. The aforementioned services fall under the personal information management (PIM) umbrella and refer to the tools used to manage the user's personal and professional lives. One approach would be to implement the PIM services in your own application, which would quickly become daunting. Also from a user perspective, providing functionality already covered by the core applications would be less than ideal. A better approach would therefore be to reuse the preexisting PIM services provided by the BlackBerry 10 core applications and leverage them in your own apps. You can essentially achieve this in two ways:

- *Use service APIs*: All BlackBerry 10 PIM applications provide an API for interfacing with their data stores. To leverage the APIs, you will have to link your application against the `bbpim` library and use service classes to access the PIM functionality.

- *Use the invocation framework*: Use this to invoke core applications from your own app.

I will cover the PIM service APIs in this chapter. The invocation framework will be the subject of Chapter 10. After having read this chapter, you will

- Understand how user accounts are linked to service providers on the BlackBerry 10 device.

- Have a good overview of the APIs used for interfacing to the BlackBerry 10 PIM applications.

Personal Information Management

In a broad sense, "personal information management" refers to the tools used by the user to organize his personal and professional lives. The following are the corresponding BlackBerry 10 core applications:

- *Contacts*: Enables the user to manage his contacts and store relevant information such as a picture, work number, mobile number, e-mail, and so forth.

- *Calendar*: Enables the user to manage meetings, appointments, and events.

- *Messaging*: Enables the user to send and receive e-mail and short text messages.

- *Notebooks*: Provides a productivity app for collecting, managing, and organizing information that the user wants to remember. Information is organized in folders.

In this chapter, I will cover the Contacts, Calendar, and Messaging APIs, which correspond to the PIM services used most often. You can also use this chapter as a reference for the PIM APIs.

PIM APIs

This section describes the APIs used for accessing the PIM applications described in the previous section. You will see that the APIs always provide a service class, which corresponds to the API's interface to the target application's database. The material will be presented in a top-down approach by always starting with the service interface, and then explaining the remaining classes used in calling the interface.

> **Note**   To use the PIM APIs, you will have to add `LIBS += -lbbpim` to your application's `.pro` file.

Service Types

The PIM APIs define service types, which correspond to broad categories of services such as messaging, calendars, contacts, geolocation, phone, and so on. The `Service` class encapsulates this information in the `Service::Type` enumeration (the values corresponding to PIM services are as follows):

- `Service::Calendars`: Represents a calendar service type. A calendar service can be used to manage meetings and appointments.

- `Service::Contacts`: Represents a contacts service type. A contact service can be used for managing user contacts, including data such as e-mail, phone numbers, and so forth.

- `Service::Messages`: Represents a message service type. A message service can be used for sending and receiving messages. A message could be an e-mail message, a short text message, or even a tweet.

- `Service::NoteBook`: Represents a notebook service type, which contains a list of items. A notebook could be something as simple as a grocery list.

As you will see in the next section, the actual services are implemented by *service providers*, which are linked to accounts on the device (for example, the caldav service provider can be used for accessing calendar services).

Service Providers

A service provider typically implements a service type. Note that a given service type can be implemented by multiple service providers, which in turn can correspond to multiple accounts on the device (for example, the calendar service is implemented by the localcalendar provider, which corresponds to the device's "local" calendar account, and the caldav service provider, which could be linked to a Google calendar account). In C++, you can use the QList<Provider> AccountService::providers() method call to retrieve the list of all service providers available on the device. You can then determine additional information about a service provider using the Provider class:

- QString Provider::id(): Returns this provider's id. Typical examples of provider ids are localcalendar, localcontacts, sms-mms, facebook, caldav, imapemail, and so forth.

- QString Provider::name(): Returns this provider's name. You can use the name property to display a user-friendly string to the user.

- bool Provider::isServiceSupported(Service::Type service): Returns whether or not the service type is supported by the provider.

- bool Provider::isSocial(): Returns whether this service provider is a social networking service.

- bool Property::EnterpriseType Provider::isEnterprise(): Returns whether or not this service provider is an enterprise service. Possible values for EnterpriseType are EnterpriseUnknown, NonEnterprise, and Enterprise.

- QList<QString> Provider::settingsKeys(): Returns this provider's settings keys. You can consider the settings keys as a generic way of specifying the parameters required for creating a new account linked to the corresponding service provider. In other words, each provider will define its own set of keys that you will have to use when linking an account to the provider.

- QVariant Provider::settingsProperty(const QString& key, Property::Field property): Returns metainformation for the given settings key. For example, you can use this method to determine the type of a given key using Property::Type as the second parameter. The returned QVariant will contain a string describing the type. The possible values are number, boolean, string, and email).

Accounts

An Account object represents a user account stored on the device. Using the Account class, you can retrieve information such as the account's id, and most importantly, to which provider the account is linked. Important Account methods are summarized as follows (the next section will show you how to retrieve user accounts stored on the device):

- `Account(const Provider& provider)`: Instantiates a new account object linked to the given provider. All the account properties are set to the default values as defined by the provider.

- `AccountKey Account::id()`: Returns this account's ID. Note that you will need the AccountKey to use service classes such as the CalendarService and MessageService.

- `Provider Account::provider()`: Returns the provider associated to this account.

- `void Account::setSettingsValue(const QString& key, const QVariant& value)`: Assigns value to the corresponding key. The key is defined by the provider linked to this account (also see `Provider::settingsKeys()`).

AccountService Class

You can use the AccountService class to determine the service providers registered on the user's device, as well as the corresponding accounts. The following list reviews important AccountService methods:

- `Result AccountService::createAccount(const QString& providerId, Account& accountData)`: Creates a new account linked to the service provider given by providerId.

- `QList<Account> AccountService::accounts()`: Retrieves the list of all accounts stored on the device.

- `QList<Account> AccountService::accounts(Service::Type service, const QString& providerId)`: Retrieves the list of accounts stored on the device for a given service type and provider. The providerId string is given by `Provider::id()` (see the description in the "Service Providers" section).

- `Account AccountService::defaultAccount(Service::Type type)`: Returns the default account for a given service type. The Service::Type enumeration can take the following values: Calendars, Contacts, Notebook, Geolocations, Linking, Memos, Messages, Tags, Tasks, and Phone.

- `QMap<Service::Type, Account> AccountService::defaultAccounts()`: Returns a map of default accounts by service type.

- `QList<Provider> AccountService::providers()`: Retrieves the list of all provider objects.

- `QList<Account> AccountService::accounts(Service::Type service)`: Retrieves the list of Account objects currently synchronizing data for the given service type.

Creating a New Account

You can use the AccountService class to create a new account linked to a given service provider by performing the following steps:

1. Retrieve the provider's keys, which correspond to the account parameters that you will have to set.

2. Instantiate an Account object by passing the provider object to the Account object's constructor. Update the Account object using the provider keys.

3. Create the actual account using the AccountService::createAccount(const QString& providerId, Account) method.

Listing 8-1 outlines the process in practice (note that the getKeyValue() method, which is used to retrieve a key value, is not shown. In practice, the key values could be provided by a user-entered QML form or loaded using app settings at application start-up).

Listing 8-1. Account Creation

```
const QString providerId = "imapemail";
const Provider provider = m_accountService->provider(providerId);

Account account(provider);

// Iterate over all of the provider's settings keys
foreach (const QString &key, provider.settingsKeys()) {
    QVariant value = getKeyValue(key);
    account.setSettingsValue(key, value);
}

m_accountService->createAccount(provider.id(), account);
```

Searching for Accounts

As illustrated in Listing 8-2, you can use the AccountService class to search accounts linked to a given provider.

Listing 8-2. Account Creation

```
#include <bb/pim/account/AccountService>

using namespace bb::pim::account;

AccountService accountService;
QList<Account> accounts = accountService.accounts(Service::Messages,"emailemap");
for (int i = 0; i < accounts.size(); i++) {
    cout << "display name: " + accounts[i].displayName().toStdString() << endl;
}
```

In a similar way, if you wanted to retrieve the accounts linked to the `caldav` provider, you could use the following method call: `accountService.accounts(Service::Calendar, "caldav")`

In practice, as you will see in the following sections, you will need the Account ID to update the corresponding PIM app.

Contacts API

You can use the Contacts API to create, update, and delete contacts stored on the device. Typically, when you add a new contact, you can set the contact's attributes such as e-mails, postal addresses, phone numbers, pictures, and so on. Using the `ContactService` class, the following sections will illustrate basic operations of the Contacts database.

> **Note**   To access the Contacts database, you need to add the `access_pimdomain_contacts` permission in your project's `bar-descriptor.xml` file.

ContactService

As with accounts and the `AccountService` class, the `ContactService` class is the central interface for manipulating contacts stored on the device. The following summarizes `ContactService` methods:

- `Contact ContactService::createContact(const Contact& contact, bool isWork)`: Creates a new contact and adds it to the Contacts database. If `isWork` is `true`, the contact will be created in the enterprise perimeter; otherwise, the contact will be created in the personal perimeter.

- `Contact ContactService::contactDetails(ContactId id)`: Retrieves the full details of the contact given by id.

- `ContactService::updateContact(const Contact& contact)`: Updates an existing contact. Note that you need to be sure that you have retrieved the contact using `ContactService::contactDetails(ContactId id)`. Only contacts retrieved with the previous method return the full contact data. Other methods return partial contact information and the call to `ContactService::updateContact(const Contact& contact)` might then overwrite the database with incomplete data.

- `QList<Contact> ContactService::searchContacts(const ContactSearchFilters& filters)`: Retrieves a list of contacts based on the given search filter. The default search fields are first name, last name, company name, phone, and e-mail.

- `QList<Contact> ContactService::contacts(const ContactListFilters& filters)`: Retrieves a list of contacts based on the given list filters.

- `void ContactService::deleteContact(ContactId contactId)`: Deletes the contact whose `ContactId` is id.

Creating a New Contact

Listing 8-3 shows you how to create a new contact in the Contacts database.

Listing 8-3. Creating a New Contact

```
#include <bb/pim/contacts/ContactService>
#include <bb/pim/contacts/Contact>
#include <bb/pim/contacts/ContactAttributeBuilder>
#include <bb/pim/contacts/ContactBuilder>

using namespace bb::pim::contacts;

ContactService contactService;

QString firstName("Anwar");
QString lastName("Ludin");
QDateTime birthday(QDate(1973, 1, 21));
QString email("anwar@aludin.com");

ContactBuilder builder;

// Set the first name
builder.addAttribute(ContactAttributeBuilder()
                    .setKind(AttributeKind::Name)
                    .setSubKind(AttributeSubKind::NameGiven)
                    .setValue(firstName));

// Set the last name
builder.addAttribute(ContactAttributeBuilder()
                    .setKind(AttributeKind::Name)
                    .setSubKind(AttributeSubKind::NameSurname)
                    .setValue(lastName));

// Set the birthday
builder.addAttribute(ContactAttributeBuilder()
                    .setKind(AttributeKind::Date)
                    .setSubKind(AttributeSubKind::DateBirthday)
                    .setValue(birthday));

// Set the email address
builder.addAttribute(ContactAttributeBuilder()
                    .setKind(AttributeKind::Email)
                    .setSubKind(AttributeSubKind::Work)
                    .setValue(email));

// Set the postal address
builder.addPostalAddress(ContactPostalAddressBuilder().setCity("Geneva")
                    .setCountry("Switzerland")
                    .setLine1("2 rue de la Muse")
                    .setPostalCode("1205")
                    .setSubKind(AttributeSubKind::Work));
```

```
// Set photo
builder.addPhoto(ContactPhotoBuilder()
                 .setOriginalPhoto("/accounts/1000/shared/photos/aludin.jpg"));

// Save the contact to persistent storage
contactService.createContact(builder, false);
```

The code is relatively straightforward. The easiest way to create a new contact is to use a `ContactBuilder` instance. You can also assign attributes to the contact using a `ContactAttributeBuilder` instance (as illustrated in Listing 8-2, you can specify the attribute's kind, subkind, and value). For adding a postal address, you should use a `ContactPostalAddressBuilder`. You can also assign a photo to the contact using a `ContactPhotoBuilder`. Finally, once the contact's attributes have been set, you can call the `ContactService::createContact(Contact contact, bool isWork)` method to add the new contact to the Contacts database (note that you can pass the `ContactBuilder` instance directly to the `ContactService::createContact()` method because it provides a conversion operator, which will create a `Contact` object from the `ContactBuilder` object).

Note   To access the contact's photo in a shared folder on the file system, you must add the Shared Files permission to your project's `bar-descriptor.xml` file.

And finally, Figure 8-1 illustrates the newly created contact displayed in the BlackBerry 10 Contacts app.

Figure 8-1. Newly created contact

Updating a Contact

You can also update an existing contact using the `ContactService::updateContact()` method, as illustrated in Listing 8-4.

Listing 8-4. Updating a Contact

```
#include <bb/pim/contacts/ContactService>
#include <bb/pim/contacts/Contact>
#include <bb/pim/contacts/ContactAttributeBuilder>
#include <bb/pim/contacts/ContactBuilder>

ContactService contactService

int ContactId = 100;    // alternatively use a search to get the contact

Contact contact = contactService->contactDetails(contactId);
if (contact.id()) {
    // Create a builder to modify the contact
    ContactBuilder builder = contact.edit();
```

```
    // Update the single attributes
    updateContactAttribute<QString>(builder, contact,
                                    AttributeKind::Name, AttributeSubKind::NameGiven,
                                    "Jack");
    updateContactAttribute<QString>(builder, contact,
                                    AttributeKind::Name, AttributeSubKind::NameSurname,
                                    "Smith");
    updateContactAttribute<QDateTime>(builder, contact,
                                    AttributeKind::Date, AttributeSubKind::DateBirthday,
                                    QDateTime(QDate(1980,3,21)));
    updateContactAttribute<QString>(builder, contact,
                                    AttributeKind::Email, AttributeSubKind::Other, "jsmith@aludin.com");

    // Save the updated contact back to persistent storage
    contactService->updateContact(builder);
}
```

As shown in Listing 8-4, you need to first retrieve the contact's full details using the
ContactService::ContactDetails(ContactId id) method before updating the contact. You can
then use the ContactBuilder returned by the Contact::edit() method to update the contact's
attributes (the code uses the templated updateContactAttribute<T>() helper function to update
the contact's attributes (see Listing 8-5).

Listing 8-5. Updating Contact Attributes

```
template<typename T>
static void updateContactAttribute(ContactBuilder &builder,

const Contact &contact, AttributeKind::Type kind,
    AttributeSubKind::Type subKind, const T &value)
{
    // Delete previous instance of the attribute
    QList<ContactAttribute> attributes = contact.filteredAttributes(kind);
    foreach (const ContactAttribute &attribute, attributes)
    {
        if (attribute.subKind() == subKind)
            builder.deleteAttribute(attribute);
    }

    // Add new instance of the attribute with new value
    builder.addAttribute(ContactAttributeBuilder().setKind(kind)
                        .setSubKind(subKind).setValue(value));
}
```

Note how the code first deletes all previous instances of the attribute in the contact's entry,
and then updates the builder to include the new attribute value.

Searching for Contacts

Besides creating and updating contacts, you can also use the ContactService class to search for contacts by matching search criteria. There are two ways to perform a search. First, you can create a ContactSearchFilters instance that you pass to the ContactService::searchContacts(const ContactSearchFilters& filter) method. In this case, you must at least specify a search value, which is a string, but you can also further refine the search criteria by specifying search fields using the SearchField::Type enumeration (if you don't specify any search fields, the default first name, company name, phone, and email fields will be used for matching the search value). Besides search fields, you can also specify whether an attribute is present or not in the contact's entry.

Alternatively, you can use a ContactListFilters instance and pass it to the ContactService::contacts(const ContactListFilters& filter) method. In both cases, you can control the number of returned search results by using the ContactSearchFilters::setLimit() and the ContactListFilters::setLimit() methods (if you don't specify a search limit, 20 values will be returned at most; note that you can also choose to retrieve all the results corresponding to a search by setting the limit to 0).

The following summarizes important ContactSearchFilters methods (for a detailed description of ContactSearchFilters and ContactListFilters, consult BlackBerry's online documentation):

- ContactSearchFilters& ContactSearchFilters::setSearchValue(const QString& value): Sets the string to search in the list of contacts.

- ContactSearchFilters& ContactSearchFilters::setSearchFields(const QList<SearchField::Type>& fields): Sets the search fields that the search applies to. These fields are searched for the value set by the previous method.

- ContactSearchFilters& ContactSearchFilters::setHasAttribute(Attribute Kind::Type present): Filters the search results to contain only contacts with the provided attribute kind.

- ContactSearchFilter& ContactSearchFilter::setShowAttributes(bool value): Specifies whether or not to include attributes in the search results. If true, attributes are returned. If true along with ContactSearchFilter::setHasAttribute(), then only the matching attributes are returned.

- ContactSearchFilters& ContactSearchFilters::setLimit(int limit): Sets the maximum number of results returned by the search.

- ContactSearchFilters& ContactSearchFilters::setAnchorId(ContactId anchor, bool inclusive): Sets the current anchor for paging. If inclusive is true, anchor is included in the search results; otherwise, the contact after anchor is returned in the search results (see the next section about paging).

The code shown in Listing 8-6 illustrates how to perform a search in practice (the code is adapted from the BlackBerry 10 address book sample app and is used to update a ListView data model with the search results).

Listing 8-6. AddressBook::filterContacts()

```
void AddressBook::filterContacts()
{
    QList<Contact> contacts;

    if (m_filter.isEmpty()) {
        // No filter has been specified, so just list all contacts
        ContactListFilters filter;
        filter.setLimit(0)
        contacts = m_contactService->contacts(filter);
    } else {
        // Use the entered filter string as search value
        ContactSearchFilters filter;
        filter.setSearchValue(m_filter);

        contacts = m_contactService->searchContacts(filter);
    }

    // Clear the old contact information from the model
    m_model->clear();

    // Iterate over the list of contact IDs
    foreach (const Contact &idContact, contacts) {
        // Fetch the complete details for this contact ID
        const Contact contact = m_contactService->contactDetails(idContact.id());

        // Copy the data into a model entry
        QVariantMap entry;
        entry["contactId"] = contact.id();
        entry["firstName"] = contact.firstName();
        entry["lastName"] = contact.lastName();

        const QList<ContactAttribute> emails = contact.emails();
        if (!emails.isEmpty())
            entry["email"] = emails.first().value();

        // Add the entry to the model
        m_model->insert(entry);
    }
}
```

In the previous example, if the filter string given by m_filter is empty, the code simply retrieves all contacts using the ContactService::contacts() method. Otherwise, a ContactSearchFilter instance is created with the search criteria and passed to the ContactService::searchContacts() method. Finally, the ContactService::contactDetails() method is used to retrieve a given contact's full attributes (as mentioned previously, the search results will only return a partial list of attributes; if you need the full list of attributes, you must call ContactService::contactDetails()).

Paging

You can use paging to navigate through a partial list of contacts. In practice, paging is important for performance reasons because it avoids the search to block the UI thread (as a good rule of thumb, if your search criteria returns more than 200 values, you should consider paging). Listing 8-7 illustrates how to use paging in practice.

Listing 8-7. Paging

```
ContactSearchFilters filter;
filter.setSearchValue("Anwar");
filter.setLimit(20);
QList<Contact> contactPage;
do
{
    contacts = service.searchContacts(filter);
    process(contactPage);
    if (contactPage.size() == maxLimit)
    {
        filter.setAnchorId(contactPage[maxLimit-1].id());
    }
    else
    {
        break;
    }
} while (true);
```

The previous code uses a do-while loop to process search results in pages of size 20. Note that you need to update during an iteration the anchor id, which corresponds to the last element returned by the previous page, in order to move to the next logical page. Finally, you know that you are processing the last page when the current page size is less than the maximum page limit. At this point, you need to break out of the loop.

Asynchronous Search

An alternative to paging is to use an asynchronous search to avoid blocking the main UI thread (the golden rule for building enticing Cascades apps is a nonblocking responsive UI). As mentioned in Chapter 3, to perform an asynchronous operation, you need to create a worker object and start it in a separate thread from the main UI thread.

To illustrate how you can perform an asynchronous search in practice, Listing 8-8 gives you the AsynchSearch class definition.

Listing 8-8. Asynchronous Search

```
#include <QObject>
#include <QString>
#include <QList>

#include <bb/pim/contacts/ContactService>
#include <bb/pim/contacts/Contact>
#include <bb/pim/contacts/ContactSearchFilters>
```

```cpp
using namespace bb::pim::contacts;

class AsynchSearch: public QObject {
    Q_OBJECT
public:
    AsynchSearch(QObject* parent = 0) : QObject(parent) {};
    virtual ~AsynchSearch() {};
public slots:
    void doSearch();
public:
    void setFilter(QString filter) {
        m_filter = filter;
    }
    QString filter() {
        return m_filter;
    }

signals:
    void searchFinished(QList<Contact>);

private:
    QString m_filter;
    ContactService m_contactService;
};
```

> **Note**   You can download a modified version of the AddressBook sample app using asynchronous searches
> from this book's GitHub repository at `https://github.com/aludin/BB10Apress`.

As illustrated in the AsynchSearch class definition, the class returns its search results using
the searchFinished(QList<Contact> contacts) signal. The actual search is performed in the
AsynchSearch::doSearch() method shown in Listing 8-9.

Listing 8-9. AsynchSearch::doSearch()

```cpp
#include "AsynchSearch.h"

void AsynchSearch::doSearch() {
    QList<Contact> contacts;
    QList<Contact> contactsDetails;
    if (m_filter.isEmpty()) {
        // No filter has been specified, so just list all contacts
        ContactListFilters filter;
        filter.setLimit(0);
        contacts = m_contactService.contacts(filter);
        foreach (Contact c, contacts)
```

```
        {
            // Fetch the complete details for this contact ID
            const Contact contact = m_contactService.contactDetails(c.id());
            contactsDetails.append(contact);
        }
        emit searchFinished(contactsDetails);
    } else {
        // Use the entered filter string as search value
        ContactSearchFilters filter;
        filter.setSearchValue(m_filter);
        contacts = m_contactService.searchContacts(filter);
        foreach (Contact c, contacts)
        {
            // Fetch the complete details for this contact ID
            const Contact contact = m_contactService.contactDetails(c.id());
            contactsDetails.append(contact);
        }
        emit searchFinished(contactsDetails);
    }
}
```

Here again, the code uses the m_filter variable to retrieve the search results in a similar way to Listing 8-6 (the main difference comes from the fact that the contact details are not used to update a data model). Finally, as mentioned, when the search has completed, the searchFinished() signal is emitted with the list of contacts corresponding to the search criteria. The updated version of AddressBook::filterContacts(), which performs an asynchronous search, is given in Listing 8-10.

Listing 8-10. AddressBook::filterContacts(), Updated

```
void AddressBook::filterContacts() {
    QThread* thread = new QThread;
    AsynchSearch* asynch = new AsynchSearch;
    asynch->setFilter(m_filter);
    asynch->moveToThread(thread);

    bool result = connect(thread, SIGNAL(started()), asynch, SLOT(doSearch()));
    Q_ASSERT(result);
    result = connect(asynch, SIGNAL(searchFinished(QList<Contact>)), this,
                     SLOT(onSearchFinished(QList<Contact>)));
    Q_ASSERT(result);

    result = connect(asynch, SIGNAL(searchFinished(const QList<Contact>)),
                     thread, SLOT(quit()));
    Q_ASSERT(result);
    result = connect(asynch, SIGNAL(searchFinished(const QList<Contact>)),
                     asynch, SLOT(deleteLater()));
    Q_ASSERT(result);
    result = connect(thread, SIGNAL(finished()), thread, SLOT(deleteLater()));
    Q_ASSERT(result);

    thread->start();
}
```

As illustrated in Listing 8-10, the updated version of AddressBook::filterContacts() creates a new Thread and initializes an AsynchSearch object so that it will be run in the separate Thread by moving the AsynchSearch instance to the new thread context.

The signals and slot connections are configured as follows:

- The QThread::started() signal is connected to the AsynchSearch::doSearch() slot to perform the search when the thread is started.

- The AsynchSearch::searchFinished() signal is connected to the AddressBook:: onSearchCompleted() slot to return the search results to the main UI thread.

- The same AsynchSearch::searchFinished() signal is also connected to the secondary thread's QThread::quit() slot, which will in turn emit the QThread::finished() signal.

- Memory management and cleanup is handled by the AsynchSearch::searchFinished() and QThread::finished() signals, which call their corresponding deleteLater() slots.

Finally, the AddressBook::onSearchCompleted() slot, which is used to update the data model, is shown in Listing 8-11.

Listing 8-11. AddressBook::onSearchFinished()

```
void AddressBook::onSearchFinished(QList<Contact> contacts) {

    // Clear the old contact information from the model
    m_model->clear();

    // Iterate over the list of contact IDs
    foreach (Contact c, contacts)
    {
        // Copy the data into a model entry
        QVariantMap entry;
        entry["contactId"] = c.id();
        entry["firstName"] = c.firstName();
        entry["lastName"] = c.lastName();

        const QList<ContactAttribute> emails = c.emails();
        if (!emails.isEmpty())
            entry["email"] = emails.first().value();
            // Add the entry to the model
        m_model->insert(entry);
    }
}
```

Also note that you need to register with the Qt type system the QList<Contact> type used as a parameter in the *interthread* signal (in interthread signals, slots are not called immediately. but at a "later stage" in the emitting thread's event loop; therefore, the parameters passed to a slot located in a different thread need to be saved and restored by the Qt type system); see Listing 8-12.

Listing 8-12. main.cpp

```
qRegisterMetaType< QList<Contact> >( "QList<Contact>" );
```

Using a ContactsPicker

You can include the ContactsPicker control in your app if you want to provide a search interface similar to the core Contacts app (the ContactPicker control uses a Card behind the scenes to display its UI; you will find out about Cards when we cover the invocation framework in Chapter 10). As you will see shortly, you can specify whether the ContactsPicker is configured in single-selection or multiselection mode. To use the ContactsPicker in QML, you must first register the corresponding C++ type with the QML type system (note that you must also register the ContactSelectionMode class, which is used for setting the selection mode; see Listing 8-13 and Listing 8-14).

Listing 8-13. main.cpp

```
qmlRegisterType<ContactPicker>("bb.cascades.pickers", 1, 0, "ContactPicker");

qmlRegisterUncreatableType<ContactSelectionMode>("bb.cascades.pickers", 1, 0,
    "ContactSelectionMode", "Can't instantiate enum");
```

And finally, Listing 8-14 shows you how to use the ContactPicker control in QML.

Listing 8-14. ContactPicker

```
import bb.cascades 1.2
import bb.cascades.pickers 1.0
Page {
    Container {
        Button {
            text: "Open contact picker"
            onClicked: {
                picker.open();
            }
        }
        Label {
            id: result
            text: "You chose contact: "
        }

        attachedObjects: [
            ContactPicker{
                id: picker
                mode: ContactSelectionMode.Multiple
                onContactsSelected:{
                    for(var i=0; i< contactIds.length; i++){
                        console.log(contactIds[i]);
                    }
                }
            }
        ]
    }
}
```

When the ContactPicker control is displayed, the user can select multiple contacts (see Figure 8-2). When the user completes his selection and touches the Done button, the contactsSelected() signal is emitted with a list of selected contact ids (if you don't want the user to be able to select multiple contacts, you can change the selection mode to ContactSelectionMode.Single and respond to the contactSelected(id) signal).

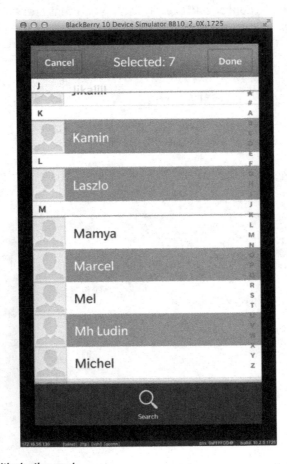

Figure 8-2. ContactPicker in multiselection mode

Calendar API

You can use the CalendarService class to add, update, and delete events in the Calendar database. Each event is represented by a CalendarEvent object, which should contain at least the following mandatory fields:

- Account ID: The account used for accessing the calendars. As mentioned previously, an account is linked to a service provider, which is either localcalendar or caldav.

- Folder ID: Each user account can in turn include multiple calendars identified by a folder ID. Therefore the "account ID, folder ID" pair uniquely identifies a user calendar on the device.

- Start time: The start time for this event (in C++ you can use a QDateTime object to specify this parameter; in QML you can use a DatePicker).

- End time: The end time for this event.

- Subject: The event's subject specified as a QString.

> **Note**   To access the Calendar database, you need to set the access_pimdomain_calendars permission in your project's bar-descriptor.xml file.

CalendarService

The CalendarService class is the API entry point for accessing the Calendar database. You can use a CalendarService instance to manage calendars, events, attendees, and event locations. Note that all CalendarService methods provide a Result::Type parameter to indicate to the client application whether or not the API call was successful.

The following summarizes important CalendarService methods:

- QList<CalendarFolder> CalendarService::folders(Result::Type* result): Returns all calendars folders from all calendar accounts (including remote calendars such as caldav; a CalendarFolder object's represents a distinct calendar).

- QPair<AccountId, FolderId> CalendarService::defaultCalendar(Result:: Type* result): Returns a pair of IDs that specify the default calendar (the default calendar is set by the user during device configuration. The setting is available using the Set Defaults action located under Settings ➤ Account Settings).

- Result::Type CalendarService::createEvent(const CalendarEvent& event, const Notification& notification=0): Creates a new event in the Calendar database. You can optionally specify whether a notification should be sent to attendees.

- QList<CalendarEvent> CalendarService::events(const EventSearchParameters& params, QResult::Type* result=0): Retrieves a list of events that match a specific search criteria identified by params. Note that depending on the search criteria, this method can potentially take a few seconds to complete. It would therefore be preferable not to call this method in the UI's main thread; use an asynchronous search instead.

- Result::Type CalendarService::deleteEvent(const CalendarEvent& event, const Notification& notification): Deletes and removes an event from the Calendar database.

CalendarFolder

A `CalendarFolder` is a container for calendar events. You can use this class to determine calendar information such as name, type, owner e-mail address, and color (you can only update the calendar's color in the Calendar database).

CalendarEvent

A `CalendarEvent` object represents an event or meeting in the user's calendar. Apart from the mandatory fields discussed at the start of this section, you can add additional information to the event, including attendees, location, event details, whether the event is a birthday, and so on.

The following summarizes important `CalendarEvent` setters:

- `CalendarEvent::setAccountId(AccountId accountId)`: Sets the account ID for this CalendarEvent.

- `CalendarEvent::setFolderId(FolderId folderId)`: Sets the folder ID for this CalendarEvent.

- `CalendarEvent::setStartTime(const QDateTime& startTime)`: Sets the start time for this CalendarEvent.

- `CalendarEvent::setEndTime(const QDateTime& endTime)`: Sets the end time for this CalendarEvent.

- `CalendarEvent::setBody(const QString& body)`: Sets the body of this CalendarEvent. The body provides further details about the event.

- `CalendarEvent::setAllDay(bool allDay)`: Sets whether or not this CalendarEvent is an all-day event.

- `CalendarEvent::setAttendees(const QList<Attendee>& attendees)`: Sets the list of attendees for this CalendarEvent.

- `CalendarEvent::setLocation(const EventLocation& eventLocation)`: Sets the location for this CalendarEvent. EventLocationis a defined as a typedef QString EventLocation.

Attendee

An *attendee* is a participant to a meeting. You can use the `Attendee` class to specify information about the participant, such as his name, e-mail, and his role in the meeting (chair, required participant, optional participant, or nonparticipant included for information only).

The following summarizes important `Attendee` properties:

- `Attendee::setContactId(ContactId contactId)`: Sets the contact ID for this Attendee.

- `Attendee::setEmail(const QString& email)`: Sets the e-mail of this Attendee.

- `Attendee::setName(const QString& name)`: Sets the name of this `Attendee`.

- `Attendee::setRole(AttendeeRole::Type role)`: Sets the role of this `Attendee` (the possible values are `AttendeeRole::Invalid`, `AttendeeRole::Chair`, `AttendeeRole::ReqParticipant`, `AttendeeRole::OptParticipant`, and `AttendeeRole::NonParticipant`).

Creating a New Event

Putting all the pieces together, Listing 8-15 shows you how to create new events in the default calendar.

Listing 8-15. CalendarService

```cpp
#include <bb/pim/calendar/CalendarService>
#include <bb/pim/calendar/CalendarEvent>
#include <bb/pim/calendar/CalendarFolder>

#include <bb/pim/calendar/Attendee>

using namespace bb::pim::calendar;

// Create the calendar service object
CalendarService calendarService;

// Create the calendar events
CalendarEvent firstEvent;

// Retrieve the IDs of the default calendar on the device
QPair<AccountId, FolderId> defaultCalendar = calendarService.defaultCalendarFolder();

// Specify information for the first event
firstEvent.setStartTime(QDateTime(QDate(2014, 03,11), QTime(10,00,00)));
firstEvent.setEndTime(QDateTime(QDate(2014, 03,11), QTime(11,00,00)));
firstEvent.setSensitivity(Sensitivity::Normal);
firstEvent.setAccountId(defaultCalendar.first);
firstEvent.setFolderId(defaultCalendar.second);
firstEvent.setSubject("Dentist");

// create first event in database
calendarService.createEvent(firstEvent);

CalendarEvent secondEvent;

// Create the attendees for the second event
Attendee firstAttendee;
Attendee secondAttendee;

firstAttendee.setName("John Smith");
firstAttendee.setRole(AttendeeRole::ReqParticipant);
```

```
secondAttendee.setName("Anwar Ludin");
secondAttendee.setRole(AttendeeRole::OptParticipant);

// Add the attendees to the second event, and specify other
// information for the event
secondEvent.setStartTime(QDateTime(QDate(2014, 03, 11), QTime(15, 0, 0)));
secondEvent.setEndTime(QDateTime(QDate(2014, 03, 11), QTime(18, 00, 0)));
secondEvent.setSensitivity(Sensitivity::Confidential);
secondEvent.setAccountId(defaultCalendar.first);
secondEvent.setFolderId(defaultCalendar.second);
secondEvent.setSubject("Annual Results");
QList<Attendee> attendees;
attendees << firstAttendee << secondAttendee;
secondEvent.setAttendees(attendees);

// Add the events to the database
calendarService.createEvent(secondEvent);
```

In practice, you should let the user choose the specific calendar where he wants to add the new event (for example, you could display a list of available calendars to the user by using the list returned by the `CalendarService:folders()` method; note that the method will also return remote calendars, which can be quite handy).

You can also use the `CalendarService::folders()` method to iterate by name over all of the user's calendars; for example, Listing 8-16 shows you how to add a new event in the user's "Hobbies" calendar.

Listing 8-16. Creating Events

```
#include <bb/pim/calendar/CalendarService>
#include <bb/pim/calendar/CalendarEvent>
#include <bb/pim/calendar/CalendarFolder>

using namespace bb::pim::calendar;

QList<CalendarFolder> folders = calendarService.folders();
foreach(CalendarFolder folder, folders){
    if(folder.name() == "Hobbies"){
        CalendarEvent sailingEvent;
        sailingEvent.setStartTime(QDateTime(QDate(2014, 03,12), QTime(14,00,00)));
        sailingEvent.setEndTime(QDateTime(QDate(2014, 03,12), QTime(18,30,00)));
        sailingEvent.setSensitivity(Sensitivity::Normal);
        sailingEvent.setAccountId(folder.accountId());
        sailingEvent.setFolderId(folder.id());
        sailingEvent.setSubject("Sailing competition");
        sailingEvent.setLocation("Geneva Yatch club");
        calendarService.createEvent(sailingEvent);
    }
}
```

Finally, you can check that the previous event has been successfully added to the Calendar app (see Figure 8-3). Besides, if the folder is linked to a `caldav` service provider, the corresponding event should also appear on the remote calendar.

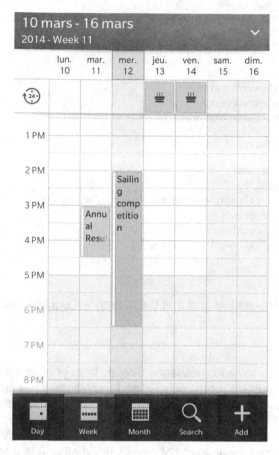

Figure 8-3. Events added to calendar

Searching for Calendar Events

You can define search criteria to search for particular events in a calendar by using the EventSearchParameters class.

The following summarizes important EventSearchParameters properties:

- EventSearchParameters::setPrefix(const QString& prefix): Sets this search's prefix string. The search will return events whose subject or location string starts with the prefix string.

- EventSearchParameters::setStart(const QDateTime& start): Sets the start date and time for this search.

- EventSearchParameters::setEnd(const QDateTime& end): Sets the end date and time for this search.

- EventSearchParameters::addFolder(const FolderKey& folder): Adds a folder key for this search. A FolderKey defines the account ID and folder ID to search (you can use FolderKey::setAccountId(AccountId id) and FolderKey::setFolderId(FolderId id) to define the calendar to be searched).

For example, Listing 8-17 shows you how to search the calendar database for the event created in Listing 8-16.

Listing 8-17. Searching Events

```
#include <bb/pim/calendar/CalendarService>
#include <bb/pim/calendar/CalendarEvent>
#include <bb/pim/calendar/EventSearchParameters>

using namespace bb::pim::calendar;

EventSearchParameters searchParams;
searchParams.setPrefix("sailing");
QList<CalendarEvent> events = calendarService.events(searchParams);
foreach(CalendarEvent event, events){
    qDebug() << "subjet: " << event.subject();
    qDebug() << "start time: " << event.startTime();
    qDebug() << "end time: "  << event.endTime();
}
```

Note that the prefix is case-insensitive and that the search will equally match "sailing" or "Sailing".

Message API

The Message API enables you to send messages directly from your application. A message can include information such as subject, body, sender, and recipients. You can also include attachments to messages. Messages can take various forms, such as text or e-mail, and they can be grouped together in a conversation. Finally, some message types can be organized in folders (for example, Inbox, Sent, Trash, Deleted, and so on). A very convenient aspect of the Message API is that you can use a common interface to manage any kind of message, whether it is a text message or an e-mail. The Message API's entry point is the MessageService class, which is described in the next section.

MessageService

MessageService is the interface to the messaging service. You can use MessageService to perform operations such as sending, saving, updating, removing, and retrieving messages. The following describes MessageService methods of interest:

- MessageKey MessageService::send(bb::pim::account::AccountKey accountId, const Message& message): Sends a message. The accountId is given by Account::id().

- QList<Message> messages(bb::pim::account::AccountKey accountId, const MessageFilter& filter): Retrieves a list of messages using the search criteria given by filter.

- int MessageService::messageCount(bb::pim::account::AccountKey accountId, const MessageFilter& filter): Returns the number of messages with the provided accountId and corresponding to the search criteria given by filter. You can use this method to predetermine the number of messages that will be returned using the search filter.

- QList<MessageFolder> MessageService::folders(bb::pim::account::AccountKey accountId): Returns all message folders associated with this accountId.

- bool MessageService::isFeatureSupported(bb::pim::account::AccountKey accountId, MessageServiceFeature::Type feature): Returns whether or not the indicated feature is supported by an account. In particular, you can use this method to determine if folder management is supported by passing MessageServiceType::FolderManagement to the method.

- QList<Conversation> MessageService::conversation(bb::pim::account:: AccountKey accountId, const MessageFilter& filter): Retrieves a list of conversations that fit the provided criteria.

Sending Messages

Sending messages, whether it is an e-mail or a short text message (SMS), is amazingly simple using the Message API. Listing 8-18 shows you the basic steps for creating a new message and sending it using the MessageService class.

Listing 8-18. Sending Messages

```
#include <bb/pim/account/AccountService>
#include <bb/pim/account/Account>

#include <bb/pim/message/Message>
#include <bb/pim/message/MessageBuilder>

AccountService accountService;
MessageService messageService;
QList<Account> accounts = accountService.accounts(Service::Messages, "imapemail");
if(accounts.size() > 0){
    Account account = accounts.first();  // use the first imapemail account available.

    MessageBuilder* builder = MessageBuilder::create(account.id());
    MessageContact recipient(-1, MessageContact::To, "Anwar Ludin", "anwar@aludin.com");

    builder->subject("Hello world");
    builder->body(MessageBody::PlainText, QString("This is the message body").toUtf8());
    builder->addRecipient(recipient);

    messageService.send(account.id(), *builder);

    delete builder;
}
```

Listing 8-18 creates a new MessageBuilder instance by passing an account corresponding to an imapemail service provider (as mentioned previously, you can potentially have multiple accounts corresponding to the same service provider and the code simply uses the first one returned by the AccountService). Next, you need to create a message recipient, which is represented by the MessageContact class and has to be added to the MessageBuilder instance. As illustrated, the

MessageContact instance is created using recipient's name, e-mail address, and the fact that he is the primary recipient (this is reflected by the Message::To parameter; if the message was copied, you should have used Message::CC instead). Finally, when all message parameters have been specified using the MessageBuilder instance, you can send the message using the MessageService instance.

Sending a short text message is similar to sending e-mails, except that you must use the sms-mms service provider and include your text message in a *conversation* (a conversation is essentially a grouping of related messages between recipients). The updated version of the code for sending text messages is shown in Listing 8-19.

Listing 8-19. Sending a Short Text Message

```
AccountService accountService;
MessageService messageService;

QList<Account> accounts = accountService.accounts(Service::Messages, "sms-mms");

    if(accounts.size() > 0){
        Account account = accounts.first();

        ConversationBuilder* conversationBuilder = ConversationBuilder::create();
        conversationBuilder->accountId(account.id());

        MessageContact recipient(-1, MessageContact::To, "Anwar Ludin", "0041766271***");

        QList<MessageContact> participants;
        participants << recipient;

        conversationBuilder->participants(participants);

        Conversation conversation = *conversationBuilder;
        ConversationKey conversationKey = messageService.save(account.id(), conversation);

        MessageBuilder* builder = MessageBuilder::create(account.id());

        builder->conversationId(conversationKey);

        builder->subject("Hello world");
        builder->body(MessageBody::PlainText, QString("This is the message body").toUtf8());
        builder->addRecipient(recipient);

        messageService.send(account.id(), *builder);

        delete conversationBuilder;
        delete builder;

    }
```

You can use the following `MessageService` signals to track new messages and message updates:

- `MessageService::messageAdded(bb::pim::account::AccountKey accountId, bb::pim::message::ConversationKey conversationId, bb::pim::message::MessageKey message)`: Emitted when a single message is added to the message service.

- `MessageService::messageUpdated(bb::pim::account::AccountKey accountId, bb::pim::message::ConversationKey conversationId, bb::pim::message::MessageKey messageId, bb::pim::message::MessageUpdateD ata data)`: Emitted when a message is updated in the message service.

Searching for Messages

You can use the message service to search for messages corresponding to specific search criteria. For example, you can specify that you are interested in messages sent to a specific recipient or messages containing a given text in their body. You can also search messages by status. To perform a search, you need to use a `MessageSearchFilter` instance:

- `MessageSearchFilter::addSearchCritera(SearchFilterCriteria::Type criteria, const QString& value)`: Adds a search criteria to this message search filter.

- `MessageSearchFilter::addStatusCriteria(SearchStatusCriteria::Type criteria)`: Adds a status criteria to this message search filter. For example, if you want to apply the search to inbound (received) messages, you can use `SearchStatusCriteria::Received`.

Listing 8-20 illustrates how to use a search filter in practice.

Listing 8-20. Searching Messages

```
// Create the message service object
MessageService service;

// Create the search criteria
MessageSearchFilter filter;
filter.addSearchCriteria(SearchFilterCriteria::Subject, "BlackBerry 10 book");
filter.addSearchCriteria(SearchFilterCriteria::Body, "Chapter 8");
filter.addStatusCriteria(SearchStatusCriteria::Received);
filter.setLimit(20);

// Perform a local search using the filter criteria
QList<Message> localMessageResults = service.searchLocal(1, filter);

// Perform a remote search using the filter criteria
QList<Message> remoteMessageResults = service.searchRemote(1, filter);
```

As illustrated in Listing 8-20, you can also specify whether the search should be performed locally on the device or remotely on the messaging server.

Message API Summary

This section provides you with a brief summary of the Message APIs.

MessageBuilder

The `MessageBuilder` class lets you create a new `Message` object or edit an existing one. The following summarizes important `MessageBuilder` methods:

- `MessageBuilder& MessageBuilder::addRecipient(const MessageContact& recipient, bool* ok=0)`: Adds the recipient to the message. You can check if the operation was successful by using the ok flag.

- `MessageBuilder& MessageBuilder::body(MessageBody::Type, const QByteArray& data)`: Sets the body of this message, which can be either plain text (`MessageBody::PlainText`) or HTML (`MessageBody::Html`).

- `MessageBuilder& MessageBuilder::addAttachment(const Attachment& attachment, bool* ok=0)`: Adds an attachment to this message.

- `MessageBuilder::operator Message()`: Casts this `MessageBuilder` into a `Message`.

MessageContact

A `MessageContact` object represents a recipient or sender of a message and includes the contact id, contact type, name, and e-mail address. The following summarizes `MessageContact` methods of interest:

- `MessageContact::MessageContact(MessageContactKey, MessageContact::Type type, const QString& name, const QString& address, unsigned char ton=0, unsigned char npi=0)`: Constructs a message contact. `MessageContactKey` corresponds to the id of a Contact retrieved from the Contacts database. You can set this value to –1 if the message contact is not located in the Contacts database. `MessageContact::Type` can take the following values: `MessageContact::To`, `MessageContact::Cc`, `MessageContact::Bcc`, `MessageContact::From`, and `MessageContact::ReplyTo`. The last two parameters are optional and are used only in alphanumeric addresses in SMS. Finally, in the case of SMS messages, you can simply pass the contact phone number in the name and address fields.

- `QString MessageContact::displayableName()`: Returns the displayable name of this contact, which includes the contact name, friendly name, and e-mail address.

ConversationBuilder

A conversation is a set of related messages between recipients. The main purpose of organizing messages in conversations is to display them together in your UI (for example, as a thread of related messages). The following summarizes important ConversationBuilder methods:

- ConversationBuilder* ConversationBuilder::create(): Starts a new conversation.

- ConversationBuilder& ConversationBuilder::accountId(bb::pim::account::AccountKey accountId): Associates this conversation with the user account given by accountId.

- ConversationBuilder& ConversationBuilder::name(QString string): Sets the name of this conversation.

- ConversationBuilder& ConversationBuilder::participants(QList<Message Contact> participants): Sets the participants of this conversation.

- ConversationBuilder::operator Conversation(): Casts this ConversationBuilder into a Conversation object.

Summary

Personal information management (PIM) is an important aspect of writing applications for the BlackBerry 10 platform. This chapter reviewed the BlackBerry 10 PIM APIs and showed you how to use them in your own applications. The APIs provide a service interface, which can be used to update and search the corresponding PIM data stores. A PIM data store contains items such as contacts, calendars, messages, and notebooks. The BlackBerry 10 PIM APIs use service types such as Messages, Calendars, and Contacts to describe groups of services. Service providers provide the actual implementation. The service providers are in turn linked to accounts on the device, which provide access to the target systems. This chapter covered mostly the PIM service providers, but in practice, the BlackBerry 10 device uses a wide range of service providers (such as social networking providers, for example).

Chapter 9

Sensors

Sensors enable your BlackBerry 10 device to collect information about the outside world and to react to physical events. With some imagination, you can use the sensors API to build highly immersive apps that respond to the device's position, accelerations, and rotations. Gaming is an obvious area that benefits from using sensors, but the majority of apps have yet to tap into the potential of using sensors. There are really no limits to what you can achieve, and as mobile devices continue adding new types of sensors, the number of applications that use sensor data will experience exponential growth in the years to come.

Cascades leverages the Qt Mobility module for the sensors API (this is a good example of how BlackBerry 10 is built using a layered architecture where Cascades uses the underlying Qt modules when necessary; see Chapter 1). As illustrated in Figure 9-1, the sensors architecture is designed around a front end and a back end. The front end, a QSensor instance or subclass, is what you call to access data provided by the back end (which can be considered as a low-level wrapper to the actual hardware sensor; in other words, a glorified device driver). The advantage of splitting sensors into a back end and front end is that you can use a common abstraction to access data, regardless of the sensor type. I will show you how to use QSensor in a generic way. In most cases, I will directly instantiate a subclass to do the actual data reading (the data is returned to the application as an instance of QSensorReading or one of its subclasses).

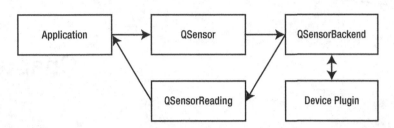

Figure 9-1. *Sensor architecture*

Finally, you can also directly access sensors from QML, which is important if you want to design sensor-aware applications entirely in QML/JavaScript.

The purpose of this chapter is to give you an overview of the BlackBerry 10 sensor types, as well as show you how to use them in your own applications. You will also learn how to handle sensor readings in C++ and QML/JavaScript.

Sensor Types

At the time of writing, the following sensors types are supported by the BlackBerry 10 platform. (Note that for a given device, not all sensor types are supported. The next section will show you how to detect the availability of a given sensor type at runtime. You can also check the BlackBerry web site for device specifications, which also lists supported sensors).

- *Ambient light sensor*: Returns a constant representing the current brightness of the external environment. You can use it to adjust the backlight, thus optimizing battery power consumption.

- *Light sensor*: Returns a value representing the light intensity measured in lux.

- *Accelerometer*: Returns the device acceleration in three dimensions. You can also specify which acceleration component should be reported by the sensor (gravity, user, or combined). For example, only the gravity component is relevant if you want to detect if the device is falling.

- *Compass*: Returns the device's azimuth, which is the angle between the device's current orientation when it is pointing toward the horizon and the magnetic north (the sensor reading is a clockwise angle measured in degrees).

- *Gyroscope*: Returns the device's angular velocity in three dimensions measured in degrees per second.

- *Holster sensor*: Returns a Boolean value indicating whether the device is in the holster or not.

- *Proximity sensor*: Returns a Boolean value, which indicates whether an object is close to the device.

- *Infrared proximity sensor*: Returns the measured reflectance, which is a percentage of the emitted infrared light returned by an object. Note that in practice it is easier to use the proximity sensor than to try to detect an object's presence with the infrared proximity sensor.

- *Magnetometer*: Returns the current magnetic field measured in Teslas.

- *Orientation*: Reports the device orientation. For example, you can use this sensor to detect whether the device is pointing up or down.

- *Rotation*: Returns a reading containing three angles—measured in angles—that define the orientation of the device in space (the device coordinate system will be explained shortly).

All sensors essentially work in the same way, as follows:

1. Instantiate a QSensor or one of its subclasses.

2. Set the sensor's properties according to your application's requirements. For example, you can specify that the sensor should not send you duplicate values or that it should not be active when the application is running in the background.

3. Optionally, add filters to the sensor in order to provide a more efficient way of notifying data changes. (For example, the accelerometer readings are very susceptible to noise. You can use a filter to smooth out the noisy signal and notify your application when a reading has truly changed).

4. Connect the QSensor::readingChanged() signal to a slot in your application in order to receive sensor readings.

5. Once the initial setup has been completed, you can start the sensor readings with a call to QSensor::start().

6. Handle the sensor data using the slot you have configured for the QSensor::readingChanged() signal.

7. When you are done using the sensor, call QSensor::stop() to end data notifications.

Sensors in C++

Determining Sensors Types

Not all of the sensors described in the previous section are available on a given device. You will therefore have to determine the availability of a sensor by using the QSensor::sensorTypes() method, which returns a list of sensors. For example, Listing 9-1 shows you how to check for the presence of an accelerometer.

Listing 9-1. Sensors Check

```
bool checkForAccelerometer(){
    QList<QByteArray> sensorTypes = QSensor::sensorTypes();
    return sensorTypes.contains(QAccelerometer::type);
}
```

You need to add the following two lines to your application's `.pro` file in order to use sensors:

```
Config += mobility
MOBILITY += sensors
```

You can access the Sensors project presented in this chapter by cloning the BB10Apress repository (https://github.com/aludin/BB10Apress).

Using Sensors in C++

The sensors API blends in with the rest of the QtCore APIs, and as usual in the world of Qt, it is all about connecting signals to slots. To illustrate how sensors work in practice, let us put together a very simple application displaying multiple sensor values. The application illustrated in Figure 9-2 combines acceleration readings with light readings.

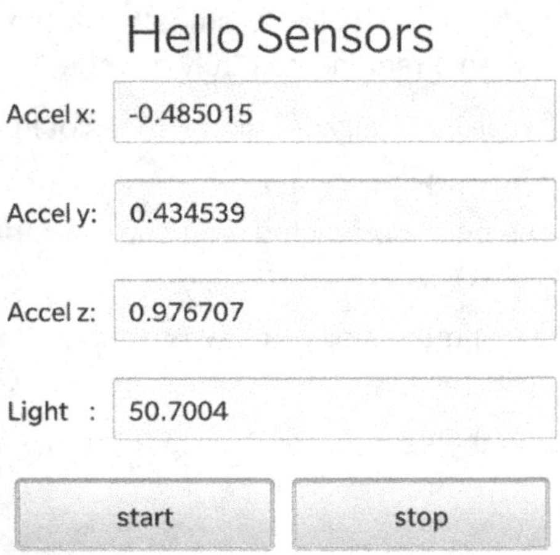

Figure 9-2. Sensors view

When the Start button is touched, the application starts receiving data from the accelerometer and light sensors, and updates the corresponding UI text fields. The Stop button interrupts the data flow from the sensors. The corresponding QML document is show in Listing 9-2.

Listing 9-2. main.qml

```
import bb.cascades 1.2
Page {
    Container {
        leftPadding: 10
        rightPadding: 10
        Label {
            text: "Hello Sensors"
            textStyle.base: SystemDefaults.TextStyles.BigText
```

```
            horizontalAlignment: HorizontalAlignment.Center
    }
    Container {
        bottomMargin: 50
        layout: StackLayout {
            orientation: LayoutOrientation.LeftToRight
        }
        Label {
            text: "Accel x:"
            verticalAlignment: VerticalAlignment.Center
        }
        TextField {
            text: _app.sensor.accelX
        }

    }
    Container {
        bottomMargin: 50
        layout: StackLayout {
            orientation: LayoutOrientation.LeftToRight
        }
        Label {
            text: "Accel y:"
            verticalAlignment: VerticalAlignment.Center
        }
        TextField {
            text: _app.sensor.accelY
        }
    }
    Container {
        bottomMargin: 50
        layout: StackLayout {
            orientation: LayoutOrientation.LeftToRight
        }
        Label {
            text: "Accel z:"
            verticalAlignment: VerticalAlignment.Center
        }
        TextField {
            text: _app.sensor.accelZ
        }
    }
    Container {
        bottomMargin: 50

        layout: StackLayout {
            orientation: LayoutOrientation.LeftToRight
        }
        Label {
            text: "Light    :"
            verticalAlignment: VerticalAlignment.Center
        }
```

```
                TextField {
                    id: light
                    text: _app.sensor.lux
                }
            }
        Container {
            layout: StackLayout {
                orientation: LayoutOrientation.LeftToRight
            }
            horizontalAlignment: HorizontalAlignment.Center
            Button {
                text: "start"
                onClicked: {
                    _app.sensor.start();
                }
            }
            Button {
                text: "stop"
                onClicked: {
                    _app.sensor.stop();
                }
            }
        }
    }
}
```

The preceding QML code is fairly straightforward. Three text fields are used to display the device's current acceleration in three-dimensional space and a fourth text field displays the current luminosity. Note how the text fields' text properties have been bound to corresponding _app.sensor properties. You will see shortly how the _app.sensor variable is defined.

HybridSensor

The HybridSensor class encapsulates the sensors reading logic (see Listing 9-3).

Listing 9-3. ApplicationUI.hpp

```cpp
#ifndef HYBRIDSENSOR_H_
#define HYBRIDSENSOR_H_

#include <QObject>
#include <QtSensors/QAccelerometer>
#include <QtSensors/QLightSensor>

class HybridSensor : public QObject {
    Q_OBJECT
    Q_PROPERTY(qreal accelX READ accelX NOTIFY accelChanged)
    Q_PROPERTY(qreal accelY READ accelY NOTIFY accelChanged)
    Q_PROPERTY(qreal accelZ READ accelZ NOTIFY accelChanged)
    Q_PROPERTY(qreal lux READ lux NOTIFY luxChanged)
```

```
public:
    HybridSensor(QObject* parent = 0);
    virtual ~HybridSensor();

signals:
    void accelChanged();
    void luxChanged();

public slots:
    void start();
    void stop();
    void onAccellerationChanged();
    void onLightChanged();

public:
    double accelX();
    double accelY();
    double accelZ();
    double lux();

private:
    QtMobility::QAccelerometer* m_accelerometer;
    QtMobility::QLightSensor* m_lightSensor;

    double m_accelX;
    double m_accelY;
    double m_accelZ;
    double m_lux;
};

#endif /* HYBRIDSENSOR_H_ */
```

As illustrated in Listing 9-3, the HybridSensor class declares four properties intended to be accessed from QML (accelX, accelY, accelZ, and lux). These are the same properties that will be bound to the corresponding QML text fields. The m_accelerometer and m_lightSensor member variables provide the actual sensor readings (m_accelerometer is an instance of the QAccelerometer class and m_lightSensor an instance of QLightSensor). Both variables are initialized in the HybridSensor class constructor, which is shown in Listing 9-4. The start() and stop() slots are used respectively for initiating and halting sensor readings. The onAccelerationChanged() slot is called by the accelerometer sensor when a new reading is available, and the onLightChanged() slot is called by the light sensor when a new light reading is available (as you will see shortly, the slots "propagate" the sensor signals using the corresponding HybridSensor notify signals in order to update the QML bindings).

Listing 9-4. HybridSensor Constructor

```
HybridSensor::HybridSensor(QObject* parent) :
                QObject(parent),
                m_accelerometer(new QAccelerometer(this)),
                m_lightSensor(new QLightSensor(this)),
                m_accelX(0), m_accelY(0), m_accelZ(0), m_lux(0) {
```

```
m_accelerometer->setAccelerationMode(QAccelerometer::User);
m_accelerometer->setSkipDuplicates(true);
m_accelerometer->setAlwaysOn(false);
m_accelerometer->setAxesOrientationMode(QAccelerometer::FixedOrientation);

bool result = QObject::connect(m_accelerometer, SIGNAL(readingChanged()), this,
                SLOT(onAccellerationChanged()));
Q_ASSERT(result);

result = QObject::connect(m_lightSensor, SIGNAL(readingChanged()), this,
                SLOT(onLightChanged()));
Q_ASSERT(result);
}
```

As usual, you need to handle memory management correctly by setting the "parent-child" ownerships of all dynamically allocated member variables (in the code shown in Listing 9-4, the parent object is the HybridSensor instance). There are a few interesting points to consider in the way the accelerometer sensor is initialized. Setting QAccelerometer::setSkipDuplicat es() to true results in the sensor notifying the application only when data has changed. This eliminates duplicate updates when successive readings are identical or very similar. Setting QAccelerometer::setAlwaysOn() to false ensures that the application will not receive sensor data when it's running in the background (this is the default behavior, but I prefer making it explicit in the code). You should be aware that if you decide to override the default behavior, running sensors such as the accelerometer in the background will drain the device's power quickly.

Next, we proceed by specifying the way the sensor should report the data to the application: the call to QAccelerometer::setAccelerationMode(QAccelerometer::User) tells the sensor to only report the acceleration caused by the user moving the device (i.e., the effect of gravity is discarded). The call to QAccelerometer::setAxesOrientation(QAccelerometer::FixedOrientation) fixes the coordinate system so that axes are not reoriented when the device orientation changes (I will tell you more about coordinate systems shortly).

Next, you connect the accelerometer's readingChanged() signal to HybridSensor's onAccelerationChanged() slot. As mentioned previously, the accelerometer sensor will call the slot when a new reading is available. In a similar way, the light sensor's readingChanged() signal is connected to the application's onLightChanged() slot. Finally, the code for HybridSensor's slots is given in Listing 9-5.

Listing 9-5. HybridSensor Slots

```
void HybridSensor::start() {
    m_accelerometer->start();
    m_lightSensor->start();
}

void HybridSensor::stop() {
    m_accelerometer->stop();
    m_lightSensor->stop();
}
```

```
void HybridSensor::onAccellerationChanged() {
    QAccelerometerReading* reading = m_accelerometer->reading();

    double x = reading->x();
    double y = reading->y();
    double z = reading->z();

    if(x*x+y*y+z*z > 0.1){
            m_accelX = x;
            m_accelY = y;
            m_accelZ = z;
            emit accelChanged();
    }
}

void HybridSensor::onLightChanged() {
    QLightReading* reading = m_lightSensor->reading();
    m_lux = reading->lux();
    emit luxChanged();
}
```

The code is relatively self-explanatory. The start() and stop() slots call the corresponding sensor methods. The onAccelerationChanged() slot is triggered by the accelerometer when a new reading is available: the method retrieves a pointer to a QAccelerometerReading instance and uses the x, y, and z components to update the corresponding HybridSensor member variables. The QML bindings are also updated with the new acceleration values when the accelChanged signal is emitted (note that the accelChanged signal is emitted only if the reading's magnitude is higher than a predefined threshold, which is defined by x*x+y*y+z*z > 0.1). The onLightChanged() slot works in a similar way by retrieving a pointer to a QLightReading instance.

The Application Delegate

You still need to access a HybridSensor instance from QML. The application delegate takes care of this by providing a QML property for the HybridSensor instance (see Listing 9-6).

Listing 9-6. ApplicationUI.hpp

```
class ApplicationUI : public QObject
{
    Q_OBJECT
    Q_PROPERTY(HybridSensor* sensor READ sensor CONSTANT)
public:
    ApplicationUI(bb::cascades::Application *app);
    virtual ~ApplicationUI() { }
private:
    HybridSensor* sensor();
    HybridSensor* m_hybridSensor;
};
```

The application delegate's constructor proceeds by registering the HybridSensor class with the QML type system. (The constructor also sets the application delegate as a QML document context property. The sensor property will therefore be accessible as _app.sensor from QML. See Listing 9-7.)

Listing 9-7. ApplicationUI.cpp

```cpp
#include <bb/cascades/Application>
#include <bb/cascades/QmlDocument>
#include <bb/cascades/AbstractPane>
#include "applicationui.hpp"

using namespace bb::cascades;

ApplicationUI::ApplicationUI(bb::cascades::Application *app) :
        QObject(app), m_hybridSensor(new HybridSensor(this))
{
    qmlRegisterType<HybridSensor>();
    // Create scene document from main.qml asset, the parent is set
    // to ensure the document gets destroyed properly at shut down.
    QmlDocument *qml = QmlDocument::create("asset:///main.qml").parent(this);

    qml->documentContext()->setContextProperty("_app", this);

    // Create root object for the UI
    AbstractPane *root = qml->createRootObject<AbstractPane>();

    // Set created root object as the application scene
    app->setScene(root);
}

HybridSensor* ApplicationUI::sensor(){
        return m_hybridSensor;
}
```

Filters

Some sensors, such as the accelerometer, are particularly sensible to a noisy signal. You can therefore recourse to a filter as a way of removing spikes out of the signal. A filter permits you to do the following:

- Modify the reading values.
- Suppress the reading altogether.
- Process readings in a pipeline. The filters will be called in turn by the sensor and each filter can modify the current reading.

Filters must subclass the QSensorFilter class and implement the following pure virtual method:

- bool QSensorFilter::filter(QSensorReading* reading)=0: This function is called by the sensor when the reading changes. If the filter returns true, the next filter in the chain will handle the reading; otherwise, the reading will be dropped. When the last filter in the chain returns true, the readingChanged signal is emitted.

Note that you can greatly optimize your application by using filters and avoiding triggering the readingChanged signal unnecessarily. Also, instead of subclassing QSensorFilter directly, you can use one of its subclasses corresponding to a particular sensor type. For example, you can subclass the QAccelerometerFilter class for accelerometer readings, as follows:

```
bool QAccelerometerFilter::filter(QAccelerometerReading* reading) = 0.
```

Finally, you can add a filter to a sensor using the QSensor::addFilter(QSensorFilter* filter) method.

To illustrate the previous points, let's modify HybridSensor by adding filtering capabilities to the class (see Listing 9-8).

Listing 9-8. HybridSensor.hpp

```
class HybridSensor : public QObject, public QtMobility::QAccelerometerFilter{
Q_OBJECT
// properties omitted
public:
    virtual bool filter(QtMobility::QAccelerometerReading *reading);
// remaining class members
};
```

Next, you need to update the HybridSensor constructor (see Listing 9-9).

Listing 9-9. HybridSensor.cpp

```
HybridSensor::HybridSensor(QObject* parent) :
            QObject(parent), m_accelerometer(new QAccelerometer(this)),
            m_lightSensor(new QLightSensor(this)), m_accelX(0), m_accelY(0), m_accelZ(0),
            m_lux(0) {
    // code omitted. See Listing 9-4
    m_accelerometer->addFilter(this);
}
```

And finally, Listing 9-10 gives the filter method.

Listing 9-10. HybridSensor.hpp

```
bool HybridSensor::filter(QAccelerometerReading *reading) {
    double x = reading->x();
    double y = reading->y();
    double z = reading->z();
    if (x * x + y * y + z * z > 0.1) {
        return true;
```

```
    } else {
        return false;
    }
}
```

Sensors in QML

Using sensors in QML is deceptively simple. All you need to do is declare the sensor as an attachedObject property of a control in the scene graph. You can then handle the sensor's readingChanged signal in the usual QML way by defining an onReadingChanged slot. To illustrate this, I have rewritten the QML document from Listing 9-1 so that it uses sensors directly (see Listing 9-11).

Listing 9-11. main.qml

```
import bb.cascades 1.0
import QtMobility.sensors 1.3
Page {
    Container {
        leftPadding: 10
        rightPadding: 10

        Label {
            text: "Hello Sensors"
            textStyle.base: SystemDefaults.TextStyles.BigText
            horizontalAlignment: HorizontalAlignment.Center
        }
        Container {
            bottomMargin: 50
            layout: StackLayout {
                orientation: LayoutOrientation.LeftToRight
            }
            Label {
                text: "Accel x:"
                verticalAlignment: VerticalAlignment.Center
            }
            TextField {
                id: x
            }

        }
        Container {
            bottomMargin: 50
            layout: StackLayout {
                orientation: LayoutOrientation.LeftToRight
            }
            Label {
                text: "Accel y:"
                verticalAlignment: VerticalAlignment.Center
            }
```

```
        TextField {
            id: y
        }
    }
    Container {
        bottomMargin: 50
        layout: StackLayout {
            orientation: LayoutOrientation.LeftToRight
        }
        Label {
            text: "Accel z:"
            verticalAlignment: VerticalAlignment.Center
        }
        TextField {
            id: z
        }
    }
    Container {

        bottomMargin: 50

        layout: StackLayout {
            orientation: LayoutOrientation.LeftToRight
        }
        Label {
            text: "Light    :"
            verticalAlignment: VerticalAlignment.Center
        }
        TextField {
            id: light
        }
    }
    Container {
        layout: StackLayout {
            orientation: LayoutOrientation.LeftToRight
        }
        horizontalAlignment: HorizontalAlignment.Center
        Button {
            id: start
            text: "start"
            onClicked: {
                accel.start();
                lux.start();
            }
        }
        Button {
            id: stop
            text: "stop"
```

```
            onClicked: {
                accel.stop();
                lux.stop();
            }
        }
    }
    attachedObjects: [
        Accelerometer {
            id: accel
            active: false
            // Don't change sensor axis on screen rotation.
            axesOrientationMode: Accelerometer.FixedOrientation
            // Remove gravity, detect only user movement.
            accelerationMode: Accelerometer.User
            skipDuplicates: true
            // Called when a new accel reading is available.
            onReadingChanged: {
                if(reading.x*reading.x+reading.y*reading.y+reading.z*reading.z > 0.1)
                {
                    x.text = reading.x;
                    y.text = reading.y;
                    z.text = reading.z;
                }
            }
        },
        LightSensor {
            id: lux
            active: false
            onReadingChanged: {
                light.text = reading.lux;
            }
        }
    ]
    }
}
```

Before referencing sensors in QML, you need to import the QtMobility.sensors namespace (this is achieved with the second import statement). You also have to declare the sensor objects as attachedObjects properties of the root container. Note that the signal handlers are similar to their C++ counterparts and behave in exactly the same way.

Sensors Coordinate System

Sensors such as the accelerometer, gyroscope, and magnetometer use a right-handed coordinate system to report their readings. The x-axis, or *abscissa*, increases as you move toward the right of the screen, and the y-axis, or *ordinate*, increases as you move toward the top of the screen. Finally, the z-axis is perpendicular to the screen (see Figure 9-3).

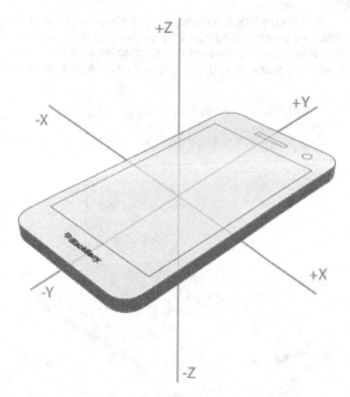

Figure 9-3. Right-handed coordinate system (image source: BlackBerry web site)

Sensors inheriting from QOrientableSensorBase (such as the accelerometer) can react to screen orientation changes. Therefore, these sensors can report their readings differently according to the screen's orientation. Their reporting behavior is controlled by the QOrientableSensorBase::axesOrientationMode property, which can take the following values:

- QOrientableSensorBase::FixedOrientation: This is the default behavior and the readings remain unaffected by the screen's orientation change. When the screen orientation changes, the application will have to "compensate" the returned values in order to take into account the new screen orientation (the application will also need to detect screen orientation changes).

- QOrientableSensorBase::AutomaticOrientation: The sensor readings are automatically remapped based on the current screen orientation. Therefore, the application need not worry about screen orientation changes (this is the recommended value to use in your application).

- QOrientatableSensorBase::UserOrientation: This is similar to the previous setting except that the readings are rotated by fixed angles of 0, 90, 180, and 270 degrees (no intermediate values).

Notice that applying the device rotation to the sensor readings is equivalent to rotating the coordinate system when the screen orientation changes.

Finally, angular displacements around the coordinate system's axes are also reported as right-hand rotations. You can visualize this by imagining that you are holding an imaginary screwdriver in your hand along a coordinate system axis. Positive rotations along an axis are then defined by using the screwdriver so that an imaginary screw would move toward increasing values along the axis (see Figure 9-4).

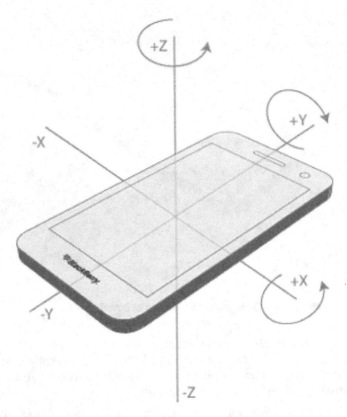

Figure 9-4. Right-handed rotations around coordinate system (image source: BlackBerry web site)

Accelerometer and Gyroscope

Before finishing this chapter, I want to give you some tips on how to process the data readings provided by the accelerometer and gyroscope sensors. As you noticed throughout the chapter, receiving sensor readings is quite simple. The difficulty lies in the handling and interpretation of the data. I don't intend to give you a comprehensive treatment of the data processing, but hopefully this section will put you on the right track should you need to implement more advanced techniques in your own applications.

Accelerometer

As implied by its name, an accelerometer measures acceleration; in our case, it measures your device's *linear* acceleration in three-dimensional space. So how do you define acceleration exactly? You might recall from high-school physics that acceleration is a *vector* giving the rate of change of velocity per unit of time (a vector is a quantity having direction and magnitude). Velocity in turn is the rate at which an object changes position per unit of time. Expressing this mathematically, we can write the following:

$$a = \frac{dv}{dt} = \frac{d}{dt}\left(\frac{dx}{dt}\right) = \frac{d^2x}{dt^2}$$

An accelerometer can therefore be used in order to measure

■ Velocity and displacement by integrating the accelerometer readings.

■ A vibration or impact indicator (for example, when you shake or jolt the device).

So how should you proceed to integrate accelerometer values to obtain the device's velocity and position in practice? You will first need to capture accelerometer readings at regular time intervals, as previously illustrated using the QTimer technique. You will then need to integrate twice. The first integration step is acceleration with respect to time in order to obtain the device's velocity. You will then integrate velocity with respect to time in order to obtain the device's displacement. To illustrate this, let us consider the acceleration readings given in Figure 9-5.

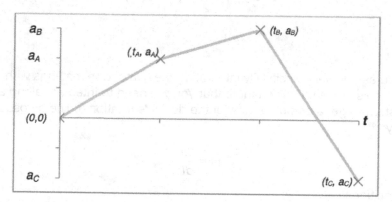

Figure 9-5. Acceleration readings with linear interpolation

You will notice that I am using linear interpolation for acceleration, which also makes the integration trivial. The velocity's value at time t_A is therefore given by:

$$v_a = \int_0^{t_A} \frac{a_A}{t_A} t\, dt = \frac{a_A}{t_A} \frac{t^2}{2}\Bigg]_0^{t_A} = \frac{a_A}{2} t_A$$

Repeating the same procedure at time t_B, we get (I am going to consider here that the time samples are equally spaced and $t_B = 2t_A$) the following:

$$v_b - v_a = \int_{t_A}^{t_B} \left[\frac{a_B - a_A}{t_A} t + 2a_A - a_B \right] dt = \frac{1}{2} t_A (a_B + a_A)$$

In the general case, the following recursion stands:

$$v_n = v_{n-1} + \frac{1}{2} t_A (a_n + a_{n-1})$$

In other words, you can calculate your device's velocity at any time by sampling the acceleration and applying this recursive relation.

You can measure displacement applying the same technique, but this time by integrating velocity, as follows:

$$x_A = \int_0^{t_A} \frac{v_A}{t_A} t \, dt = \frac{a_A}{2} \frac{t^2}{2} \bigg]_0^{t_A} = \frac{a_A}{4} t_A^2$$

You will then also get a recursive relation of the following form:

$$x_n = x_{n-1} + \frac{1}{2} t_A (v_n + v_{n-1})$$

Gyroscope

A gyroscope measures angular velocity. By integrating the gyroscope readings with respect to time, you will get the device's angular position (note that you will need to integrate along all three axes of the coordinate system to get a complete view of the device's rotations). The gyroscope's angular velocity is given by:

$$\omega = \frac{d\theta}{dt}$$

And the angular position is given by:

$$\theta = \int_0^t \omega \; dt \cong \sum_0^N \omega \Delta t$$

If you want to use the relation in recursive form, it is given by:

$$\theta_n = q_{n-1} + \omega_n \Delta t$$

Combining Readings

In practice, you will combine the gyroscope and accelerometer readings to measure your device's displacement using six degrees of freedom (i.e., three translations measured by the accelerometer and three rotations measured by the gyroscope).

The first application that comes to mind is gaming. For example, let us consider the infamous first person shooter: you could use the gyroscope in order to "aim" with your weapon at various targets. A tap on the screen would fire that weapon, and then jolting the device would reload the weapon.

Summary

This chapter introduced you to the rich world of sensors and their applications in mobile computing. I showed you how to write sensor-aware applications by using the QtMobility module, which is part of the BlackBerry 10 platform. You also saw how easily you could obtain sensor readings in C++ and QML by using the sensor types supported by BlackBerry 10. I emphasized the fact that obtaining those readings is extremely simple and that the real difficulty lies in the data post-processing.

The obvious application of sensors is in game programming by combining the accelerometer and gyroscope. However, as the BlackBerry 10 platform evolves and new sensor types are introduced in the future, the potential applications will grow exponentially. Applications in domains such as personal health management have huge potential. For example, imagine an application using sensors capable of monitoring your heart and stress levels and capable of playing a specific playlist on your device in order to lower your stress.

Sensor-aware applications are a largely untapped market at the moment and this is something you should definitely consider when designing your next BlackBerry 10 killer app.

Chapter 10

Invocation Framework

You discovered in Chapter 8 how to access the PIM databases using the BlackBerry 10 PIM APIs. This chapter shows you another way of accessing third-party functionality using the invocation framework. The *invocation framework* is a very powerful way of integrating external applications directly into your own app (including UI elements called *cards*). The invocation framework is a two-sided coin: you can also use it to expose some of your own application's functionality to client apps. This is an extremely important concept because it provides seamless integration between applications, thus avoiding the necessity to develop from scratch functionality that is already available in a core or third-party app. Here are some typical scenarios where you should consider using the invocation framework:

- Invoking core BlackBerry 10 apps for displaying or updating information
- Viewing files such as images and documents in PNG, PDF or DOC format
- Playing multimedia content

You should also consider making your own app invocable if it can handle very specific MIME types. For example, a medical-imaging application capable of handling X-ray images would be an ideal invocable target for displaying DICOM images. The invocation framework gives you all the means for registering your application, as well as your app's supported MIME types with the BlackBerry 10 OS. As a result, when your users try to open a document with a MIME type managed by your application, the invocation framework will transparently call your app and display the corresponding application card.

After having read this chapter, you will be able to

- Use the invocation framework to call other applications from your own app, including the BlackBerry 10 core applications.
- Make your own application invocable.

Invoking Core Applications

Before getting into the details of invoking other applications from your own app, I want to introduce some terminology that will help you understand the concepts behind the invocation framework:

- A client application invokes a target application with some content and, optionally, metadata. The target can be either launched as a separate app or as a UI fragment such as a Page or a Sheet, which will be displayed in your application. If the target application is launched independently, your application will be minimized and the target app will come to the foreground.

- The UI fragment "exposed" by the target app is called a card. It is displayed on top of your application's main UI. When you are finished with the card, your application's main UI is displayed again. It is important to keep in mind that a card is not part of your app's UI, but something provided by the target app (note that the user can also reveal your app's UI by "peeking" behind the card).

- A client invocation can be bound or unbound. In the case of a *bound invocation*, the client app specifies the exact target application to be called (this is achieved by setting a target application ID in the request). In the case of an *unbound invocation*, the invocation framework chooses the most appropriate application for handling the request using *brokering*.

The parameters passed in an invocation request are summarized as follows:

- *Target ID*: Sets the identity of the invocation receiver. The invocation is bound if you set the target ID and it is unbound if you don't.

- *Action ID:* Defines the action to perform on the invocation data. Examples of default actions are bb.action.View or bb.action.OPEN. For an unbound invocation, the framework uses the action ID to select the most suitable target app in a process called *brokering*.

- URI: Indicates where the content is located (for example, file:///accounts/1000/shared/photos/palance.png).

- MIME *type*: Sets the format of the data sent to the target application (for example, "image/png"). The MIME type is usually a mandatory field but you can omit it in the special case of a URI pointing to a file where the MIME type can be inferred from the file extension (and only if the file extension is known by the framework).

- *Data*: Defines additional data that might or might not be used by the target (note that you are limited to about 16KB of data). If you don't specify the data, the MIME type, action, and URI must be sufficient for the target to complete the request.

- *MetaData*: Additional information, usually in JSON format, passed to the invocation request. For example, if a target application accepts multiple files, the URI could specify the root folder where the files are located and the metadata could be a JSON array of file names. As you will see in the following section about the InvokeRequest object, the JSON object is created using a QVariantMap.

To illustrate how the previous parameters are used in practice, the code samples given in Listings 10-1 and 10-2 show you how to perform a bound invocation (in other words, the target application ID is specified and no brokering is involved by the invocation framework).

Listing 10-1. AppInvoker::viewImage

```
void AppInvoker::viewImage(QString fileName){
    InvokeRequest request;
    request.setTarget("sys.pictures.card.previewer");
    request.setAction("bb.action.VIEW");
    request.setUri(fileName);
    InvokeTargetReply *reply = m_invokeManager->invoke(request);
    if(reply){
        bool result = connect(reply, SIGNAL(finished()), this,
                              SLOT(onInvocationFinished()));
        Q_ASSERT(result);
    }else{
        // error handling goes here
    }
}
```

Note The code samples presented in this chapter are located in the Invoker and InvokerTarget projects in the BB10Apress GitHub repository (https://github.com/aludin/BB10Apress). Invoker is the client app for performing invocations and InvokerTarget is the corresponding target app. Deploy both apps on the simulator and use Invoker to perform the invocations.

The AppInvoker class can be used to call target applications from you own app (in the code samples shown in this chapter, the Invoker app is used to perform the invocations). For example, the AppInvoker::viewImage(QString fileName) method is used to view a picture from your app using the picture viewer card. To call a target app, you need to initialize an InvokeRequest object and pass it to an InvokeManager instance using the InvokeManager::invoke(InvokeRequest request) method. The return value for the method is a pointer to an InvokeTargetReply object, which will emit the finished signal when the invocation has completed. You can use the signal to check for any errors, as well as get the opportunity to cleanup all allocated resources. Finally, note that the call to InvokeManager::invoke() is asynchronous and will return immediately.

The AppInvoker::onInvocationFinished() slot, which is called when a InvokeTargetReply message is received, is given by Listing 10-2.

Listing 10-2. AppInvoker::onInvocationFinished()

```
void AppInvoker::onInvocationFinished(){
    InvokeTargetReply* reply = qobject_cast<InvokeTargetReply*>(sender());
    if(reply->error()){
            // error handling goes here
    }
    reply->deleteLater();
}
```

Note the call to reply->deleteLater(), which "schedules" the reply object for deletion once the event loop has completed. (If you don't call reply->deleteLater(), you will effectively have a memory leak. Also, as mentioned in Chapter 3, you can't delete the InvokeTargetReply object immediately from a slot using operator delete because other slots might need to reference the object).

Let's include the possibility to view an HTML page by adding an openBrowser method to the AppInvoker class (see Listing 10-3).

Listing 10-3. AppInvoker::openBrowser()

```
void AppInvoker::openBrowser(const QString& url) {
    InvokeRequest request;
    request.setAction("bb.action.OPEN");
    request.setTarget("sys.browser");
    request.setUri(url);

    InvokeTargetReply* reply = m_invokeManager->invoke(request);
    if (reply) {
        bool result = connect(reply, SIGNAL(finished()), this,
                              SLOT(onInvocationFinished()));
        Q_ASSERT(result);
    } else {
        // error handling goes here
    }
}
```

Note that AppInvoker::openBrowser () and AppInvoker::viewImage() methods are very similar. As a matter of fact, you could very easily refactor them in a single generic method taking the action, target and uri parameters and capable of invoking any kind of target application.

It is now time to call AppInvoker from QML. As usual, you can either register the class with the QML type system and use it as an attached object in QML, or set an AppInvoker instance as a QML document context property. I have chosen the former approach by registering AppInvoker with the QML type system in main.cpp (see Listing 10-4).

Listing 10-4. main.cpp

```
Q_DECL_EXPORT int main(int argc, char **argv)
{

    Application app(argc, argv);
    qmlRegisterType<AppInvoker>("com.ludin.utils", 1, 0, "AppInvoker");

    // Create the Application UI object, this is where the main.qml file
    // is loaded and the application scene is set.
    new ApplicationUI(&app);

    // Enter the application main event loop.
    return Application::exec();
}
```

Make sure to register the `AppInvoker` type *before* instantiating the application delegate (the type needs to be known by the QML declarative engine before the app delegate instantiates the QML scene graph). As illustrated in Figure 10-1, the Invoker app's UI is mostly designed using buttons.

Figure 10-1. Invoker UI (main.qml)

Each button triggers a different invocation target. For the moment you can focus on the Invoke Picture Viewer button (see Listing 10-5).

Listing 10-5. main.qml

```
import bb.cascades 1.2
import bb.cascades.pickers 1.0
import com.ludin.utils 1.0
Page {
    Container {
        leftPadding: 10
        rightPadding: 10
        topPadding: 10
        bottomPadding: 10
        Button {
            text: "Invoke Picture Viewer"
            horizontalAlignment: HorizontalAlignment.Fill
```

```
            onClicked: {
                filePicker.open();
            }
        }
        Button {
            text: "Invoke Browser"
            horizontalAlignment: HorizontalAlignment.Fill
            onClicked: {
                appInvoker.openBrowser("http://www.apress.com");
            }
        }
        Button {
            text: "Create Calendar Event"
            horizontalAlignment: HorizontalAlignment.Fill
            onClicked: {
                var participants = [ "aludin@riskcetera.com", "jsmith@riskcetera.com" ];
                appInvoker.createEvent("Ride", "Specs for the R cloud editor", participants);
            }
        }
        Button {
            text: "Take Picture"
            horizontalAlignment: HorizontalAlignment.Fill
            onClicked: {
                appInvoker.takePicture();
            }
        }
        Button {
            text: "Invoke com.riskcetera.card.previewer"
            horizontalAlignment: HorizontalAlignment.Fill
            onClicked: {
                appInvoker.invokeTargetWithUri("com.riskcetera.card.previewer",
                    "bb.action.VIEW", "file:///accounts/1000/shared/photos/leevancleef.jpg")
            }
        }
        Button {
            text: "Invoke com.riskcetera.card.picker"
            horizontalAlignment: HorizontalAlignment.Fill
            onClicked: {
                appInvoker.invokeTargetWithUri("com.riskcetera.card.picker", "bb.action.VIEW",
                    "file:///accounts/1000/shared/photos/leevancleef.jpg")
            }
        }
    }
    attachedObjects: [
        AppInvoker {
            id: appInvoker
            onTargetsChanged: {
                for (var i = 0; i < appInvoker.targets.length; i ++) {
                    var targetId = appInvoker.targets[i];
                    console.log(targetId);
                }
            }
        },
```

```
        FilePicker {
            id: filePicker
            type: FileType.Picture
            title: "Select Picture"
            directories: [ "/accounts/1000/shared/photos" ]
            onFileSelected: {
                //make sure to prepend "file://"
                appInvoker.viewImage("file://" + selectedFiles[0]);
            }
        }
    ]
  }
}
```

When you press the Invoke Picture Viewer button, a FilePicker is launched by the application so that you can select a picture (see Figure 10-2).

Figure 10-2. *FilePicker*

Note that, at this point, the target invocation has not yet occurred. When you actually select an image, the picture viewer application's card is invoked and displayed on top of the Invoker app's UI (see Figure 10-3).

Figure 10-3. Picture viewer card displayed

You can check that the main UI is still running in the background by partially sliding the picture viewer's card to the right in order to reveal your Invoker's UI (this is called *peeking*). You can also press the Back button to close the card and return to your application's main UI. Note that while the card is open, you can effectively leverage the previewer app's functionality (for example, by sharing a picture by pressing the Share button)!

Going back to the Invoker application, you can try to launch the browser app by pressing the Invoke Browser button. You will notice that unlike the picture viewer example, the browser does not provide a displayable card. Instead, your application is minimized and the browser appears with the HTML content at the foreground.

Now that you have got the gist of calling apps using the invocation framework, let's delve into the details.

InvokeManager

The InvokeManager object plays the role of dispatcher between client and target applications. The invocations methods are all asynchronous and return immediately. You will therefore have to check for a signal to determine whether the invocation has completed successfully.

InvokeRequest

The InvokeRequest class encapsulates all the information required for performing an invocation. The class methods are summarized as follows:

- InvokeRequest.setTarget(const QString& name): Sets the identity of the target receiver as defined in the target's bar-descriptor.xml.

- InvokeRequest.setAction(const QString& action): Sets the operation the client is asking the target to perform. If omitted, the invocation framework will use the MIME type to determine the action.

- InvokeRequest.setMimeType(const QString& mimeType): Sets the format of the data sent to the target application.

- InvokeRequest.setUri(const QUrl& url): Sets the URI sent to the target application. If omitted, the data, MIME type, and action must be sufficient for the target to do its work.

- InvokeRequest.setMetaData(const QVariantMap& metaData): sets the metadata sent to the target. The metadata usually specifies additional information required in order to handle the invocation. The metaData parameter is encoded as a JSON object before being sent to the target. As mentioned in Chapter 3, a QVariantMap is defined as a map of (key,value) pairs. The keys are QString objects and the values are QVariants. You can basically build an arbitrarily complex JSON object using a QVariantMap.

Target IDs, Actions, URIs, and MIME Types

A target ID uniquely identifies an invocable application that has been previously registered with the invocation framework. For your own applications, you should prefix your application's name with your company's reverse DNS name (for example, com.riskcetera.Ride). Some common IDs for the BlackBerry core apps are com.rim.bb.app.adobeReader (Adobe Reader), sys.browser (BlackBerry Browser), and sys.pictures.card.previewer (Picture Viewer). Note that the same target application can potentially have different target IDs, depending on the kind of action and cards it will provide to the client application.

Actions also use the reverse DNS style (for example, com.riskcetera.action.OPEN) and have to be unique across all actions registered with the invocation framework. You can register your own actions and verbs with the invocation framework. However, you are encouraged to use the standard built-in actions for common tasks such as viewing or editing content (the built-in actions all start with bb.action followed by a verb in capital letters; for example, bb.action.OPEN). A list of standard actions is given below:

- bb.action.VIEW: Used for viewing content such as a picture, calendar entry, or a contact's details (this is also the default action when you don't specify an action in the invocation request.)

- bb.action.OPEN: Used for opening (for example, an HTML document).

- bb.action.CREATE: Used for creating new content.

- bb.action.EDIT: Used for editing or updating existing content.

You can either transfer data "in-memory" to the target application using the
InvokeRequest::setData(const QByteArray& data) method or specify a URI with a MIME type. When
you specify a URI, you are actually telling the invocation framework to transfer the data identified by
the URI to the target application's private inbox (for more details, see the following section about data
transfer). Depending on the target application and action, the URI can either specify a single item
upon which the action is invoked (for example, a file; see Listing 10-1), or a list of items, upon which
the action should be carried out (in this case, the URI will define a base directory containing multiple
files; the specific files are provided as additional metadata in JSON format). To further illustrate the
points discussed earlier, let us consider invocation attributes for the calendar and camera core apps.

Creating a Calendar Event

To create a new event in the Calendar database, you need to do the following:

1.   Set the target ID of the InvokeRequest object to
     sys.pim.calendar.viewer.event.create.

2.   Set the action ID to bb.action.CREATE.

3.   Set the MIME type to text/calendar.

4.   Provide the event details as PPS-encoded in-memory data (see Listing 10-6).

Listing 10-6. AppInvoker::createEvent()

```
void AppInvoker::createEvent(const QString& subject, const QString& body,
             const QVariantList& participants) {
   QPair<AccountId, FolderId> defaultAccount =
       m_calendarService.defaultCalendarFolder();

   QVariantMap map;
   map.insert("accountid", defaultAccount.first);
   map.insert("folderid", defaultAccount.second);
   map.insert("participants", participants);
   map.insert("subject", subject);
   map.insert("body", body);

   QByteArray requestData = bb::PpsObject::encode(map, NULL);

   InvokeRequest request;
   request.setTarget("sys.pim.calendar.viewer.event.create");

   request.setAction("bb.action.CREATE");
   request.setMimeType("text/calendar");
   request.setData(requestData);

   InvokeTargetReply* reply = m_invokeManager->invoke(request);
   if (reply) {
       bool result = connect(reply, SIGNAL(finished()), this,
                              SLOT(onInvocationFinished()));
```

```
        Q_ASSERT(result);
    } else {
        // error handling goes here
    }
}
```

To test the invocation, you can use the Create Calendar Event button in the Invoker application.

Listing 10-7. Create Calendar Event Button

```
Button {
    text: "Create Calendar Event"
    horizontalAlignment: HorizontalAlignment.Fill
    onClicked: {
        var participants = ["aludin@riskcetera.com", "jsmith@riskcetera.com"];
        appInvoker.createEvent("Ride","Specs for the R cloud editor", participants);
    }
}
```

When you touch the Create Calendar Event button, the Calendar app's card is displayed on top of Invoker's main UI. You can then use the card to create a new event (as soon as you have completed and saved the event, the card is closed and once again Invoker's main UI is displayed, see Figure 10-4).

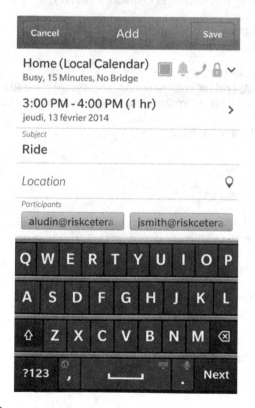

Figure 10-4. Calendar card displayed

Taking a Picture

The next example shows you how to use the camera card in order to take a picture. You will also see how to handle a response from the card using a CardDoneMessage instance.

To take a picture with the camera card, you need to:

- Set the target ID of the InvokeRequest object to sys.camera.card.
- Set the action ID to bb.action.CAPTURE.
- Set the data attribute to photo.

Once the picture has been taken by the user, you need to handle the InvokeManager::childCardDone signal in order to determine the picture's path on the file system (see Listing 10-8 and Listing 10-9).

Listing 10-8. AppInvoker::takePicture()

```
void AppInvoker::takePicture() {
    InvokeRequest request;
    request.setTarget("sys.camera.card");
    request.setMimeType("image/jpeg");
    request.setAction("bb.action.CAPTURE");
    request.setData("photo");
    InvokeTargetReply* reply = m_invokeManager->invoke(request);
    if (reply) {
        bool result = connect(reply, SIGNAL(finished()), this,
                              SLOT(onInvocationFinished()));
        Q_ASSERT(result);
        result = connect(m_invokeManager,
                         SIGNAL(childCardDone(const bb::system::CardDoneMessage&)),
                         this, SLOT(onCardDone(const bb::system::CardDoneMessage&)));
    } else {
            // error handling goes here
    }
    }
}
```

Listing 10-9. AppInvoker::onCardDone()

```
void AppInvoker::onCardDone(const CardDoneMessage& message){
    if(message.reason() == "save"){
        QString picturePath = message.data();
        // handle picture
        qDebug() << picturePath;
    }
}
```

You can test the invocation using the Take Picture button (see Listing 10-10).

Listing 10-10. Take Picture Button

```
Button {
    text: "Take Picture"
    horizontalAlignment: HorizontalAlignment.Fill
    onClicked: {
        appInvoker.takePicture();
    }
}
```

Figure 10-5 illustrates the resulting card displayed on top of Invoker's UI. You can either take a picture by touching the screen or touch the back button. In both cases the card will be closed and Invoker's main UI will be displayed again.

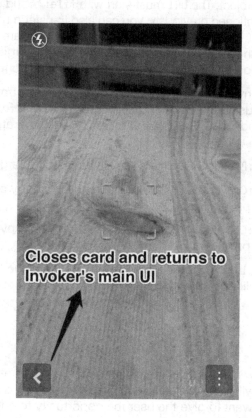

Closes card and returns to Invoker's main UI

Figure 10-5. Camera card displayed

> **Note**   You can use the URL shown below to determine the parameters for invoking the BlackBerry 10 core apps from your own application: http://developer.blackberry.com/native/documentation/cascades/device_platform/invocation/invoking_core_apps.html

Data Transfer

I have informally described data transfer during an invocation. This section gives you further details about the process. The invocation framework essentially supports two data transfer modes. You can either transfer data in-memory using the InvokeRequest's data property, or use a file transfer (when you transfer data in-memory, the invocation request URI is automatically set to data://local for you but you still have to specify the data's MIME type). Note that you have seen both transfer methods in action in the examples provided in the previous sections.

File Transfer

To transfer a file to the target application, you need to specify the file's location by setting the URI property of the InvokeRequest object. The URI must start with file:// and provide the file's full path, including the extension. As mentioned previously, you can also transfer multiple files to the target application. In this case, the URI identifies a base directory and the files are given by additional metadata encoded in JSON format (since the JSON format is very specific to each target application, you will have to consult the online BlackBerry documentation to see how to create the corresponding QVariantMap).

You can also control how the invocation framework handles the file(s) transferred to the target application's private inbox by using the InvokeRequest::setFileTransferMode(FileTransferMode:: TypefileTransferMode) method. The FileTransferMode::Type enumeration can take one of the following values:

- FileTransferMode::Preserve: Delivers the file as-is to the target application.

- FileTransferMode::CopyReadOnly: Creates a read-only copy of the file in the target application's private inbox.

- FileTransferMode::CopyReadWrite: Creates a read/write copy of the file in the target application's private inbox.

- FileTransferMode::Link: Creates a hard link to the file in the target application's private inbox. The client application must own the file and set read-write permissions on it.

Target Discovery

The examples shown until now have always specified the target application for a given invocation. At some point, however, you will want to query all targets available for a given URI and/or MIME type (perhaps because you would want to give the user the opportunity to choose the appropriate target application for a given invocation). To achieve this, you must create an InvokeQueryTargetsRequest object and pass it to the InvokeManager::queryTargets() method. You can then use the InvokeQueryTargetsReply::finished signal to handle the results (see Listing 10-11).

Listing 10-11. Querying targets

```
void AppInvoker::queryTargets(const QString& mimeType, const QString& action) {
    InvokeQueryTargetsRequest request;
    request.setMimeType(mimeType);
    request.setAction(action);
    InvokeQueryTargetsReply* reply = m_invokeManager->queryTargets(request);
```

```
    if (reply) {
        bool result = connect(reply, SIGNAL(finished()), this,
                            SLOT(onQueryTargetsResponse()));
        Q_ASSERT(result);
    }

}
```

As shown below, the query results are returned in the InvokeQueryTargetsReply object (see Listing 10-12).

Listing 10-12. QueryTargetsResponse

```
void AppInvoker::onQueryTargetsResponse() {
    InvokeQueryTargetsReply* reply = qobject_cast<InvokeQueryTargetsReply*>(sender());
    if(!reply->error()){
        m_targetIDs.clear();
            QList<InvokeAction> invokeActions = reply->actions();
            for(int i=0; i<invokeActions.size(); i++){
                QList<InvokeTarget> targets = invokeActions[i].targets();
                for (int j=0; j < targets.size(); j++){
                    QString targetId = targets[j].name();
                    m_targetIDs.append(targetId);
                }
            }
            emit targetsChanged();
    }
        reply->deleteLater();
}
```

Unbound Invocations

An unbound invocation lets the invocation framework figure out the most appropriate target application. In other words, you don't need to specify a target ID for the invoked application. You can even omit the target action. If you do not specify the target action, the invocation framework will try to find a target application for the bb.action.VIEW action. If no target application is found, the framework will fall back to the bb.action.OPEN action. If once again no suitable application is found, the invoke request fails. As mentioned previously, the MIME type can also be omitted, but only if the URI is pointing to a file with an extension known to the invocation framework.

Invocable Applications

Now let's turn our attention to the flip side of the coin and see how you can make your own applications invocable. For your application to be invocable, you need to handle the following steps:

1. Register your application with the BlackBerry 10 operating system so that it can receive invocations (this is done by declaring an invocation target in your application's bar-descriptor.xml file).

2. Listen for the invoked signal to handle invocations in your application.

3. Check whether your application was launched by an invocation or if the user launched your application and displayed the corresponding UI (you will find out more about this in the following section about cards).

Declaring an Invocation Target

The first step in making your application invocable is to declare one or several invocation targets in your application's `bar-descriptor.xml` file. For example, Listing 10-13 illustrates how to add an invocation target for viewing images.

Listing 10-13. Invocation Target Definition in bar-descriptor.xml

```xml
<invoke-target id="com.riskcetera.app.previewer">
    <invoke-target-type>application</invoke-target-type>
    <filter>
        <action>bb.action.VIEW</action>
        <action>bb.action.OPEN</action>
        <mime-type>image/png</mime-type>
        <mime-type>image/jpeg</mime-type>
        <property var="uris" value="file://,data://local"/>
    </filter>
</invoke-target>


<invoke-target id="com.riskcetera.card.previewer">
<invoke-target-type>card.previewer</invoke-target-type>
        <filter>
            <action>bb.action.VIEW</action>
            <action>bb.action.OPEN</action>
                <mime-type>image/png</mime-type>
                <mime-type>image/jpeg</mime-type>
                <property var="uris" value="file://,data://local"/>
        </filter>
</invoke-target>


<invoke-target id="com.riskcetera.card.picker">
    <invoke-target-type>card.picker</invoke-target-type>
    <filter>
        <action>bb.action.VIEW</action>
        <action>bb.action.OPEN</action>
        <mime-type>image/png</mime-type>
        <mime-type>image/jpeg</mime-type>
        <property var="uris" value="file://,data://local"/>
    </filter>
</invoke-target>
```

An invocation target defines a target ID, an invocation type, and one or more filters. The `invoke-target-type` is by default an application, but you can also define card types, which I will explain shortly (for example, the second `invoke-target-type` definition is a card). The `filter` definition essentially tells the invocation framework which kind of actions, MIME types, and URIs your application can handle through invocation. By adding invocation target definitions to your application's `bar-descriptor.xml` file, you are registering them with the BlackBerry 10 OS but you still need to handle the actual invocation in your application's code, which is the topic of the next section.

Handling Invocations

The first step in handling invocations in your application is to connect the `InvocationManager::invoked(const bb::system::InvokeRequest&)` signal to a corresponding slot in your application. Listing 10-14 illustrates how to setup this in the application delegate's constructor.

Listing 10-14. Application Delegate Constructor

```
ApplicationUI::ApplicationUI(bb::cascades::Application *app) :
            QObject(app), m_invokeManager(new InvokeManager(this)), m_uri("") {

    // Listen to incoming invocation requests
    bool result = connect(m_invokeManager,
                    SIGNAL(invoked(const bb::system::InvokeRequest&)), this,
                    SLOT(onInvokeRequest(const bb::system::InvokeRequest&)));
    Q_ASSERT(result);

    result = connect(m_invokeManager,
    SIGNAL(cardResizeRequested(const bb::system::CardResizeMessage&)),
    this, SLOT(onCardResized(const bb::system::CardResizeMessage&)));
    Q_ASSERT(result);
    result = connect(m_invokeManager,
                    SIGNAL(cardPooled(const bb::system::CardDoneMessage&)), this,
                    SLOT(onCardPooled(const bb::system::CardDoneMessage&)));
    Q_ASSERT(result);

    switch (m_invokeManager->startupMode()) {
    case ApplicationStartupMode::LaunchApplication:
        this->initFullUI();
        break;
    default:
        // Wait for the invoked signal to initialize UI
        break;
    }

}
```

You can safely ignore the other signals for the moment. You should however notice that unlike the previous examples in this book, where the default main UI was created in the application delegate's constructor, this time the application delegate checks the app's start-up mode and only creates the main UI if the startup mode is `ApplicationStartupMode::LaunchApplication`. The ability to check the application's start-up mode essentially gives you the possibility to customize your UI. If the user launches the application, you can display the entire UI, otherwise if the application is launched by a target invocation, you can display a subset of the UI.

Let's now turn our attention to the `ApplicationUI::onInvokeRequest()` slot implementation given in Listing 10-15.

Listing 10-15. ApplicationUI::onInvokeRequest

```
void ApplicationUI::onInvokeRequest(const bb::system::InvokeRequest& request) {
    QString target = request.target();
    QString action = request.action();
    QString mimeType = request.mimeType();
    if (target == "com.riskcetera.app.previewer") {
        this->initFullUI();
        this->m_uri = request.uri().toString();
        emit uriChanged();
    } else if (target == "com.riskcetera.card.previewer") {
        this->initPreviewerUI();
        this->m_uri = request.uri().toString();
        emit uriChanged();
    } else if (target == "com.riskcetera.card.picker") {
        this->initPickerUI();
    }
}
```

To find out whether the application has been invoked as a card or a target application, the `ApplicationUI::onInvokeRequest()` method retrieves the target attribute of the invocation request and compares it with the values defined in the `bar-descriptor.xml` file. The UI is also initialized differently, depending on the invocation method: if the invocation is a target application invocation, the method loads the application's full UI from `main.qml`; otherwise, a card UI is created using `previewer.qml` or `picker.qml`. Note that both QML documents are located in the assets folder of the application (see Listing 10-16 and Listing 10-17).

Listing 10-16. previewer.qml

```
import bb.cascades 1.2
NavigationPane {
    backButtonsVisible: true
    peekEnabled: true
    Page {
        titleBar: TitleBar {
            title: "Previewer Card"
        }
        Container {
            Layout: DockLayout{}
            ImageView {
                horizontalAlignment: HorizontalAlignment.Center
                verticalAlignment: VerticalAlignment.Center
                imageSource: _app.uri
                scalingMethod: ScalingMethod.AspectFit
            }
        }
    }
}
```

Listing 10-17. picker.qml

```
import bb.cascades 1.2

Page {
    Container {
        layout: StackLayout {
            orientation: LayoutOrientation.LeftToRight
        }
        leftPadding: 10
        ImageButton {
            horizontalAlignment: HorizontalAlignment.Fill
            verticalAlignment: VerticalAlignment.Center
            id: palance
            defaultImageSource: "file:///accounts/1000/shared/photos/jackpalance.jpg"
            preferredWidth: 300
            preferredHeight: 300
            onClicked: {
                _app.onPickDone(eastwood.defaultImageSource.toString());
            }
        }
        ImageButton {
            topMargin: 10
            horizontalAlignment: HorizontalAlignment.Fill
            verticalAlignment: VerticalAlignment.Center
            id: vancleef
            defaultImageSource: "file:///accounts/1000/shared/photos/leevancleef.jpg"
            preferredWidth: 300
            preferredHeight: 300
            onClicked: {
                _app.onPickDone(vancleef.defaultImageSource.toString());
            }
        }

    }
}
```

Note that for a picker, when the user selects an image, the application's onPickDone slot is called (see Listing 10-18).

Listing 10-18. picker.qml

```
void ApplicationUI::onPickDone(const QString& uri) {

        CardDoneMessage message;
        message.setData(uri);
        message.setDataType("text/plain");
        message.setReason("Success!");

        // Send message
        m_invokeManager->sendCardDone(message);
}
```

The method creates a CardDoneMessage, which is sent back to the client using the InvokeManager instance, thus notifying the client that the card should be closed (the data passed to the client contains the URI of the selected image, as well as an indication on whether the invocation was successful).

Cards

You can expose three card styles to the client application: composers, pickers, and previewers (for example, Listing 10-13 defined both a previewer and a picker using the <invoke-target-type/> tag). You can use a composer for creating content, a picker for choosing existing content, and a previewer for viewing existing content. Each style defines a different transition between your application's main UI and the card. For example, previewers slide in from the right side, whereas composers and pickers slide in from the bottom of the screen. Figure 10-6 illustrates all three styles.

Figure 10-6. Picker, composer, and previewer

Pooling Cards

To optimize usage, the BlackBerry 10 OS can pool cards and reuse them when required, instead of creating new instances of your application. You must therefore be ready to handle the InvokeManager::cardPooled(const bb::system::CardDoneMessage&) signal and clear your application's internal state, as illustrated in Listing 10-19.

Listing 10-19. ApplicationUI::onCardPooled()

```
void ApplicationUI::onCardPooled(
    const bb::system::CardDoneMessage& cardDoneMessage) {
    m_uri = "";
    emit uriChanged();
}
```

Sandbox Data Synchronization

When a target is invoked as an application, there can only be a single instance of the app running. In other words, if the application has already been launched and is minimized, the app will go back to the foreground and the InvokeManager will emit the invoked signal. When a card is invoked, a new instance of the application is created and launched (unless, of course, the card is pooled). You could therefore potentially have multiple instances of the target application running at the same time (for example, when multiple client applications invoke the same card). Since the application sandbox is shared by all running instances of an application, you should take extra care by correctly synchronizing sandbox data access (for additional information about the application's sandbox, see Appendix).

Summary

This chapter showed you how to use the invocation framework in order to leverage services provided by target applications in your own apps. Target invocation is an extremely powerful concept because not only does it enable you to leverage another app's functionality, but also to use UI elements called cards directly in your own application. Application invocation can be bound or unbound. In the case of a bound invocation, you specify the target application ID. In the case of an unbound invocation, you basically let the framework figure out the most appropriate target for you. You can also use the invocation framework to expose your app's functionality, including UI fragments.

Device File system

You can use the BlackBerry 10 device's file system in order to store your application's data and share files with other apps running on the device. This appendix gives you an overview of your application's home directory's structure and the corresponding directory permissions.

File system structure

When you deploy a Cascades app on a device, an application working directory or *sandbox* is created for your app by the BlackBerry 10 runtime (see Figure A-1).

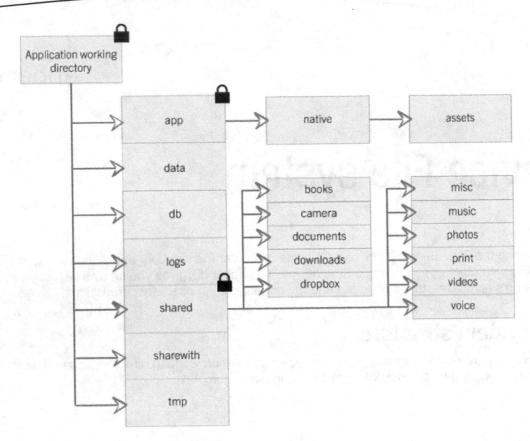

Figure A-1. Application Sandbox (image source: BlackBerry)

The following list gives you a description of the directory structure created for your app by the BlackBerry 10 runtime:

- The application's working directory, or sandbox, is the directory where your application is started. When you deploy your app on the device, additional sub-directories are also created for you by the BlackBerry 10 runtime. Depending on the sub-directory, your app has either read-only or read-write access.

- app: The app directory is where your application's binaries and resources such as QML files are deployed. You have read-only access to this directory (your app's QML files are located under app/native/assets).

- data: The data directory is where you can store your application's data, including new data created by your app. Your app has read-write access to this directory. Your app can also create new sub-directories in order to organize its data. Note that when the user removes your app, the contents of this directory will be also removed.

- db: You can store database files in this directory (note that the directory will not always be created for you automatically). In practice, and for convenience reasons, you can simply store your database files in the data directory instead.

This is a read-only directory (in other words even if you store database files here, you can't update their contents).

- `logs`: Your application's logs, including the `stderr` and `stdout`, are written in this directory. Your app has read-write access to the directory.

- `shared`: This directory will be created for you if your app has the `access_shared` permission specified in its bar-descriptor.xml file (the directory is in fact a link to the /accounts/1000/shared folder on your device). This is a read-only directory; however your app can write in its sub-directories. The different sub-directories correspond to locations where other apps share their own files (for example, shared/camera is where the Camera app stores images taken with the device's camera). Note that when the user removes your app from the device, the files stored in this folder's sub-directories by your app are not removed.

- `sharewith`: Contains files that your app can pass to other apps using the Invocation Framework (see Chapter 10).

- `tmp`: This is a folder where your app can store temporary data. The BlackBerry 10 OS can delete the contents of this folder without notification when your app is closed.

You can use the QDir class in C++ in order to update your application's sandbox directories (of course your app must have read-write permissions on the updated directories. Also note that a default-constructed QDir instance will always point to the app's working directory).

- `QString QDir::currentPath()`: Returns the application's sandbox absolute path. This is a static method that you can also use in order to determine the absolute path of directories located under the application sandbox (for example, to get the absolute path of the data directory, you can use the following method call: `QString dataPath = QDir::currentPath()+"/data"`. You can also use this method in order to build URLs pointing to resources located on the file system. For example: `QUrl("file://"+QDir::currentPath()+"/shared/camera/file001.jpg");`

- `bool QDir::mkpath(conts QString& path)`: Creates the directory path located under the app's working directory. All parent directories required to create the child directory will also be created if necessary. Returns true if successful.

Finally, to access files in the app sandbox, you can use the C++ QFile class. For example, this can be very useful if you want to download or upload files using the Qt networking classes (see Chapter 7; note that you can always pass a QFile as a second parameter to the QNetworkAccessManager::post() method).

Note   You can find additional information about QFile and QDir at the following URLs:

http://developer.blackberry.com/native/reference/cascades/qfile.html

http://developer.blackberry.com/native/reference/cascades/qdir.html

Index

■S

Get the eBook for only $10!

Now you can take the weightless companion with you anywhere, anytime. Your purchase of this book entitles you to 3 electronic versions for only $10.

This Apress title will prove so indispensible that you'll want to carry it with you everywhere, which is why we are offering the eBook in 3 formats for only $10 if you have already purchased the print book.

Convenient and fully searchable, the PDF version enables you to easily find and copy code—or perform examples by quickly toggling between instructions and applications. The MOBI format is ideal for your Kindle, while the ePUB can be utilized on a variety of mobile devices.

Go to www.apress.com/promo/tendollars to purchase your companion eBook.

Apress®
THE EXPERT'S VOICE™